THE REAL ESTATE INVESTOR AND THE FEDERAL INCOME TAX

Real Estate for Professional Practitioners
DAVID CLURMAN, Editor

CONDOMINIUMS AND COOPERATIVES
by David Clurman and Eda L. Hebard

THE BUSINESS CONDOMINIUM
by David Clurman

HOW TO PROFITABLY BUY AND SELL LAND
by Rene A. Henry, Jr.

REAL ESTATE LIMITED PARTNERSHIPS
by Theodore S. Lynn, Harry F. Goldberg, and Daniel S. Abrams

THE REAL ESTATE INVESTOR AND THE FEDERAL INCOME TAX
by Gaylon E. Greer

The Real Estate Investor and the Federal Income Tax

GAYLON E. GREER
DePaul University

A RONALD PRESS PUBLICATION
John Wiley & Sons • New York • Chichester • Brisbane • Toronto

This publication is designed to provide accurate and authoritative information in regard to the subject matter covered. It is sold with the understanding that the publisher is not engaged in rendering legal, accounting, or other professional service. If legal advice or other expert assistance is required, the services of a competent professional person should be sought.
From a Declaration of Principles jointly adopted by a Committee of the American Bar Association and a Committee of Publishers.

Library of Congress Cataloging in Publication Data:

Greer, Gaylon E
The real estate investor and the Federal income tax.

(Real estate for professional practitioners)
"A Ronald Press publication."
Includes index.
1. Real property and taxation–United States.
2. Real estate investment–Taxation–United States.
I. Title.
KF6540.G7 343'.73'054 78-569
ISBN 0-471-01882-1

Printed in the United States of America

10 9 8 7 6 5 4 3 2 1

To Jane
because a promise made
is a debt unpaid

SERIES PREFACE

Since the end of World War II, tremendous changes have taken place in the business and residential real estate fields throughout the world. This has been evidenced not only by architectural changes, exemplified by the modern shopping center, but also in the many innovative financing responses that have enabled development of new structures and complexes, such as multiuse buildings. It can be expected that real estate development will speed in new directions at an ever increasing pace to match the oncoming needs of our time. With this perspective, The Real Estate for Professional Practitioners series has been developed in response to professional needs.

As real estate professional activities have become divided into specialties, because of intensive demand for expertise at all stages, so has there developed an increasing need for extensive training and continual education for persons directly involved or dealing in business ventures requiring detailed knowledge of realty procedures.

Perhaps no field of business endeavor is more in need of a series of professional books than real estate. Working in the practical world of business and residential construction and space utilization, or at advanced levels of college training covering these areas, one is constantly aware that too little of existing creative thinking has been transcribed into viable books. Many of the books that have been written do not thoroughly enough encompass both the practical and theoretical aspects of complex subjects. Too often the drive for immediate answers has led to the overlooking of fundamental purposes and technical know-how that might lead to much more favorable results for the persons seeking knowledge.

This series will be made up of books thoroughly and expertly expounding existing procedures in the many fields of real estate, but searching as well for innovative solutions to current and future problems. These books are intended to offer a compendium of each author's wide experience and knowledge to aid the seasoned professional.

The series is addressed to professionals in all walks of realty endeavor. These include business investors and developers, urban affairs specialists, attorneys, accountants, and the many others whose work involves real estate creativity and investment. Just as importantly, the series will present to advanced students in many realty fields the opportunity to review professional thinking that will help to stimulate their own thoughts on modern trends in housing and business construction.

We believe these goals can be achieved by the outstanding group of authors who will create the books in the series.

DAVID CLURMAN

PREFACE

Though now Professor of Finance at a major university, I was for several years engaged as a property consultant and real estate broker. I vividly recall widespread ignorance and misapprehension regarding the income-tax implications of real estate transactions. My concern with this state of affairs prompted me to compile a comprehensive, nontechnical source of relevant tax information for brokers, dealers, and investors in real estate, information that I have for some time offered as an upper-division and graduate-level course in real estate investment analysis and taxation. Lecture notes form that course form the core of this book.

Most tax manuals and reference works are useful only to professionals in the field of taxation. They are often so complex that one must be knowledgeable in accounting and law to understand the explanations. The available nontechnical literature, on the other hand, tends to be so vague as to be almost useless as an aid to tax planning and decision making. Participants in the real estate market need a tax reference source that is comprehensible to one not versed in the general field of taxation. It should not attempt to encompass the entire tax code but should concentrate instead on offering broad "single source" coverage of tax laws affecting dealers and investors in real property. Tax rules should be presented in sufficient detail to enable the reader to know when they apply and to be aware of any special provisions that might render a particular rule inapplicable to his circumstances.

This is such a book. It provides the tax information investors need, while eliminating or relegating to appendices technical references or computational details and refinements not of general interest. It is written in nontechnical language and in a literary style designed to enhance readability and comprehension.

It stops where professional and technical treatises begin. It will have served its purpose if it makes the real estate investor or practitioner aware of tax situations requiring professional attention. Although procedures are suggested for tax-saving, these should be considered as preliminary ideas subject to review by expert counsel.

Acknowledgments

A number of people have helped make this book possible. The assistance of Mrs. Peach Henry of DePaul University was of particular value. She corrected faulty grammar and spelling and typed numerous drafts and revisions of the material. Without her courteous and persistent help, the manuscript might never have been accepted for publication.

The students in my real estate investment classes have served as unwitting guinea pigs for both the style and content of the book. To this group belongs credit for on-the-spot correction of pedagogical and factual errors that might otherwise have been extended to the manuscript.

Finally, a note of gratitude is due to DePaul University, which expedited the writing of the book by providing a skilled manuscript typist and by releasing me from many of the duties normally expected of a college professor.

Chicago, Illinois
December 1977

GAYLON E. GREER

CONTENTS

THE REAL ESTATE INVESTOR AND THE FEDERAL INCOME TAX

CHAPTER 1

WHAT THIS BOOK CAN DO FOR YOU

Crafty men condemn studies; simple men admire them; and wise men use them.

Sir Francis Bacon

A recent book on the relationship between income and the federal income tax contains an apology to the "nonpropertied, salaried employee . . . [because] little can be done to save him significant amounts of taxes."* The operative words in this disclaimer are "nonpropertied." But no law requires anyone to remain propertyless. A multitude of tax-saving opportunities become available when one joins the property-owning class. These opportunities result from provisions of the Internal Revenue Code, both deliberate and unintentional, that either exempt some revenue from taxation altogether or provide for taxation at rates significantly below that levied on income derived from wages and salaries.

This book demonstrates how one can benefit from these special tax provisions. Some of the opportunities are available only to owners of certain kinds of real estate, such as residential income property. Others are available to the knowledgeable taxpayer whose only real property is his own home.

Whether special provisions are called tax shelters or tax loopholes generally depends upon whether they are being praised or damned. The popu-

* Ray M. Summerfeld, *Federal Taxes and Management Decisions.* Homewood, Ill.: Richard D. Irwin, 1974, p. 2.

lar literature often leaves the impression that such arrangements are designed to enable the rich to shift the tax burden onto the middle class. That middle-class wage earners often pay a larger portion of their income as taxes than do the wealthy, however, springs more from lack of knowledge than from lack of access to tax savings.

Many of the tax shelter opportunities offered by real estate ownership are particularly beneficial to those in relatively low income-tax brackets. A careful study of the tax rate tables reveals why this is so. The rate tables in effect in 1976 are reproduced as an appendix to this chapter.

Note first of all that the rates are highly progressive. This means taxpayers earning higher levels of income pay a progressively greater percentage of their additional income as taxes. But note also that most of the progression takes place in the first $50,000 or so of taxable income. The incremental rate (the rate applicable to the last increment of taxable income) for a single taxpayer, for example, moves from 14% to 62% as earnings move from $500 to $50,000. But the rate increases by only eight additional percentage points on the second $50,000 of taxable income. The same reduction in taxable income through tax-sheltered real estate investment, therefore, enables the taxpayer earning an income of say $30,000 to "step down" to a much smaller effective incremental tax rate than is the case for one earning say twice that amount.

Expressed another way, the low-bracket taxpayer may be able to reduce his income-tax liability by at least the same proportion as the high-bracket person, by reducing his taxable income by the same percentage. Example 1–1 illustrates the point.

This example demonstrates that low-income taxpayers can benefit just as much from tax-shelter opportunities as the wealthy can. The difficulty, of course, is that many tax-sheltered investments require a far larger initial investment than the low-income investor can muster. This is where real estate really comes to the fore. Because investment opportunities in real estate come in all sizes, they present a shelter opportunity not restricted to the high-bracket investor. By employing "sweat equity" (investing one's own labor and time in the property) and exploiting various government-assisted financing opportunities, almost anyone can invest in real estate. Additional opportunities may be available by pooling funds with other like-minded investors in a joint venture such as those discussed in Chapter 11.

Our demonstration used the taxes applicable to a single person, but the reader can satisfy himself that the same principles are effective for heads of households or married persons filing joint returns by duplicating Example 1–1 using the appropriate tax tables.

Example 1–1

Taxpayer A, who is single, has taxable income of $100,000 and finds that he can, through judicious use of the tax principles associated with real estate and other tax-sheltered investments, cut this in half. Taxpayer B, who has taxable income of only $32,000, can also cut his taxable income in half by investing in tax-sheltered real estate ventures. Taxpayer B is also single. What is the percentage saving each taxpayer enjoys? The computations, using tax data from Table 1–3 in Appendix A, follow:

	Taxpayer A		*Taxpayer B*	
	Taxable Income	Income Tax	Taxable Income	Income Tax
Before investing	$100,000	$53,000	$32,000	$10,290
With investment	50,000	20,190	16,000	3,830
Reduction	$ 50,000	$32,900	$16,000	$ 6,460
Percentage change	50%	62%	50%	63%

We hasten to assure dubious readers of the legality of the tax avoidance opportunities to which they are about to be introduced. Justice Learned Hand, though presenting a dissenting opinion, eloquently expressed the prevailing legal opinion when he wrote: ". . . there is nothing sinister in so arranging one's affairs as to keep taxes as low as possible."

WHO CAN BENEFIT

This book is intended for all current or would-be owners of real estate, whether the property be a simple cottage or a massive regional shopping center. The principles we demonstrate are applicable at both these extremes and at all intermediate points. Whether property is intended for one's personal use or for investment or business use, careful planning with an eye toward the tax consequences of every decision pays large dividends.

Brokers and salesmen also find the book helpful. Their ability to point to the tax implications of property purchase or sale proves a powerful marketing tool. The good will attendant to helping clients avoid needless tax liability builds valuable client loyalty.

How Investors and Owners Can Benefit. Tax shelter opportunities were generally created intentionally either as a break for special interest groups or as encouragement for types of economic activity considered to be in the public interest. A goodly portion of these special opportunities involve investment in real estate. But failure to fully understand the provisions of the Internal Revenue Code and Internal Revenue Service regulations pertaining to transactions in real property can result in an income-tax liability far in excess of that intended by the framers of the code.

Many tax-avoidance opportunities are missed due to insufficient attention to the need to comply with the often complex details of the code. Some of these missed opportunities can be salvaged by timely filing of an amended tax return, but in many cases an election once made (or missed) represents an irrevocable decision affecting one's tax liability. A prudent and knowledgeable investor can, by careful planning, avoid the anguish of realizing too late that he has needlessly incurred thousands of dollars in tax liabilities at the time of disposal of his real estate, due to decisions made (or not made) when the property was purchased 10 or 20 years earlier.

How Brokers and Salesmen Can Benefit. Knowledgeable real estate brokers often find that special provisions of the tax code contain the key to closing a deal when all else has failed to bring buyer and seller together. The tax implications of financing methods, for example, may enable the deal to be improved for one party without doing violence to the position of the other. The seller gets his price, the buyer gets his property and the broker gets his commission, because of the broker's tax savvy.

Allocation of the purchase price between land and buildings by agreement between the parties is an example of how tax knowledge can often serve the best interests of the broker's client. This allocation affects the division of the seller's gain between ordinary income and tax-favored capital gains. It also affects the extent of the tax shelter available to the buyer. But failure to specify what part of the total purchase price applies to the raw land and what part to the purchase of the improvements means the allocation has to be made in a manner that may be less favorable to the broker's client.

Where a deal is in trouble due to difficulty in obtaining financing, a broker may be able to salvage the deal by demonstrating to the seller the tax advantages of taking back a purchase money mortgage in part payment. The seller benefits by deferring recognition of a substantial portion of the taxable gain to a date when he may be in a much lower tax bracket. The buyer benefits by acquiring the property with a minimal down payment. The broker benefits by collecting a commission. All this is made possible because the broker did his income-tax homework.

To belabor the point, a broker may find he can obtain a listing not otherwise available by showing how the owner can move into another real estate investment without incurring a tax liability for his gain on disposal of the property currently owned. This can be accomplished with a like-kind exchange, as is discussed in Chapter 10.

These few examples demonstrate the potential value to a salesman or broker of a knowledge of tax law applicable to real estate ownership. The possible variations are limited only by the initiative of the person structuring the deal.

HOW THE BOOK IS ORGANIZED

This book is divided into two major sections. The first of these, comprising Chapters 2 and 3, deals with the tax implications of property held exclusively for one's personal use. But many of the rules discussed require advance rather than post hoc planning. Homeowners, therefore, should study carefully these two chapters. Likewise, the ideas contained in Chapters 2 and 3 will prove invaluable aids to brokers in listing and selling residential property.

The main thrust of the book, however, is the tax consequence of acquisition, ownership, and sale of real estate held for investment or business purposes. The balance of the book is organized in the chronological sequence of events normally associated with such activity. Chapters 5 and 6 deal with the acquisition and financing of property, whereas Chapter 7 explains the tax consequences of decisions involved in ownership and operation. Chapters 8 through 10 consider the tax consequences of disposition under various circumstances. The final three chapters are concerned with special circumstances and problems the investor may encounter.

Tax specialists find the book lacking in computational details. This is an unavoidable consequence of attempting to make the book comprehensible to investors and to specialists in other fields. A wide range of alternative information sources are available to the tax specialist, while the nonspecialist has been largely ignored.

The structure and style of the book follow naturally from the intended audience. Technical language has been avoided wherever possible. Where this is not practical, or where technical language may actually contribute to clarity of exposition or facilitate the reader's grasp of concepts, the terms are explained in detail, and in layman's language. While this approach often sacrifices precision, the benefits in terms of simplicity are well worth the cost.

A tax specialist reviewing the book might be appalled at the lack of references to the code and to court decisions upon which tax rules are based. Once again, this departure from the conventional format of tax treatises reflects an attempt to better serve the nonspecialists for whom the book is intended. Reference to the applicable section of the code is generally incorporated into the explanation of each tax rule. Readers seeking more detailed coverage or technical references are invited to refer to any of several fine reference services available at most university and public libraries.

Consistent with the nontechnical treatment of the subject, chapter bibliographies are limited to those articles and books written generally for the nonspecialist. In many instances, references are skimpy if not altogether absent. This is a consequence of the Tax Reform Act of 1976, which rendered much of the available literature obsolete. References include only topics not changed by the 1976 revision, or articles published since that date.

THE BASIC STRUCTURE OF THE TAX SYSTEM

It seems reasonable to assume that those sufficiently interested to read this far already have a basic understanding of the income-tax system. This section serves as a review and may amplify understanding. If what follows seems too elementary to justify working through the examples, skip to a chapter that holds more interest. Otherwise, bear with us while we work our way through some fundamentals.

Our discussion centers first on the tax law as it affects the individual taxpayer. Having established these rules, we close the discussion with a comprehensive example.

What Income Is Taxable. The starting point for computing taxable income is the taxpayer's *gross income*. Gross income consists of revenue from all sources and is reduced by certain adjustments, deductions, and exemptions to arrive at *taxable income*. The distinction between adjustments, deductions, and exemptions is somewhat subtle, but becomes clear when the forms and schedules provided by the Internal Revenue Service are used.

Gross income, once again, is simply all income not specifically excluded by statute. Typical sources are wages and salaries, dividends and interest, pensions and annuities, rents, royalties, sales and exchanges of assets, and revenue from the operation of a business or a farm.

Adjusted gross income is simply gross income minus all *adjustments*. There are specific types of adjustments applying to each possible source of gross income. Sick pay, moving expenses, and unreimbursed business expenses, for example, are subtracted from salaries and wages. The cost of operations is subtracted from revenue from a business or firm. Acquisition and selling costs are subtracted from proceeds from the sale of assets.

From adjusted gross income, the taxpayer subtracts deductions and exemptions to arrive at *taxable income*. Deductions are certain expenditures made during the taxable year that are allowed by law to be offset against adjusted gross income to reduce the portion of one's earnings subject to taxation. These itemized deductions include certain medical expenses, contributions to qualified charities, interest expenses not incurred in one's income-generating activities, taxes to states and political subdistricts, and so forth. The list of allowable deductions is lengthy and should be studied carefully.

Exemptions are based upon the number of persons dependent upon the taxpayer for support. There are additional exemptions for taxpayers who are elderly or blind.

The Standard Deduction. The distinction between an adjustment and a deduction is not trivial. If it proves beneficial to the taxpayer, he may elect to take a minimum standard deduction instead of itemizing his specific deductions. The standard deduction is based upon the amount of adjusted gross income reported, with a maximum that varies with the taxpayer's domestic status. It is advantageous for a taxpayer using the standard deduction to include in adjustments all items that qualify, since he loses the benefit of itemization when he takes the standard deduction. Adjustments are often referred to as "above-the-line" items whereas deductions are "below-the-line."

Computing the Tax Liability. Having subtracted all adjustments, deductions, and exemptions to arrive at taxable income, the result is divided into ordinary income and what we summarily refer to at this point as capital gains. One must also determine the portion of income, if any, that qualifies as tax-exempt. Finally, one must determine if any of the income falls into special provisions enabling its recognition to be deferred until some future date. Each of these factors merits separate consideration.

Capital gains (and losses) result from the sale or other disposition of assets not held specifically for resale. Capital gains that are classified as long-term are given preferential treatment, which results in their generally being taxed at a rate about one-half that of ordinary income. Gains and losses on the disposition of real estate qualify as capital items unless the seller is deemed to be a dealer in real estate who was holding the property specifically for resale. Capital-gains computations are explained in Chapter 8.

Tax-exempt income includes interest on bonds or certain other obligations of states, cities, and other political subdivisions of a state. Such income is not directly subject to taxation but it does figure in the computation of the taxpayer's minimum tax liability, explained on page 59.

It is also possible to structure certain transactions so that the gain may be deferred until a later date, or perhaps never be taxed at all. Examples include sales reported on the installment method and like-kind exchanges. Installment-method reporting enables the seller to defer paying taxes on the gain until he collects the proceeds from the sale, where the collection is in a subsequent taxable period. When there is an exchange of like-kind property, it is often the case that no gain or loss is recognized on the transaction, no matter what the amount of such gain or loss. Installment sales are discussed in Chapter 9, and like-kind exchanges, in Chapter 10.

The balance of taxable income is *ordinary income* and is taxable according to the tax rate tables on pages 15 through 17. Note that different rates apply depending upon whether the taxpayer is married and filing a joint return with his spouse, married and filing separately, single, or an unmarried head of household.

Example 1–2

An unmarried taxpayer has income from a salary of $12,000 and gross revenue from operation of a part-time business enterprise of $8000. His business operating expenses are $6000, and he has unreimbursed expenses in connection with his full-time job of $500. He has no other adjustments. He has deductions of $1200. Also, he has two dependents. His tax liability is computed as follows:

Step 1. Determine gross income.

Salaries and wages		$12,000
Business income		8,000
Total (gross income)		$20,000

Step 2. Determine adjusted gross income.

Gross income (from *Step 1*)		$20,000
Less adjustments–business expenses:		
Unreimbursed from full-time job	$ 500	
From business operation	6,000	6,500
Adjusted gross income		$13,500

Step 3. Determine taxable income.

Adjusted gross income (from *Step 2*)		$13,500
Less:		
Deductions (standard deduction)*	$2,160	
Exemptions (3 at $750)†	2,250	4,410
Taxable income		$ 9,090

Step 4. Compute tax liability. In this example, we have simply assumed there is no tax-exempt income and that there were no transactions involving capital assets. These issues are introduced at a later stage in the discussion. All the taxpayer's taxable income is, therefore, taxable as ordinary income. We can determine his liability by reference to the tax rate tables at the end of the chapter.

If the taxpayer is married and filing separately from his spouse, or if he is unmarried and does not qualify as head of household, his tax is computed with reference to Table 1–3, page 17.

We have assumed our taxpayer is an unmarried head of household, so the appropriate reference is Table 1–2, page 16.

Tax on first $8000	$1,480
Plus 25% of income in excess of $8000	
(0.23 × $1090)	251
Total tax liability	$1,731

* The standard deduction (in 1977) is 16% of adjusted gross income or $2,400, whichever is less. Sixteen percent of adjusted gross is $2,160, so this is the maximum standard deduction. This exceeds the itemized deductions, so the taxpayer elects to take the standard deduction.

† The exemptions are $750 for oneself and $750 for each dependent. We have assumed for simplicity that the taxpayer is neither blind or over 65.

Special Tax Limit on Personal Services Income. The tax rate tables in Appendix A reflect a maximum incremental tax rate of 70%. This rate applies to all income over $200,000 for married taxpayers filing joint returns, and to much lower incomes for everyone else.

Responding to the number of professionals who were incorporating their practice to escape these almost confiscatory rates, the Congress provided that a maximum rate of 50% will apply to income from rendering personal services. This includes salaries and wages and all other compensation for personal services. It also includes pensions, annuities, and deferred compensation. All other income is subject to the incremental rates indicated in the tax tables.

Computational problems arise in connection with the maximum tax on personal-service income when it is subject to the 50% rate, and where there is also income from other sources that is subject to taxation at rates about 50%. The computation involves discontinuity in the application of the rate tables. This problem is explained in detail in Chapter 4.

Minimum Tax on Preference Items. A second complication often encountered by taxpayers who invest in real estate involves obligation for a minimum tax arising from certain items called "tax preferences." These preference items are deductions that reduce taxable income without requiring a current cash outlay. This subject is also covered in Chapter 4.

SOME FUNDAMENTAL IDEAS

The tax literature is cluttered with legal and technical terms having special definitions that foil the reader not schooled in legal and accounting terminology. This book has been written with a constant view toward its general readability. Accordingly, we have tried to avoid the more abstruse terms with which the literature abounds. It remains necessary, however, to resort to certain concepts that form a convenient "shorthand" language in taxation. These are introduced where needed to enhance the clarity of the text. Several such fundamental ideas are set forth in this chapter before proceeding to a discussion of the basic tax factors involved in real estate transactions.

The Meaning and Importance of the Property "Basis." The term "basis" as used in the tax literature can be thought of as the constructive cost of property. This includes all costs incurred in acquiring and defending title to the property. It does not, however, include any cost of arranging financing.

Example 1–3

Smith agrees to pay $30,000 for property intended for his personal use. He pays an attorney $450 for representation at the closing and incurs the following additional expenses: survey, $90; documentary tax, $2; loan origination fee, $275; insurance, $65. His share of the property tax proration is $80. Smith's basis is $30,542, comprised of the purchase price, attorney's fee, survey, and documentary tax. The loan origination fee, insurance, and property taxes are not involved in procuring and defending his title and, therefore, are not a part of the constructive cost.

Special rules apply for determining the basis of property acquired by gift or inheritance, or received in trade. These special rules are explained in Chapter 3.

The Adjusted Basis. The basis is adjusted for subsequent expenditures that are considered to be capital items and for deductions that decrease the value or useful life. This adjusted basis is then used to compute the gain or loss when the property is ultimately disposed of. The adjusted basis is subtracted from the amount realized to find the gain or loss on disposal.

Subsequent expenditures that have the effect of increasing the adjusted basis of the property include all outlays that increase the property's market value, extend its useful life, or convert it to an alternative use. Certain events that reduce the market value or useful life of the property have the effect of decreasing the owner's tax basis. Examples include the sale of a part of the property, as well as casualty losses or involuntary conversions as discussed in Chapter 2. All these changes represent adjustments to the owner's tax basis. The adjusted basis is employed to compute the gain or loss on a sale or exchange.

Example 1–4

Brown purchases a home for $30,000 and incurs closing costs of $350 that are includable in his basis. He subsequently adds a patio at a cost of $850. A shed representing $400 of the original cost is destroyed by a storm. Brown collects insurance on this loss. Brown then sells the property, realizing $35,000 on the sale. His adjusted basis at the time of sale is computed as follows:

Original purchase price	$30,000
Closing costs included in basis	350
Brown's basis at the time of purchase	$30,350
Add expenditures increasing the value of the property (new patio)	850
Deduct compensated involuntary conversion (shed destroyed by storm)	(400)
Brown's adjusted basis at the time he sells	$30,800

Amount Realized from Conversion. The term "amount realized" is employed repeatedly in discussions concerning the computation of a gain or loss on a sale of exchange. This is the net amount of money and the fair market value of any other property or service received, plus net debt relief, minus all selling costs. Detailed instructions for computing the amount realized are presented in Chapters 3 and 9.

What Is a Purchase or Sale? For tax purposes, a purchase or sale is a transaction in which property is transferred between persons for money. The money may be payable either at the time of title transfer or at some future date. That is, a sale or purchase involves a transfer of property for either cash or a promise to pay cash. If the consideration is in some form other than money or evidence of indebtedness, then there has been an exchange rather than a purchase or sale. This is an important distinction in terms of the tax liability arising from transactions involving property held for income or business purposes. Whether a transaction involves a sale or an exchange is of less significance in the case of property held for personal use.

Example 1-5

Jones agrees to convey his property for $32,000 payable as follows: $5000 in marketable securities plus $3200 in cash to be delivered at the time of closing, the balance to be paid in equal monthly installments over 20 years as evidenced by a note and first mortgage on the property. The transaction is defined for tax purposes as an exchange, because it involves the transfer of property other than money or a promise to pay money in exchange for the real property (i.e., marketable securities).

When Is a Transaction Completed? In general, a taxable event does not occur until the sale has been closed, ordinarily upon delivery of the deed. Note that it is not necessary for the purchaser to have taken physical possession of the property, only that there has been delivery of the deed and an unqualified right of the seller to receive compensation. Even in the absence of delivery of the deed, it is possible to satisfy the requirements of the tax code for a taxable event to have occurred. If the buyer secures possession and exercises all the rights of ownership under an unconditional contract of purchase that absolutely obligates the seller to deliver a deed and the purchaser to tender the agreed compensation, the Internal Revenue Service holds that a transaction has occurred.

Capital Gain or Loss? A capital gain or loss is the difference between the amount realized on disposal and the adjusted basis of a capital item, or any property to the extent treated as a capital item. This classification is sufficiently broad to include all real estate.

A basic determinant of the treatment accorded capital gains is the length of time the property was owned. Gains on the sale of property held for 12 months or less are classified as "short-term." If the gain stems from the sale or exchange or property held for *more than* 12 months, there is a "long-term" capital gain.

The distinction between long- and short-term capital gains is important because only one-half the long-term gain need be reported as taxable income. This is accomplished on the tax form (Schedule D) provided for reporting sales of real property. The taxpayer is instructed to deduct 50% of the "excess" (i.e., of the net long-term gain) before reporting the balance from Form D on his tax return, Form 1040. The practical effect is that long-term capital gains are taxed at approximately one-half the rate of ordinary income.

The analysis is more complex when there are both capital gains and losses, or when the taxpayer is in a very high tax bracket. A discussion of the more complex situation is included in Chapter 8.

A NOTE OF CAUTION

It has been observed that all of the words in the Internal Revenue Code make sense until they are combined into sentences! The code includes approximately 18 pages telling what income is taxable. This is followed by about 3000 pages of exceptions, qualifications, loopholes, and attempts to close loopholes.

Compounding the problem, the taxpayer faces over 5000 pages of explanations and implementation regulations issued by the Treasury Department. Not to be outdone, the Internal Revenue Service has "explained" the Treasury Department explanations and published rulings to spell out the tax effects of numerous types of transactions.

Their profuseness notwithstanding, Treasury Department and Internal Revenue Service publications are perhaps a minor portion of the authority for federal taxation. They are overshadowed by a massive judicial outpouring. Resulting from litigation of disputes between taxpayer and tax collector, these judicial decisions form the basis for subsequent decisions and comprise several volumes of extremely small print. In keeping with the general lack of order and logic in much of the area of taxation, not all federal courts agree on the issues. The result is that what is allowable in one part of the country may involve the taxpayer in litigation elsewhere.

Although this book concerns itself with only a small portion of the total income-tax law, even that minute segment can be handled in only a precursory fashion in a single volume of this size. The attempt to treat the tax rules in a manner comprehensible to those untutored in law and accounting forces us to ignore some of the finer points of the law. The reader should heed well, therefore, the caveat that the book is intended primarily to alert him to the tax implications of real estate ownership and transactions. Competent tax counsel should always be sought prior to committing oneself in any real estate deal. The book should prove invaluable as a reference source for tax planning and as an aid in recognizing tax-avoidance opportunities. It is manifestly not intended as a primary source of tax-computation guidance.

The reader should also avoid the trap of becoming so enamored of the tax-shelter possibilities of a proposed investment that he loses sight of the basic investment quality of the opportunity.

As this book is being written, the financial press is awash with horror stories of fortunes lost in cattle-feeding operations and limited partnerships involved in luxury condominium construction. In some instances, these losses have resulted from investing in well-structured tax-shelter opportunities that have run afoul in the current economic climate. But many of them were poorly conceived deals that would probably have failed even under the best economic conditions. Their appeal was founded almost entirely on the basis of the tax shelter offered the investor. The unfortunate result has been, all too often, that there is no income left to shelter.

APPENDIX A: TAX RATE TABLES

The following tax rate tables were in effect in 1976. They indicate the tax liability associated with different levels of net taxable income (after all deductions and exemptions). They are not adjusted to reflect temporary tax credits or other adjustments intended to function as temporary inflation or recession countermeasures.

TABLE 1-1. TAX RATE TABLE FOR MARRIED INDIVIDUALS FILING JOINT RETURNS AND SURVIVING SPOUSES

Taxable Income		
Over–	But less than–	Income Tax Liability
$ 0	$ 1,000	$ plus 14% of income over $ 0
$ 1,000	$ 2,000	$ 140 plus 15% of income over $ 1,000
$ 2,000	$ 3,000	$ 290 plus 16% of income over $ 2,000
$ 3,000	$ 4,000	$ 450 plus 17% of income over $ 3,000
$ 4,000	$ 8,000	$ 620 plus 19% of income over $ 4,000
$ 8,000	$ 12,000	$ 1,380 plus 22% of income over $ 8,000
$ 12,000	$ 16,000	$ 2,260 plus 25% of income over $ 12,000
$ 16,000	$ 20,000	$ 3,260 plus 28% of income over $ 16,000
$ 20,000	$ 24,000	$ 4,380 plus 32% of income over $ 20,000
$ 24,000	$ 28,000	$ 5,660 plus 36% of income over $ 24,000
$ 28,000	$ 32,000	$ 7,100 plus 39% of income over $ 28,000
$ 32,000	$ 36,000	$ 8,660 plus 42% of income over $ 32,000
$ 36,000	$ 40,000	$ 10,340 plus 45% of income over $ 36,000
$ 40,000	$ 44,000	$ 12,140 plus 48% of income over $ 40,000
$ 44,000	$ 52,000	$ 14,060 plus 50% of income over $ 44,000
$ 52,000	$ 64,000	$ 18,060 plus 53% of income over $ 52,000
$ 64,000	$ 76,000	$ 24,420 plus 55% of income over $ 64,000
$ 76,000	$ 88,000	$ 31,020 plus 58% of income over $ 76,000
$ 88,000	$100,000	$ 37,980 plus 60% of income over $ 88,000
$100,000	$120,000	$ 45,180 plus 62% of income over $100,000
$120,000	$140,000	$ 57,580 plus 64% of income over $120,000
$140,000	$160,000	$ 70,380 plus 66% of income over $140,000
$160,000	$180,000	$ 83,580 plus 68% of income over $160,000
$180,000	$200,000	$ 97,180 plus 69% of income over $180,000
$200,000	—	$110,980 plus 70% of income over $200,000

TABLE 1–2. TAX RATE TABLE FOR HEADS OF HOUSEHOLDS

Taxable Income		
Over–	But less than–	Income Tax Liability
$ 0	$ 1,000	$ 0 plus 14% of income over $ 0
$ 1,000	$ 2,000	$ 140 plus 16% of income over $ 1,000
$ 2,000	$ 4,000	$ 300 plus 18% of income over $ 2,000
$ 4,000	$ 6,000	$ 660 plus 19% of income over $ 4,000
$ 6,000	$ 8,000	$ 1,040 plus 22% of income over $ 6,000
$ 8,000	$ 10,000	$ 1,480 plus 23% of income over $ 8,000
$ 10,000	$ 12,000	$ 1,940 plus 25% of income over $ 10,000
$ 12,000	$ 14,000	$ 2,440 plus 27% of income over $ 12,000
$ 14,000	$ 16,000	$ 2,980 plus 28% of income over $ 14,000
$ 16,000	$ 18,000	$ 3,540 plus 31% of income over $ 16,000
$ 18,000	$ 20,000	$ 4,160 plus 32% of income over $ 18,000
$ 20,000	$ 22,000	$ 4,800 plus 35% of income over $ 20,000
$ 22,000	$ 24,000	$ 5,500 plus 36% of income over $ 22,000
$ 24,000	$ 26,000	$ 6,220 plus 38% of income over $ 24,000
$ 26,000	$ 28,000	$ 6,980 plus 41% of income over $ 26,000
$ 28,000	$ 32,000	$ 7,800 plus 42% of income over $ 28,000
$ 32,000	$ 36,000	$ 9,480 plus 45% of income over $ 32,000
$ 36,000	$ 38,000	$ 11,200 plus 48% of income over $ 36,000
$ 38,000	$ 40,000	$ 12,240 plus 51% of income over $ 38,000
$ 40,000	$ 44,000	$ 13,260 plus 52% of income over $ 40,000
$ 44,000	$ 50,000	$ 15,340 plus 55% of income over $ 44,000
$ 50,000	$ 52,000	$ 18,640 plus 56% of income over $ 50,000
$ 52,000	$ 64,000	$ 19,760 plus 58% of income over $ 52,000
$ 64,000	$ 70,000	$ 26,720 plus 59% of income over $ 64,000
$ 70,000	$ 76,000	$ 30,260 plus 61% of income over $ 70,000
$ 76,000	$ 80,000	$ 33,920 plus 62% of income over $ 76,000
$ 80,000	$ 88,000	$ 36,400 plus 63% of income over $ 80,000
$ 88,000	$100,000	$ 41,440 plus 64% of income over $ 88,000
$100,000	$120,000	$ 49,120 plus 66% of income over $100,000
$120,000	$140,000	$ 62,320 plus 67% of income over $120,000
$140,000	$160,000	$ 75,720 plus 68% of income over $140,000
$160,000	$180,000	$ 89,320 plus 69% of income over $160,000
$180,000	—	$103,120 plus 70% of income over $180,000

TABLE 1–3. TAX RATE TABLE FOR UNMARRIED INDIVIDUALS

Taxable Income		
Over–	But less than–	**Income Tax Liability**
$ 0	$ 500	$ 0 plus 14% of income over $ 0
$ 500	$ 1,000	$ 70 plus 15% of income over $ 500
$ 1,000	$ 1,500	$ 145 plus 16% of income over $ 1,000
$ 1,500	$ 2,000	$ 225 plus 17% of income over $ 1,500
$ 2,000	$ 4,000	$ 310 plus 19% of income over $ 2,000
$ 4,000	$ 6,000	$ 690 plus 21% of income over $ 4,000
$ 6,000	$ 8,000	$ 1,110 plus 24% of income over $ 6,000
$ 8,000	$ 10,000	$ 1,590 plus 25% of income over $ 8,000
$ 10,000	$ 12,000	$ 2,090 plus 27% of income over $ 10,000
$ 12,000	$ 14,000	$ 2,630 plus 29% of income over $ 12,000
$ 14,000	$ 16,000	$ 3,210 plus 31% of income over $ 14,000
$ 16,000	$ 18,000	$ 3,830 plus 34% of income over $ 16,000
$ 18,000	$ 20,000	$ 4,510 plus 36% of income over $ 18,000
$ 20,000	$ 22,000	$ 5,230 plus 38% of income over $ 20,000
$ 22,000	$ 26,000	$ 5,990 plus 40% of income over $ 22,000
$ 26,000	$ 32,000	$ 7,590 plus 45% of income over $ 26,000
$ 32,000	$ 38,000	$10,290 plus 50% of income over $ 32,000
$ 38,000	$ 44,000	$13,290 plus 55% of income over $ 38,000
$ 44,000	$ 50,000	$16,590 plus 60% of income over $ 44,000
$ 50,000	$ 60,000	$20,190 plus 62% of income over $ 50,000
$ 60,000	$ 70,000	$26,390 plus 64% of income over $ 60,000
$ 70,000	$ 80,000	$32,790 plus 66% of income over $ 70,000
$ 80,000	$ 90,000	$39,390 plus 68% of income over $ 80,000
$ 90,000	$100,000	$46,190 plus 69% of income over $ 90,000
$100,000	—	$53,090 plus 70% of income over $100,000

CHAPTER 2

ACQUISITION AND OWNERSHIP OF REAL ESTATE FOR PERSONAL USE

Almost everything an owner does from the time he acquires real estate through the point of disposal affects his income-tax liability. Many events that "just happen," such as damage to property or condemnation by the government, also have important tax implications. Yet the owner often gives little thought to the tax consequences of his decisions, other than considering the deductibility of mortgage interest payments. Opportunities to reduce his tax obligation through the timing and structure of transactions are often completely overlooked. The scale and ubiquity of income-tax consequences are such that this oversight can be very costly.

This chapter discusses the tax consequences of acquisition and ownership of real estate for the owner's personal use. All real property *not* being held as an investment or for use in a trade or business is included in this category. The chapter explores how the manner of acquisition affects the tax basis and thus the tax consequences when property is ultimately sold.

Both the immediate and the long-range tax implications of transactions affecting the property are analyzed in this chapter. Certain expenditures that can be included in the owner's tax basis during his period of ownership are discussed. The tax effects of destruction of real property by forces outside the control of the owner are also considered. The chapter concludes with an explanation of the proper tax treatment of the various elements in the "carrying costs" and a discussion of tax strategies available to the present and potential property owner.

WHEN IS PROPERTY HELD "FOR PERSONAL USE"?

Essentially, any property not held for productive use in a trade or business, or for investment, can be said to be held for personal use. It does not matter that the property also yields some income. If the primary motive for ownership is not pecuniary, the proper tax treatment is that accorded property held for personal use.

It is not always clear whether real estate is held primarily for personal, business, or investment reasons. The Internal Revenue Service has become increasingly aggressive in challenging taxpayers who, in the absence of clear substantiating evidence, claim the most advantageous usage. They have, for example, challenged the claim that a previous residence, rented out prior to being sold, qualifies for the special tax treatment accorded the disposal of a personal residence. Their argument was that the property had been abandoned as a personal residence and converted to income property. In other cases, the government has challenged deductions for expenses on property held for income or investment purposes, maintaining that the real motivation was personal use.

The actual realization of income is not necessarily essential to support a claim that property has been converted from personal to income use. Nor does the receipt of income necessarily defeat a claim that property is held for personal use. But in either instance, the taxpayer must be able to present proof of his intent.

The principle is illustrated by a case in which expense deductions were allowed for a house listed with a broker for renting and shown to several prospective renters, even though the house was not rented. The listing and showing were sufficient to establish intent. But a taxpayer who rented his former residence to the eventual purchaser until the latter party sold his own home was denied a deduction for a loss on the transaction. The deduction was denied on the basis that the property was held for personal rather than income-producing purposes. The rental agreement with the eventual purchaser was held to have been incidental to the sale, and not proof of the owner's intention to convert the property to income use.

In other cases, the courts have upheld the disallowance of an expense deduction based on the claim that property was being held for income purposes, holding that the primary motive was other than pecuniary. Property rented to relatives at less than its fair market rental value, with no attempt to rent it to outsiders, represented such a case. In another instance, deductions in excess of income were denied in the case of a vacation cottage. But the fact that the owner makes occasional personal use of property held primarily for income purposes is not sufficient in itself to defeat a claim that the property is not held for personal use.

COMPUTING THE TAX BASIS OF PROPERTY ACQUIRED BY PURCHASE OR EXCHANGE

The concept of the tax basis of real property is introduced in Chapter 1. Recall that the adjusted basis is subtracted from the selling price to compute the taxable gain when property is sold. One, of course, would like to pay as little as possible for the property when acquired. But having arrived at terms acceptable to both parties, the buyer should structure the transaction to achieve the highest possible basis, so as to incur a minimum income-tax liability when he disposes of the property.

This section discusses the effect on the basis of each step in the purchase process. It provides the guidance necessary to determine which of the numerous expenditures incident to the acquisition are properly added to the basis, which are a tax deductible expense and which have no tax consequences whatsoever.

The Purchase Offer. The typical first step in acquiring real estate is to make a written offer to purchase. This offer is (usually) accompanied by an "earnest money" deposit to be applied to the purchase price at the time title is transferred. When the transaction is completed, the deposit is considered a part of the purchase price and is included in the basis of the purchased property.

Should the prospective purchaser decide not to complete the transaction, he may be required to forfeit his earnest money deposit. To avoid this situation, the written offer should very carefully spell out the various conditions under which the buyer may decline to complete the transaction and have his deposit promptly returned.

Forfeiture of the earnest money deposit has no tax consequences to the prospective purchaser–it does not involve a tax-deductible loss. The offer and deposit were in effect an option to purchase. The loss from failure to exercise the option is treated as a loss from the sale of the option. Such a loss is considered to be from the sale or exchange of property that has the same character as the optioned property. Since a loss from sale of property held for personal use is not tax deductible, neither is the loss from forfeiture of the earnest money deposit. Note that if the optioned property were intended for revenue-generating purposes (e.g., as rental property), the loss would be deductible.

Completing the Transaction. Assuming the transaction is completed as specified in the offer and acceptance, the tax basis to the purchaser consists of the purchase price plus certain of the additional costs incurred at time of closing. Since some of the closing costs are tax deductible in the year of purchase, whereas some are included in the basis and certain others have no tax consequences, it is important to analyze carefully the nature of each item on the closing statement.

The basic rule is that all costs involved in obtaining title (but not for arranging financing) constitute costs of purchase and form the basis for computing the gain or loss on a later sale. Costs such as title examinations, property surveys, appraisals (if not for purposes of securing financing), attorney's fees, commissions and recording fees, when paid by the purchaser, increase the basis of the property. Special provisions for costs incurred in selling or buying a personal residence by persons moving as a result of a change in location of employment may enable these costs to be deducted in the year incurred. These provisions are explained in Chapter 3.

The cost of the acquired property includes payments made with borrowed funds as well as from the funds of the purchaser. It includes the fair market value of any property given in exchange and the amount of any mortgage encumbrance on the property at the time title passes to the purchaser, without regard to whether the purchaser becomes personally liable for the outstanding debt. The effect remains the same even if the outstanding debt is payable to the purchaser himself.

The thrust of the law and judicial decision seems to be that the cost includes any "economic benefit" given to acquire title. The buyer's basis has been held to include, for example, the fair market value of the right given the seller to occupy the premises for a period on a rent-free basis.

Certain other charges incurred at the time of closing are only incidental to the purchase. They are a result of ownership of the property rather than to the purchase or the financing. In this category are real estate taxes, utility bills, fire insurance premiums, heating fuels, and the like. These items typically are prorated between buyer and seller at the time of closing. The only item among them that has tax significance to the purchaser of property for personal use is real estate taxes. Section 164(d) of the code provides that taxes for the year of sale be prorated between buyer and seller on the basis of the number of days during the year that each owned the property. This approach must be used for tax purposes regardless of how the proration is handled at the closing. The buyer's share of the real estate taxes constitute a tax deductible expense to him. If the purchase contract provides that the purchaser must pay or assume liability for real estate taxes that are imposed upon the seller under the apportionment rule of Section 164(d), this becomes a part of the consideration and should be added to the purchaser's tax basis.

Financing the Acquisition. Charges by a lending institution incident to mortgage financing are not a tax-deductible item to the borrower. Neither may such expenses be added to the purchase price to increase the tax basis of the acquired property. But these incidental charges by the lender are not to be confused with the lender's origination fee, commonly called "points."

Points paid on indebtedness in connection with the purchase or improvement of a personal residence are generally deductible as interest expense in the year of payment. But this applies only if such charges are a general business practice in the area, and if the amount does not exceed that usually charged for the size and type loan being negotiated. If the purpose of the loan is other than for purchase or improvement of the residence, then the points are not currently deductible. Note also that the points are not deductible if the property is other than the taxpayer's personal residence.

Points that do not satisfy the criteria for current deductibility may be deductible as interest expense ratably over the period of the loan.

The fees charged by the Veterans Administration and the Federal Housing Administration are in the nature of a service charge rather than prepaid interest. They are, therefore, not deductible as interest expense. Chapter 3 explains special circumstances under which Federal Housing Administration and Veterans Administration charges may be included as tax-deductible moving expenses for persons buying a new home incident to a change in location of employment.

Importance of Good Records. At the time buyer and seller meet to close the transaction, the purchaser is presented with a closing statement detailing all the costs involved in the purchase. This very important document forms the basic supporting evidence for including the appropriate items of closing costs in the original tax basis of the property. Subsequent additions and improvements that increase the basis should be supported by paid in-

Example 2–1

Weems agrees to buy for his personal use a vacation lodge at a price of $43,000. At the closing, he is presented with this statement:

Charges:			
Purchase price		$43,000	
Fire insurance (remaining term of prepaid policy to be transferred to grantee)		125	
Personal property (refrigerator and drapes to be transferred by bill of sale)		875	
Finance charges:			
Survey	$ 75		
Appraisal	40		
Credit report	20		
Loan origination fee*	344	479	
Attorney's fee		300	
Recording fee		3	
Total charges			$44,782
Credits:			
Mortgage loan		$34,400	
Earnest money deposit		500	
Total credits			$34,900
Balance (due in cash at closing)			$ 9,882

Of the $479 finance charge, only $344 (the loan origination fee) is a tax-deductible expense. The remaining finance charges are "service fees" having no tax consequences. The fire insurance and the cost of the refrigerator and drapes are also personal expenses having no tax consequences. Weems's tax basis at the time of purchase is $43,303, computed as follows:

Purchase price	$43,000
Attorney's fee	300
Recording fee	3
Total (original tax basis)	$43,303

* Clearly identified as an interest charge.

voices from contractors and suppliers. All these documents must be carefully preserved to substantiate the owner's adjusted basis for computing his tax liability when he disposes of the property.

When the Internal Revenue Service challenges a tax return, the burden of proof is upon the taxpayer, not the government. The courts have in many cases denied deductions where the taxpayer failed to maintain adequate records to support his claim. It is important, therefore, to carefully document all transactions and preserve all records.

ACQUISITION OF REAL ESTATE OTHER THAN BY PURCHASE OR EXCHANGE

An open market purchase is, of course, not the only way to acquire property. Many owners receive their property as a gift or by inheritance. Special rules apply to the computation of the owner's tax basis in these instances.

The Basis of Property Received as a Gift. The basis to the recipient of a gift of real property is generally the adjusted basis of the last owner who did not acquire the property by gift, plus or minus any allowable adjustments taken while the property was held by any gift recipient since that time. This amount is increased by any gift tax paid by the donor, with the limiting provision that the adjustment for gift tax cannot increase the basis above the property's fair market value at the time of the gift. The basis of the gift to the recipient, therefore, may be a great deal less than its fair market value at the time the gift was made. If the recipient disposes of a gift and experiences a *loss* on the transaction, the basis for purposes of computing his loss is the lesser of the basis as described or the fair market value at the time the gift was made. This is a significant consideration in the case of property held as an investment, or for use in a trade or business.

Example 2–2

Smith makes a gift to his daughter of land having a fair market value of $18,000. Smith's basis was $17,900. He incurs a gift tax liability of $140 on the gift. The tax basis to his daughter is computed as follows:

Basis of donor	$17,900
Gift tax	140
Original basis plus gift tax	$18,040
Fair market value	$18,000

Since the adjustment for the gift tax would increase the basis above the fair market value of the gift, the daughter's basis is limited to the fair market value of $18,000.

The Basis of Property Received by Inheritance. The general rule is that the basis of inherited property is the same as its basis in the hands of the decedent. Exceptions to this rule apply to situations where federal and state taxes are levied based on the property's appreciated value. A second exception is the "fresh start" rule. A final exception is due to application of the "minimum carry-over basis" rule.

If the fair market value of the aggregate estate of the decedent is $60,000 or more, then the estate's aggregate carry-over basis cannot be less than $60,000, regardless of its basis in the hands of the decedent. Thus if the market value is more than $60,000, whereas the decedent's basis was less than $60,000, the aggregate carry-over basis is the lesser of $60,000 or the decedent's basis plus estate and succession taxes levied on a valuation in excess of the decedent's basis. The increased basis due to application of the minimum carry-over basis rule is allocated to the various portions of the estate in proportion to their net appreciation.

The "fresh start" rule applies to property that has substantially appreciated over the period held by the decedent. A carry-over of the decedent's basis would subject the recipient to an unfair capital-gains tax when he disposes of the property. For purposes of computing the taxable gain when the property is subsequently sold, the basis is the value of the property as of December 31, 1976, where the value on this date exceeds the decedent's adjusted basis. In determining this fresh start basis, the property is considered to have appreciated evenly over the period from the time acquired by the decedent to the time sold by the heir.

The Basis of Repossessed Property. Suppose an owner sells his property under a conditional sales contract or takes back a note and mortgage on the property. Suppose further that the buyer defaults and the seller repossesses the property. What is the basis of the repossessed property? It is the unrecovered portion of the defaulted debt plus costs incurred in repossession and any recognized gain on repossession.

If the repossessed property were the principal residence of the seller, and if he excluded all or a part of the gain on the original sale under special rules for taxpayers 65 years of age or older, or in contemplation of or actual purchase of a qualifying replacement home, then the basis of the repossessed property varies depending upon how soon it is resold. If the repossessed personal residence is sold again within 1 year after repossession, the basis is the old adjusted basis plus or minus any subsequent adjustments (e.g., improvements or involuntary conversions). The gain on the original sale and repossession and the gain or loss on the final sale are all treated as a gain on a single transaction. If the repossessed residence is not sold within 1 year, however, the special rules do not apply. In that case, the treatment is the same as for any other property.

These rules apply whether the repossession is by foreclosure sale or other means (such as voluntary conveyance in satisfaction of the related debt). It should also be noted that subsequent recovery of any part of the unsatisfied debt obligation does not affect the basis of the reposessed property. But any such sums recovered must be reported as ordinary income.

TAKING TITLE TO THE PROPERTY

For married purchasers, the question arises as to whether title should vest solely in one individual or be held by both spouses. Prudent buyers carefully consider the estate and gift-tax implications of this decision. The major alternatives to having title vest solely in one spouse are tenancy in common or joint tenancy.

Tenancy in Common. If real property held solely by one spouse is subsequently conveyed to both spouses as tenants in common, liability for gift tax may be incurred on one-half the value of the granting spouse's equity in the property. If the property was originally acquired by a couple as tenants in common but the funds of only one spouse were involved, liability for gift tax on one-half the spouse's equity in the property may similarly be incurred.

Note that the gift-tax liability is based only on the owner's equity in the property, that is, the value of his interest rather than the value of the property itself. If (as is usually the case at the time of the purchase) there is a substantial mortgage involved, the value of the spouse's interest, and thus of the gift, may be quite small. Note also that the gift-tax laws provide for an unlimited marital deduction for the first $100,000 of lifetime gifts between spouses, and a 50% deduction for lifetime gifts in excess of $200,000. In addition, there is a $3000 annual exclusion, and a liberal "lifetime credit." It is probable that these provisions would enable the parties to avoid any gift-tax liability. And by holding the property as tenants in common, the couple may reduce estate-tax liability upon the death of the wealthier spouse. Estate and gift taxes are explored more fully in Chapter 3.

Joint Tenancy. The popularity of joint tenancy springs from the right of survivorship involved. The property of the surviving spouse is removed from the estate of the deceased, and probate is avoided. The tax laws provide that creation of a tenancy by the entirety, including joint tenancy with right of survivorship, does not result in a taxable gift unless the parties elect to treat the transaction as such.

ADJUSTMENTS TO THE TAX BASIS

In this section, we consider transactions affecting the basis after the initial acquisition of property. Transactions increasing the basis are considered first. This is followed by an analysis of the major types of transactions that decrease the basis.

Capital Improvements and Betterments. Certain expenditures on property may reasonably be expected to increase its useful life or current market value. Such expenditures may properly be added to the basis of the property. Examples include roof replacement, modernized lighting, and addition of space or amenities.

Expenditures that are necessary to maintain the current usefulness of the property and that do not extend its useful life or increase its market value are considered to be repairs and have no tax consequences. They do not affect the basis of the property. And since the property is for personal use, the repairs are not a tax-deductible expense (but see Chapter 3 for instances where "fix-up" costs just prior to selling a personal residence can be treated as a reduction in the net selling price). Examples of repair expenditures having no tax consequences are repainting, replastering, and repairing roofs, gutters, and downspouts.

Since the alternative to adding expenditures to the adjusted basis (and so reducing the potential tax liability upon disposal) is to treat them as personal expenses having no income-tax consequences, prudence dictates giving oneself the benefit of any doubt as to whether an expenditure is an improvement or a repair. If an expenditure seems to fall in a grey area between the two definitions, claim it as an improvement and thus add it to the basis of the property (recall the earlier precaution in this regard, concerning the importance of preserving complete records of all transactions). If it is a legitimate expenditure of which there is room to question the proper treatment, the only penalty should it be disallowed is a modest interest charge on the additional tax liability resulting from the disallowance.

Casualty Losses. When one suffers a casualty loss of all or a part of his real estate there may be an adjustment to the basis of the property. The exact nature of this adjustment depends upon the relationship between the amount of the loss and the amount of any compensation received, and of the choice between several tax elections available to the taxpayer. Any uninsured loss in excess of $100 is a tax-deductible item in the year of the loss. Both the loss and the tax deduction affect the adjustment to the basis of the property.

The rules described here apply to losses to nonbusiness property arising from fire, storm, shipwreck, theft, or "other casualty." The exact meaning of "other casualty" is not spelled out in the code, but it has been defined to some extent by judicial decision and rulings of the Commissioner. It appears to include both acts of nature and some events such as automobile accidents, if not caused by willful acts or willful negligence on the part of the person suffering the loss. A primary determinant seems to be whether the event causing the loss is sudden rather than due to a progressive, steady causal agent.

Where a loss has been suffered on nonbusiness real estate that qualifies for the casualty loss deduction, the allowable loss is the reduction in the value of the property due to the casualty minus the insurance coverage or other loss compensation received. The deduction relates only to uncompensated losses. Remember too the first $100 of uncompensated loss must be exempted in figuring the deductible loss.

The adjustment to the tax basis of the property involved is the total change in its value. The tax basis is reduced by the sum of the compensation received for the loss (from insurance or any other source) plus the casualty deduction allowed.

Involuntary Conversions. An involuntary conversion includes the events described here as casualties. But many events other than casualties may also constitute involuntary conversions. Such a conversion occurs any time compensation (with money or other property) is received for property that has been destroyed, stolen, or taken for public use under condemnation proceedings or threat of such proceedings.

In recognition of the involuntary nature of these events, the law provides the opportunity to defer any taxable gain resulting from the conversion. If the property converted is replaced by similar or related property (related in service or use), the taxpayer may elect not to have the gain realized for tax purpose until he subsequently disposes of the related property. This rule applies only if the replacement property costs at least as much as the taxpayer received in compensation for the converted property.

To take advantage of this provision the converted property must be replaced within a specified period. For all conversions other than condemnation, the period is 2 years after the taxable year in which the conversion occurred. In the case of condemnation, the replacement property may have been acquired prior to the actual conversion providing there was a clear threat of the impending conversion at that time and may be acquired anytime within *3* years after the first taxable year in which any compensation is received for the condemnation.

Example 2–3

Browning's home, which was insured for $40,000, is completely destroyed by fire. His adjusted basis is $28,000. Browning purchases, within the prescribed time period, a replacement home costing $42,000. He need not recognize his gain on conversion, but the basis of his new home is reduced by the amount of the unrecognized gain:

Cost of new home		$42,000
Deduct gain on conversion not recognized:		
Insurance proceeds	$40,000	
Less basis of destroyed home	28,000	12,000
Basis of new home		$30,000

If replacement property is purchased that otherwise qualifies the owner for nonrecognition of a gain on conversion but that costs less than the proceeds from conversion, a part of the gain must be recognized. Nonrecognition is permitted only to the extent that the proceeds are reinvested in the replacement property. The balance is subject to the capital-gains tax.

Example 2–4

Jones receives $6000 for property converted under condemnation proceedings. The adjusted basis of the condemned property is $4000, and replacement property costs $5500. Jones must recognize $500 of the gain. The computations follow:

Gain realized on conversion ($6000 less $4000)	$2,000
Less the excess of proceeds over cost of the replacement property ($6000 less $5500)	500
Amount of gain not recognized	$1,500
Amount of gain recognized ($2000 less $1500)	$ 500

If the nonbusiness real estate involved in an involuntary conversion is the taxpayer's personal residence, then he has a further option. He may apply these rules and elect to postpone any gain, or he may treat the event as a voluntary conversion and defer the tax liability under the rules described in Chapter 3 for sale of a personal residence. If he is 65 years of age or older, this second option allows him to exclude a part of the gain without purchasing another residence.

Where only a part of one's property is taken by condemnation, a portion of the compensation may have been for the property taken and a part for damages to the remaining property (severance damages). The portion received as severance damages reduces the tax basis of the remaining property. This reduction can be avoided if the taxpayer elects not to recognize the gain as an involuntary conversion and uses the severance damage proceeds to restore the damaged property.

If compensation for an involuntary conversion is less than the adjusted basis of the property converted, the taxpayer experiences a loss on conversion. Such a loss is not a deductible item unless it falls within the category of casualty loss described earlier.

A taxpayer experiencing a gain on an involuntary conversion and acquiring a substitute property within the prescribed time limit may elect not to defer recognition of all or a part of the gain. In that case, the basis of the replacement property is that of the old property, less the amount of compensation received in excess of the cost of the replacement property, increased by any recognized gain on conversion.

Allowance for Depreciation. The basis of property held for personal use is not adjusted to account for depreciation. But if a part of the improvements is devoted to revenue-producing activity (e.g., rented out), a depreciation adjustment may be made for that portion. The rules and methods for computing the depreciation adjustment are presented in Chapter 7.

TAX STRATEGY

Tax strategy in the purchase, use, and sale of real estate held for personal use has both similarities and important differences from the optimum strategy employed when a transaction involves investment or income property or property used in a trade or business.

The main dissimilarity concerns the treatment of expenditures on the property after acquisition. Were the property held as an investment or for use in a trade or business, one would generally prefer expenditures to be classified as maintenance expenses and so be deductible in the year incurred (see Chapter 7). But maintenance expenditures on property held for personal use are a personal expense and thus nondeductible. In this latter case, it is advantageous to have the expenditures classified as capital items. This increases the adjusted basis of the property and so reduces the tax liability when the property is sold.

Whether an expenditure is a capital item or a maintenance item is for the most part a matter of fact. If it increases the life or the current value of the property, it is a capital item. If it does not increase the life or the current value, it is not a capital item.

But there is a gray area where the facts are subject to considerable interpretation. When, for example, does roof work cease to be repair and become partial replacement? It is in situations of this sort that careful planning can yield substantial tax savings. Past rulings of the Internal Revenue Service and the courts can be a valuable guide in structuring transactions so that their capitalization goes unchallenged. An oft-cited case is that of the Illinois Merchants Trust Company versus the Internal Revenue Service, wherein the court concluded in part:

> In determining whether an expenditure is a capital one, or is chargeable against operating income, it is necessary to bear in mind the purpose for which the expenditure was made. To repair is to restore to sound state or to mend, while a replacement connotes a substitution. A repair is an expenditure for the purpose of keeping the property in an ordinarily efficient operating condition. It does not add to the value of the property, nor does it appreciably prolong its life. It merely keeps the property in an operating condition over its probable life for the uses for which it was acquired. Expenditures for that purpose are distinguishable from those for replacements, alterations, improvement or additions which prolong the life of the property, increase its value, or make it adaptable to a different use. The one is a maintenance charge, while the others are additions to capital investment which should not be applied against current earnings.

Bunching Maintenance with Capital Expenditures. Where repairs or improvements are made at the same time and under a general plan of improvement, it has been held that the total expenditure must be capitalized. This presents an important tax-saving opportunity to the owner of real estate held for personal use. Replacement of rusted gutters and downspouts, for example, taken alone would not be a capital item and so would have no tax consequences. But if included in a contract for a new roof, the entire project may be capitalized as a general plan of improvement. The trick is to "bunch" small repair and maintenance items with major improvements and capitalize the lot. It is advisable to include all such items in one construction contract and to avoid an itemization of the component cost factors.

Special Treatment of Fix-Up Costs. Any repairs needed to enhance the sales value of a building prior to its sale may be deducted from the sales price in determining the owner's taxable gain on the transaction. To qualify for this treatment, the fix-up expenditure must be incurred within 6 months of the sale.

Good Records Are Essential. The taxpayer must be able to present proof of any claimed expenditure that increases the basis of his property. The Internal Revenue Service disallowed an adjustment based on an estimate of the cost of improvements because the taxpayer could not prove the claim. The courts partly affirmed the action of the service.

SUMMARY

A purchase is considered to have been completed and a taxable event to have occurred when title passes to the purchaser or when the purchaser takes physical possession under an unconditional contract of sale with title to be delivered at a fixed or determinable future date.

The purchase price of the property and all costs incident to getting and defending title form the purchaser's original tax basis for the property. This basis, after adjusting for changes during the intervening period, is used to determine the gain or loss when the property is eventually sold. Financing fees that constitute a charge for the use of borrowed money are a tax-deductible expense to the borrower. Fees incident to acquiring a loan, but that are not a charge for the use of money, are neither a tax-deductible expense nor an addition to the basis of the property. To assure acceptance by the Internal Revenue Service of legitimate tax claims associated with the transaction, it is imperative that the taxpayer adequately document all transactions and safeguard his records.

The cost of any improvements that extend the useful life or increase the fair market value of the property may be added to its tax basis. The basis is reduced by any decline in fair market value or useful life due to fire, flood, storm, shipwreck, or other casualty. Uncompensated losses in excess of $100 are tax deductible in the year incurred.

A gain arising from an involuntary conversion may be deferred. This is accomplished (at the election of the taxpayer) by purchasing replacement property within 1 or 2 years after first receipt of compensation, depending upon the nature of the conversion.

CHAPTER 3

DISPOSAL OF REAL ESTATE HELD FOR PERSONAL USE

The previous chapter introduced the tax factors involved in the acquisition and ownership of real estate held for personal use. This chapter sets forth the tax consequences of a transfer of ownership, whether by sale, gift, trade, or the death of the owner.

The chapter proceeds directly to an analysis of the tax aspects of selling real estate. It also explains how the tax liability can be spread over several years by selling property on the installment basis. The chapter then moves to a discussion of the tax consequences of disposal by gift, will, or devise. It concludes with a presentation of special provisions applicable to the sale of real property used as the owner's principal personal residence.

TAX CONSEQUENCES OF A SALE OR EXCHANGE

The original purchase price and many subsequent transactions involving the property affect its adjusted basis when traded or sold. Indeed, in many instances, the chain of significant transactions goes back far beyond the time the property was purchased. This would be the case, for instance, if the present property were a replacement for property lost in an involuntary conversion, or if it were a replacement home taking the adjusted basis of an earlier residence under the special rules for deferring capital gains under those circumstances. These special rules are explained in this chapter.

Computing the Amount Realized. The first step in calculating the gain or loss on a transaction is to compute the amount realized. This is the cash received, plus net debt relief and the fair market value of any property received (including promissory notes) or services rendered in exchange, minus all selling costs. Those items properly includable as selling costs, reducing the net amount realized from the sale, include:

1. Commissions paid to a real estate broker for procuring a buyer.
2. Title insurance, if required to be furnished by the seller.
3. Cost of abstract of title, if required to be furnished.
4. Legal and administrative fees. The seller ordinarily incurs costs for drawing a contract, a deed, and other documents and for legal representation at the closing.
5. Transfer taxes where paid by the seller.
6. Loan origination fees (points). These are usually borne by the purchaser, but must in some instances be paid by the seller. A case in point is where financing is secured by a Veterans Administration-insured loan. The discount points are required by law to be borne by someone other than the buyer–veteran. This someone, of course, is the seller, and the fees absorbed represent a reduction in the amount realized.
7. Miscellaneous closing costs. So long as costs borne by the seller are associated with the sale (as opposed, for example, to proration of taxes and insurance), they represent a reduction in the amount realized.

Computing the Tax Liability. The difference between the amount realized and the adjusted basis is the capital gain or loss on the transaction. A net loss (i.e., the adjusted basis exceeds the amount realized) has no tax consequences if the real estate has been held for personal use. Any gain is accorded the special treatment that distinguishes capital gains from ordinary income.

The tax consequences of capital gains and losses are discussed in considerable detail in Chapter 8. The following outline is vastly oversimplified but does introduce the essentials of concern to one who has no capital losses and whose only capital gains are from the sale of real estate held for personal use.

The distinction was made earlier between short- and long-term capital gains. In general, the taxpayer, of course, prefers the more favorable treatment accorded long-term gains. To achieve this, the asset must be held for more than 1 year.

The most difficult problem in computing the holding period is often the question of when the period begins. For property acquired by purchase, the holding period begins with the date of purchase. But for property acquired by any other means, the answer is less straightforward.

Property acquired by will or devise (if the decedent died after 1969) qualifies for long-term capital gain or loss treatment without reference to the period it is held by the beneficiary or the estate.

When real estate is acquired in exchange for other real property or capital assets, the holding periods of the properties involved in the exchange are summed. Thus the holding period for the property received in a trade dates back to the time of acquisition of the capital asset traded. In a series of exchanges, the holding periods of all the properties in the series are accumulated.

Example 3–1

On July 1, 1974, Smith buys a duplex as an investment. On November 1, 1974, he trades the duplex for vacant land that he sells at a gain on August 4, 1975. The gain qualifies for long-term treatment, because the sum of the two holding periods exceeds 12 months.

For property received as a gift, the holding period dates back to the time the donor acquired the property, provided that either the fair market value on the date of the gift was greater than the donor's basis or that the property is sold at a profit. But if the fair market value on the date of the gift is less than the donor's basis and the property is ultimately sold for less than its fair market value at the time of the donation, the holding period starts with the date the donation was made. In this latter case, of course, there has been a loss on disposal, and the issue is whether the loss qualifies for long- or short-term treatment. This is not a relevant issue with respect to property held for personal use, since the losses would not be tax deductible in any case.

Real estate used in the owner's trade or business is accorded special treatment reserved for a group of assets that are not considered capital items yet are treated as such with respect to any gain on disposal. These are called Section 1231 Assets and are treated more fully in Chapter 8.

REPORTING SALES ON THE INSTALLMENT BASIS

The general rule is that the entire gain on a sale must be reported in the year of the transaction. Were this rule to apply when the seller takes back a purchase money mortgage for a substantial portion of the selling price, he could be faced with a tax liability exceeding his net cash proceeds in the year of the sale. To avoid this inequity, the code provides an exception that permits the tax liability to be spread over the entire period in which payments are received by the seller.

The special rule is called the installment method. It may be used for reporting all real estate sales so long as the payments received during the year of the sale (called the "initial payments") do not exceed 30% of the selling price. The selling price is the total cost to the buyer (including cash), any debt assumed or paid by the buyer, and the fair market value of any property given or service rendered in exchange.

Advantages of the Installment Method. Gains from the sale of property under the installment method are spread over the entire period of collection. Each year the taxpayer reports as a gain a portion of the payments received that year. The part representing a gain is determined by the ratio of "gross profit" to "total contract price." This percentage, called the "gross profit ratio percentage," is applied to the collections to determine the taxable portion of the installment payments received during the year. The balance of each year's collections are considered a recovery of cost and are, therefore, not subject to income tax.

Maximum Allowable Receipts in Year of Sale. To qualify for installment method reporting, the seller cannot receive "initial payments" exceeding 30% of the "selling price." Initial payments are the payments received during the year of the sale. Attempts to use the installment basis are often defeated because of a misunderstanding of this rule. The major difficulties involve calculating the selling price and the amount of the initial payments.

The selling price includes the total amount the purchaser is to pay the seller, the fair market value of anything given in exchange, and the amount of any outstanding mortgage on the property if the buyer pays off the mortgage balance at the closing or takes the property subject to the mortgage. The selling price is not reduced by the selling expenses incurred by the seller.

Initial payments have been defined as all payments received during the year of the sale. They include any cash down payment and all subsequent payments on the principal that are made during the year of the transaction.

Note that this includes only the part of the payment applying to principal. Interest payments during the year of the transaction are not a part of the initial payments. The initial payments do include the fair market value of any asset or service received either at the time of the closing or at any other time during the year in which the transaction was consummated.

Example 3–2

Joe Frugel sells a parcel of real estate under the following terms: Purchaser to deliver $200 and a used color television set (having a fair market value of $150) at the time of closing. Purchaser to sign a note and purchase money mortgage in the amount of $6000, payable to the seller in six annual installments with interest at 7%. The property is currently subject to a mortgage of $8000, which the purchaser agrees to assume and pay. The selling price is $14,350, computed as follows:

Cash at closing	$ 200
Fair market value of television set traded	150
Note payable to seller	6,000
Mortgage assumed by purchaser	8,000
Total selling price	$14,350

Example 3–3

On July 2, Smith conveys a plot of land in exchange for $500 in cash, a used tractor (fair market value $900), and the buyer's promissory note for $8000 payable in 40 monthly installments of $200 plus interest at 6% on the unpaid balance. The first installment on the note is due on August 1 of the current year. The selling price of the land is $9400. The transaction meets the initial payments qualification for installment basis reporting, since the initial payments are not more than 30% of the selling price. The computations follow:

Cash down payment	$ 500
Fair market value of tractor traded in	900
Installment note	8,000
Total selling price	$9,400
Cash down payment	$ 500
Fair market value of tractor	900
Principal payments on installment note	1,000
Total initial payments	$2,400
Initial payments as a percent of selling price ($2400/$9400)	25.5%

When computing the amount of the initial payments, do not reduce the receipts by the amount of selling expenses. Irrespective of the other tax consequences of the selling expenses, they do not reduce the amount of the initial payments or the selling price for purposes of determining whether the transaction qualifies for installment basis reporting.

If the buyer takes property subject to an existing mortgage that exceeds the seller's adjusted basis, the excess of the mortgage over the adjusted basis must be included in the initial payments.

Example 3–4

Wylie Fox sells for $20,000 property that has an adjusted basis of $6000 and on which he owes a mortgage balance of $10,000. The buyer takes the property subject to the existing mortgage, paying $2000 cash down and agreeing to pay the $8000 balance of the purchase price in six equal annual installments, with interest at 8% per annum. He makes no further payments during the calendar year of the sale. The installment method may be used for reporting this transaction, since the initial payments do not *exceed* 30% of the selling price:

Initial payments:	
Cash down payment	$2,000
Excess of existing mortgage over seller's adjusted basis ($10,000 less $6000)	4,000
Total initial payments	$6,000
Initial payments as a percent of the selling price ($6000/$20,000)	30%

The Total Contract Price and the Taxable Gain. The portion of the annual collections on a sale that must be reported as a taxable gain is determined by the ratio of the collections during the year to the "total contract price." The total contract price is usually the amount that is actually paid to the seller. This includes the amount he receives in cash and the market value of any noncash assets received. In Example 3–3, the selling price and the total contract price are the same. This is generally the case unless the buyer assumes an existing mortgage or takes the property subject to such a mortgage.

Where there is a balance outstanding on an existing mortgage, the payments that are to be made by the buyer, the total contract price, and the selling price differ. The amount of the difference equals the outstanding balance of the old mortgage, unless the seller's adjusted basis is less than the outstanding mortgage balance. In this case, the excess of the old mortgage over the adjusted basis must be included in the total contract price.

Example 3–5

Assume the same facts as in Example 3–4. Fox must report a taxable gain of $6000 in the year of the sale, determined as follows:

Contract price	
Selling price	$20,000
Less mortgage assumed by buyer	10,000
Balance	$10,000
Add back excess of mortgage over seller's adjusted basis ($10,000 less $6000)	4,000
Contract price	$14,000
Gross profit ratio	
Sales price	$20,000
Less adjusted basis	6,000
Total gain	$14,000
Gross profit ratio ($14,000/$14,000)	100%
Taxable gain in year of sale	
Initial payments	$ 6,000
Times gross profit ratio	100%
Taxable in year of sale	$ 6,000

Example 3–6

Jones sells for $20,000 land that has an adjusted basis of $12,000 and an outstanding mortgage balance of $5000. The buyer pays Jones $4000 in cash, agrees to pay the balance of the existing mortgage when due, and signs a note for the balance of the purchase price. The note calls for 10 equal annual payments of principal, with interest at 8% per annum on the unpaid balance. No further payments are made during the calendar year of the sale.

Jones qualifies for and elects to use the installment method of reporting the transaction. He is liable for income taxes on only $2132 of the gain during the first year, determined as follows:

Gain on sale	
Sales price	$20,000
Less adjusted basis	12,000
Gain on transaction	$ 8,000

Total contract price	
Sales price	$20,000
Less existing mortgage	5,000
Total contract price	$15,000
First-year taxable gain	
Initial payments:	$ 4,000
Gross profit ratio percentage ($8000/$15,000)	53.3%
Taxable gain during first year	$ 2,132

TAX CONSEQUENCES OF DONATING REAL ESTATE

Making a gift of property does not involve a capital gain or loss for the donor. If, however, the gift is to certain types of organizations, the donor may be able to claim a tax deduction for a charitable contribution. If the gift does not qualify as a charitable contribution, the donor may incur a gift-tax liability.

Charitable Contributions. The Internal Revenue Code specifies the following types of organizations as qualifying the donor of a gift for a tax deduction for a charitable donation:

1. The government of the United States, the District of Columbia, any state or United States' possession, or any political subdivision thereof. The contribution must be a bona fide gift resulting in no special benefit to the donor, and it must be exclusively for public use.
2. A religious, charitable, scientific, literary, or educational organization founded under the laws of the United States, or of any state or possession of the United States (or the District of Columbia), or any fraternal society operating under the lodge system, provided that the contribution is used solely for the purposes already described in 1.
3. An organization of war veterans or a cemetery association having no other primary purposes, provided that no part of the earnings of the organization or association are intended to benefit any private individual.

The fair market value of the donated property at the time the gift is made forms the basis for determining the amount of the allowable deduction. Thus when property has appreciated substantially above the owner's basis, he can claim a charitable deduction in the amount of the fair market value without incurring a tax liability for the gain. In many cases, this rule makes it more advantageous to donate appreciated property than to sell the property and donate the proceeds.

This rule does not apply to gifts of property that, if sold, would have resulted in a gain taxable as "ordinary income." This includes property held for not more than 12 months, and property held for investment or business purposes that would have been subject to "recapture" rules if sold (recapture rules are explained in Chapter 9). In these cases, the deduction is limited to the taxpayer's adjusted basis.

Charitable gifts of real estate are subject to a number of rules and limitations, a discussion of which are beyond the scope of this book. One contemplating a sizeable charitable donation should consult with a competent tax authority.

Gift-Tax Liability. Gifts not qualifying as charitable contributions may give rise to a gift-tax liability. The gift tax is levied on the donor during the calendar quarter in which the gift is made and is payable on a quarterly basis. The tax is computed on the fair market value of the property at the time of the donation. As noted in Chapter 2, the tax basis of the property in the hands of the recipient is generally the donor's basis plus any gift-tax liability incurred by the donor.

The special one-time exemption of gifts during the donor's lifetime that existed prior to the 1976 Tax Reform Act has been replaced by a credit that, if not used, is available to offset estate taxes. The unified gift and estate tax credit is $30,000 in 1977. It increases in annual increments to $47,000 in 1981. The 1981 credit against taxes is the equivalent of exempting $175,625 of assets from liability for estate and gift tax. In addition to the unified gift and estate tax credit, every taxpayer may exclude annually the first $3000 of gifts made to each recipient. There is no limitation on the number of recipients to whom such gifts may be made. There is also a liberal exemption for gifts between spouses.

The first $100,000 of lifetime gifts to one's spouse are exempt from the gift tax. The second $100,000 are subject to the regular gift-tax liability. Thereafter, there is a 50% deduction allowable for gifts to one's spouse (or spouses). Remember that these marital deductions apply to cumulative amounts of gifts over the lifetime of the donor.

It should be noted also that gifts made within 3 years of the donor's death are considered to have been made in contemplation of death. All such gifts are included in the estate of the decedent and thus are subject to the estate tax.

TAX CONSEQUENCES OF TRANSFERRING REAL ESTATE BY WILL OR DEVISE

There are generally no capital-gain liabilities involved in the transfer of property due to the death of the owner. But the federal government levies a tax on the value of the taxable portion of the estate (a substantial portion of the estate transferred to the surviving spouse is deductible and so reduces the size of the taxable estate). The estate tax is a liability of the estate of the deceased; it is not levied on the heirs or beneficiaries. A detailed presentation of the rules governing estate and gift taxes is beyond the scope of this book.

SPECIAL RULES FOR THE SALE OR EXCHANGE OF A PRINCIPAL PERSONAL RESIDENCE

Home ownership has long been considered a foundation of good citizenship. The concept is rooted in our heritage that "a man's home is his castle." The favoritism bestowed upon home owners by the Internal Revenue Code reflects this national prejudice. The code provides numerous tax advantages to home owners that are not available to rent-paying tenants. Real estate taxes and mortgage interest, for example, that constitute the bulk of the monthly mortgage obligation of the home owner, are treated as tax-deductible expenses. The rent paid by the landless tenant is accorded no such favorable treatment.

Home owners are again favored when disposing of their property. Any gain on the disposal is afforded capital gains treatment, which may greatly reduce the seller's tax liability. There are several circumstances under which transactions involving one's personal residence are afforded even more favorable treatment. It is often possible to so structure the transaction as to postpone the tax liability indefinitely or to avoid it altogether. In the face of such bias favoring home ownership, it is not surprising that over 50% of all households in the United States reside in homes owned by the occupant.

What Is a Principal Personal Residence? The tax consequences incident to buying or selling a principal personal residence differ markedly from those arising from dealing in income property or property used in a trade or business. While less marked, there are significant differences between the tax treatment accorded a principal personal residence and that accorded other real estate held for personal use. It is important, therefore, to distinguish a principal personal residence from all other real property.

Ordinarily one's personal residence is simply where one lives. But where two or more residences are occupied by the same family, the special provisions apply only to the principal residence.

A single-family dwelling is considered a personal residence if the occupant has legal or equitable title to the property. The owner–occupant of a condominium unit is considered to be the owner of a personal residence and is accorded the same status as the owner–occupant of a single-family dwelling, as long as the renting of commercial space in the condominium is only incidental to its primary purpose as residential property.

Tenant–stockholders of housing cooperatives are treated as owners of personal residences if the organization conforms to the definition of a "cooperative housing corporation" specified by the code and the regulations of the Internal Revenue Service. A tenant–stockholder is one whose stock is fully paid-up. The ratio of the stockholder's capital contribution to the total value of the corporate entity must bear a "reasonable" relationship to the ratio of the space the stockholder is entitled to occupy to the total space available to stockholders. The reasonableness of the relationship is determined by the Commissioner. A cooperative housing corporation must have the following characteristics:

1. There is only one class of stock outstanding.
2. Each stockholder is entitled to occupy a dwelling or a building in an apartment house or a housing development owned or leased by the corporation.
3. No stockholder is entitled to a distribution from the corporation other than from profits or in complete or partial liquidation of the corporation.
4. Not less than 80% of the gross revenue of the corporation is from tenant–stockholders. For purposes of determination of the 80% rule, revenue from a governmental body that owns stock in the cooperative is considered to derive from tenant–stockholders.

Owners of multifamily residences, who occupy one of the units in their building, may be able to claim the unit occupied as a personal residence. In this case, any transaction involving the property must be prorated as between the unit claimed as a personal residence and the balance of the property.

Sale of an Old Residence and Purchase of a New. Recognition of a gain on the sale of a personal residence may be avoided by purchasing a replacement home that costs at least as much as the adjusted sales price of the old residence. To qualify, the new residence must be purchased within 1 year prior to or 1 year following the sale of the old. Unless the acquired residence is being newly constructed, it must be occupied as the principal personal residence within 18 months after the old residence is sold. A newly constructed personal residence must be occupied within 24 months, but construction must have begun within 18 months of the sale of the old.

So long as the new residence is purchased and occupied within the prescribed time period, it is not important whether the move was made before or after the sale of the old. Nor does it matter whether the move is before or after the purchase of the new home. The new residence may have been occupied on a rental basis, for example, and subsequently have been purchased within 18 months of the sale of the old home. Or after occupying the new residence, the old home may have been rented temporarily before being sold. These variances in timing do not affect the right of nonrecognition of the gain, if the purchase and occupancy of the new residence fall within the prescribed time period.

Example 3–7

The old home is sold for an amount in excess of its adjusted basis and the taxpayer moves into an apartment. Nine months later, he buys a new home and moves in within 18 months of the date of sale of the old residence. If the price of the new home is not less than the adjusted sales price of the old, the taxpayer may defer recognition of the gain on sale of the old residence.

Example 3–8

Jones purchases and occupies a new home, renting his old home on a short-term lease. He subsequently sells the old residence within 18 months of the date he purchased the new. The fact that Jones rented his old residence before selling it need not affect his eligibility for nonrecognition of a gain on the sale.

Example 3–9

Kline purchases land and begins construction on a new home on August 2, 1974. On July 1, 1975, he accepts a favorable offer for his old home and moves into an apartment pending completion of construction on his new residence. Construction is substantially completed, and Kline moves into his new home in January 1976. If the newly constructed home costs at least as much as the adjusted sales price of the old, Kline qualifies for nonrecognition of the gain on the sale of his old property, since construction on the new residence was begun within 18 months of selling the old home and the new one was occupied within 24 months of the sale of the old.

The nonrecognition rules apply to a single-family dwelling, a condominium unit, or stock in a cooperative housing corporation, if the unit involved is being used as the owner's personal residence. They apply to an exchange of property as well as to a sale and purchase. The rules are mandatory rather than elective in all these cases. They are not mandatory in the case of condemnation of the old residence, but the taxpayer may elect to have them apply.

In computing the cost of the new residence, include all amounts spent for buying, constructing, and improving the property within the prescribed time period. Amounts spent more than 18 months prior or 18 months after the sale of the old property (24 months after sale in the case of purchase of new construction) cannot be included in the cost of the new.

The adjusted sales price of the old residence is the amount realized from the sale itself minus fix-up costs. Remember that the amount realized is the selling price minus selling expenses. Fix-up costs are the expenses incurred on the old residence, within 90 days of sale, to enhance its salability.

Example 3–10

A taxpayer sells his old residence for $42,000, and 6 months later he purchases a new home for $41,000. He had paid $34,000 for the old home several years before. He had added a patio to the old home at a cost of $750. Thirty days before selling the old home, he spent $300 for repainting in order to enhance the sales appeal of the structure. He paid $1500 in brokerage fees on the sale. His gain on disposal is computed as follows:

Gross selling price		$42,000
Less brokerage fees		1,500
Amount realized from sale		$40,500
Less fix-up costs (paint)		300
Adjusted sales price		$40,200
Less adjusted basis:		
Cost	$34,000	
Add cost of patio construction	750	$34,750
Gain on transaction		$ 5,450

The basis of the new residence is the purchase price (including any costs properly included in the basis) minus the unrecognized gain on the old residence:

Cost of new residence	$41,000
Less unrecognized gain on sale of old residence	5,450
Basis of new residence	$35,550

If the purchase price of the new residence is less than the adjusted sales price of the old, a part of the gain must be recognized. But to the extent that the purchase price of the new residence exceeds the adjusted basis of the old, the transaction qualifies for partial nonrecognition of the gain.

Example 3–11

Assume as in Example 3–10 that the adjusted sales price of the old residence is $40,200 and the adjusted basis of the old residence is $34,750, for a gain on disposal of $5,450. Within the prescribed time period, the taxpayer purchases a replacement home costing $38,000. The extent to which the gain must be recognized and the basis of the new residence are computed as follows:

Gain to be recognized on old residence	
Adjusted sales price of old residence	$40,200
Less cost of new residence	38,000
Portion of gain to be recognized (excess of adjusted sales price over the cost of the replacement home)	$ 2,200
Basis of new residence	
Cost of new residence	$38,000
Less portion of gain on sale of old residence that was not recognized ($5450 minus $2200)	3,250
Basis of new residence	$34,750

Sale of Property by Owner Aged 65 or Older. Homeowners aged 65 or older who sell their principal personal residence for a gain may qualify for a once-in-a-lifetime exclusion of all or part of the gain. This is a special benefit intended for homes of modest value. Where the sale price of a qualifying home is $35,00 or less, the entire gain is excludable. Where the home sells for more than $35,000, only a portion of the gain (equal to the portion of the sales price represented by $35,000) may be excluded.

Example 3–12

A taxpayer of age 65 or older sells his principal personal residence for $40,000. His adjusted basis is $27,000 so he has a gain of $13,000. Since the sales price exceeds $35,000, only a part of the gain is excluded. The extent to which the gain may be excluded is found as follows:

Adjusted sales price	$40,000
Ratio of $35,000 to the adjusted sales price ($35,000/$40,000)	7/8
Portion of gain excluded (7/8 times $13,000)	$11,375
Portion of gain subject to tax (1/8 times $13,000)	$ 1,625

To be eligible for this exclusion, a taxpayer must have owned the property and used it as his principal residence for at least 5 of the 8 years immediately prior to the sale. He must, of course, meet the age requirement by being 65 or older at the time of the sale. In the case of married taxpayers who hold common title (as joint tenants, tenants by the entirety or community property), both husband and wife are treated as satisfying the rules if one of them has done so, and if they file a joint return. This exclusion is available only once in the taxpayer's lifetime.

A Sale or Purchase of a Residence Incident to a Job Change. We observed earlier that certain costs involved in the sale of real property represent an offset against the sales price to arrive at the amount realized from the sale. This reduces the tax liability if there is a gain on the sale but provides no relief for the taxpayer who suffers a loss on the sale of property held for personal use. The Tax Reform Act of 1969 provides a more favorable treatment where one's primary residence is sold incident to a move that qualifies one to claim "job-related moving expenses" on his tax return. Many costs incident to the sale that would ordinarily be offset against the selling price and many that might have no tax consequences at all are allowable deductions from current income under this special provision. Similar costs resulting from the purchase of a home incident to such a job change are accorded the same favorable treatment.

To be eligible for this highly favorable tax treatment, the purchase or sale of one's home must be incident to employment at a new location that meets prescribed distance and length-of-service requirements.

The new place of employment must be at least 35 miles further from the old residence than was the old place of employment. The distance is measured as the shortest of the more commonly traveled routes.

The length-of-service requirement differs as to employees and the self-employed. A self-employed person must work at the new location on a full-time basis for at least 78 weeks within 2 years following the move. At least 39 of these work weeks must fall within the first 12 months of arrival at the new location. Employees, to qualify, must be employed on a full-time basis for at least 39 weeks of the 12 months immediately following the start of work at the new location. Exceptions are granted only in cases of death, disability, unanticipated transfer for the benefit of the employer, or termination other than for willful misconduct.

It is important to note that the residence requirement need not have been satisfied prior to filing for the moving expense deduction. It may be claimed in anticipation of fulfilling the requirement, if the move was made in the current tax year. In that case, of course, all the requirements must subsequently be met, or an amended return must be filed.

The maximum allowable deduction under this provision is $3000. This limit applies both to single persons and married persons filing joint returns. The $3000 limit applies even if both husband and wife begin work at the new location. If a married couple files separate returns, they are each limited to $1500.

The limit of $3000 applies to all moving expense deductions claimed. The amount allowable as a deduction for expenses of selling and/or purchasing a residence must, therefore, be reduced by other allowable moving expense deductions claimed, where the total would otherwise exceed $3000.

Example 3–13

The Klucks incur selling and purchasing expenses of $3500. They also incur $1800 of expenses for house-hunting and temporary meals and lodging at the new location. Since the maximum allowance for this latter moving expense is $1500 and the limit to the total claim is $3000, the Klucks may claim $1500 of the selling and purchasing expenses along with $1500 of the other moving expenses.

Costs that qualify as moving expense deductions include those that would ordinarily be offset against the selling price of the old residence to compute the net amount realized, or added to the tax basis of a new home. Examples are appraisal fees (for arriving at a fair market value but not for purposes of arranging financing), abstracts, surveys, recording fees, attorneys' fees, and brokerage commissions. Certain other costs that would otherwise have no tax consequences may also be deducted as moving expenses. These include charges incident to procuring financing, such as credit reports, appraisals, credit insurance, lenders' attorneys' fees, and so forth. The same situation applies to Veterans Administration and Federal Housing Administration loan origination fees paid by the buyer. All these costs qualify as current deductions (even if the taxpayer also takes the standard deduction) when the sale and/or purchase qualifies as a job-related change of residence.

SUMMARY

The amount realized from the sale of property, for purposes of computing the gain or loss on a sale or exchange, is the value received, whether in money, property, or debt relief, minus the selling costs incurred. The difference between the amount realized and the adjusted basis is a capital gain or loss. Capital gains are wholly included in ordinary income if the property yielding the gain is owned for 12 months or less. If the related property is held for more than 12 months, only one-half the gain is included in ordinary income.

A gain on the sale of a principal personal residence need not be recognized if a replacement residence is purchased within 12 months and occupied within 18 months. The time limit is extended to 18 months for purchase and 24 months for occupancy if the new residence is being built, but construction must have begun within 12 months.

Homeowners aged 65 or older may exclude from taxable income any gain on the sale of their principal personal residence, provided they meet certain requirements as to the minimum period of occupancy and the maximum market value of the property. If the value of the home exceeds $35,000, only a portion of the gain is excludable.

Costs incurred in selling an old residence may be deducted as a moving expense when the sale is incident to a change in the location of the home owner's employment. Costs incident to the purchase of a new residence under these circumstances are afforded the same treatment. This deduction may be claimed even though the standard deduction is also taken. The maximum moving expense deduction is $3000, and it is subject to restrictions as to the minimum distance involved and the length of employment at the new location.

CHAPTER 4

TAX FACTORS IN BUSINESS AND INVESTMENT PROPERTY

Having devoted the last two chapters to tax factors involved in the ownership of real estate held for personal use, we move now to our central treatise. The balance of this book concerns the income-tax consequences of decisions involving business and investment property.

Recent legislation has magnified the importance of this issue by virtually eliminating the tax benefits of alternative investment opportunities. For investors seeking relief from the almost confiscatory tax burden imposed on the productive members of society, real estate remains about the only game in town.

We first explain the difference between accounting income and cash flows. This distinction makes it possible to use real estate investments as a "tax shelter" to generate tax losses that offset income from other sources. Tax "losses" are only desirable to the extent they do not represent genuine economic losses to the taxpayer.

Two very important issues that must be considered at every step in tax planning are the minimum tax on items of preference income and the maximum tax on earned income. These rules, and their impact on the tax consequences of real estate investment, are treated in the second section of the chapter.

After laying the groundwork for an understanding of the critical interrelationship between tax rules and real estate investment strategy, the chapter highlights the major tax issues confronting an investor at each stage in the investment cycle. Subsequent chapters elaborating each issue are referenced where appropriate.

ACCOUNTING FLOWS AND CASH FLOWS

Critical to understanding the special opportunities available in real estate investment is a clear distinction between taxable and "economic" gains and losses. Tax laws focus on accounting flows, whereas economic analysis is concerned with cash flows. After-tax cash flows are, of course, the investor's major concern. But accounting conventions often prescribe treatment of income and expenditures in a manner not necessarily related to the realities of these cash flows. One result is that tax liabilities are often a consequence more of how the paperwork is handled than of the economic outcome of an investment.

To illustrate this point, consider the case in Example 4–1 of an investment held for 5 years, with total before-tax cash inflows exactly equal to the before-tax cash outflows over the investment cycle.

Example 4–1

An investor purchases a parcel of real estate for $100,000, signing a $100,000 note with interest at 10% per annum. The note, with accumulated interest, is due in 5 years. At the end of the fifth year the real estate is sold for $161,050, and the note is retired with the proceeds of the sale. The cash inflow from rent receipts exactly equals the cash outflows for property tax and maintenance. There are, therefore, no net cash flows during the ownership period. At the end of the fifth year, the following cash flows result:

Transaction	Cash Flows	
	Inflow	Outflow
Proceeds from sale of real estate	$161,050	
Payment of note:		
Principal		$100,000
Interest		61,050
Totals	$161,050	$161,050

In the absence of income-tax consequences, the investment in Example 4–1 makes little economic sense. The investor is neither better-off nor worse-off as a consequence of the transaction. To see how the outcome can be altered by the income-tax consequences, compare the before-tax cash flows in Example 4–1 with after-tax cash flows from the same investment. Assume that the investor is in the 50% income-tax bracket during each year of the investment cycle. Assume further that the real estate has an estimated 40-year useful life, and is to be depreciated on a straight-line basis, with 90% of the value attributable to the depreciable improvements.

The annual (tax-deductible) depreciation allowance claimed by the investor is $2250, calculated by dividing the portion of the purchase price attributable to the improvements ($90,000) by the estimated useful life (40 years). Since the investor is in the 50% income-tax bracket, he saves $0.50 in taxes for every dollar of depreciation deduction claimed. His annual tax saving due to the allowance for depreciation is, therefore, one-half the amount of the deduction, or $1125.

The interest expense is also tax deductible. This expense is deductible in the fifth year, when it is actually paid, and represents a tax savings of 50% of the interest, or $30,525.

The assumed sales price of $161,050 represents a gain of $72,300. This is determined by deducting from the sales price an amount equal to the total of all depreciation deductions taken during the holding period. Here are the calculations:

Sales price		$161,050
Deduct undepreciated balance of original cost:		
Cost	$100,000	
Less accumulated depreciation (5 years at $2250)	11,250	88,750
Gain on disposal		$ 72,300

With the assumed marginal tax rate of 50%, there is a $36,150 tax on the gain. (Readers familiar with capital-gains tax rules are asked to suspend their knowledge for the duration of our example, accepting instead the convenient assumption that the gain is taxed as ordinary income.) This additional income-tax liability reduces the cash flow from the sale. The revised cash flow from the investment under the assumed tax rules is:

Year	Transaction	Cash Inflow	Cash Outflow
1	Tax savings due to depreciation deduction	$ 1,125	
2	Same as year 1	1,125	
3	Same as year 2	1,125	
4	Same as year 3	1,125	
5	Same as year 4	1,125	
5	Payment of note–face amount		$100,000
5	Payment of note–interest		61,050
5	Tax savings due to interest expense deduction	30,525	
5	Cash from sale of property	161,050	
5	Tax from gain on sale of property		$ 36,150
	Totals	$197,200	$197,200

So far, the introduction of income-tax consequences has not affected the equality of total cash inflows and outflows over the life cycle of the investment. What has been interjected is a difference in timing of the inflows and the outflows. To appreciate the importance of this difference, one must understand the concept of the time value of money. A dollar received today is worth more than a dollar to be received next week, while a dollar to be received next week is worth more today than is a dollar to be received in one month, and so on. The exact difference in these present values depends upon the discount rate employed. Stating the issue crudely, the present value of a sum to be received in the future is the amount one would have to invest today to have that sum in the future. The discount rate is the rate of interest one could expect to earn on the money currently invested. Assume, for example, that the appropriate discount rate is 6%. At this interest rate, $943.40 invested today would accumulate to $1000 in 1 year. Therefore, the present value of $1000 due in 1 year, with a discount rate of 6%, is $943.40.

Returning now to our example, we can apply the present value concept to the cash flows through time. The result is the present value of the cash inflows and outflows over the investment cycle. The present values of the inflows exceed the present value of the outflows, even though the total inflows and outflows over the total cycle are equal. This is because certain of the inflows (in the form of tax savings due to depreciation deductions) are experienced early in the investment cycle, whereas the outflows are deferred until the very end. And the longer a cash flow is deferred, the less present value it has. The present value calculations (discounting at 6%) are as follows:

Year	Transaction	Present Value of Cash Flows	
		Inflows	Outflows
1	$1125 tax savings due to depreciation discounted for 1 year.	$ 1,061	
2	Same tax savings discounted for two periods.	1,001	
3	Same tax savings discounted for three periods.	945	
4	Same tax savings discounted for four periods.	891	
5	Same tax savings discounted for five periods.	841	
5	$100,000 note discounted for five periods.		$ 74,726
5	$61,050 interest payment discounted for five periods.		45,620
5	$30,525 tax savings discounted for five periods.	$ 22,810	
5	$161,050 cash receipts discounted for five periods.	$120,346	
5	$36,150 tax liability discounted for five periods.		$ 27,013
	Total present values	$147,895	$147,359

Expressed another way, the effect of the depreciation allowance is to give the investor dollar-equivalents in the form of tax savings during the first 4 years that he can invest at 6% (on an after-tax basis). Assuming that such investments were actually made, the investor would be $536 better off, solely due to the combination of tax laws and the time preference value of money.

The reader should quickly see that the larger the tax deductions for depreciation during the earlier years, and the longer the investor can wait before incurring an obligation for taxes, the greater is the present value of the investment opportunity. The special magic of many real estate investments can be explained in exactly this manner. They provide large tax savings during the early years, while deferring the tax liability for an extended period of time. These accounting flows are termed *tax losses* to distinguish them from actual economic losses.

If we relax the assumption that our taxpayer is in the 50% marginal tax bracket during each year of the investment cycle, even greater profit opportunities become apparent. Claiming the deductions during years of high income (and consequent high marginal tax rates) and taking the profit during years of lower income (perhaps after retirement) causes after-tax cash inflows to exceed after-tax total cash outlays, even before discounting.

Another way to increase the differential between after-tax cash inflows and outflows is to claim the tax deductions as offsets against ordinary income while claiming the income as a capital gain. Long-term capital-gains rules (discussed more fully in Chapter 8) may permit the gain to be taxed at approximately one-half the rate applicable to ordinary income. Reducing by one-half the present value of the tax due to the gain on disposal in our example increases the excess of the present value of cash inflows over the present value of cash outflows from $536 to $14,043.

These do not nearly exhaust the tax-oriented profit opportunities offered by real estate. It may be possible to further increase the tax savings by using an accelerated depreciation method. It might also be possible to so structure the sale as to avoid immediate income-tax liability on the gain. Perceptive readers have begun to develop an appreciation for the crucial role played by the timing of cash inflows and outflows and by the income-tax consequences attaching to each. Subsequent chapters extend this analysis and apply it to the specifics of current tax laws.

But before proceeding to consider these matters in detail, we must analyze two very critical tax rules that affect virtually every real estate investment decision. Failure to consider their consequences can lead to some nasty tax surprises. Yet, because they do not fit conveniently into the analysis, they are often ignored in conventional income-tax examples and illustrations. These special rules are the tax limit on earned income and the minimum tax on preference items. In order to be aware of how they might affect subsequent analysis, the rules are explained in detail in the next two sections of this chapter.

THE TAX LIMIT ON PERSONAL-SERVICE INCOME

The special tax limit on earned income became effective with the Tax Reform Act of 1969. Pursuant to that law, and beginning in 1972, the highest tax rate on earned income is 50%. The maximum rate on ordinary income from other sources is 70%.* The 1976 Tax Reform Act extended the maximum tax rule to cover all income from "personal service."

* The lower maximum tax on personal-service income is not applicable when the taxpayer uses income averaging, or if husband and wife file separate returns.

The tax on personal-service income is computed first. Any personal-service income that, in the absence of the special limitation, would be taxed at a rate in excess of 50% is taxed instead at the 50% rate. The tax on income from other sources is based on the rates that would have applied in the absence of the special limitation. The principle is best illustrated by an example.

Example 4–2

A married taxpayer who files a joint return has total taxable income, after all deductions and exemptions, of $80,000. Of this amount, $70,000 is from sources considered to be "personal service taxable income." Married taxpayers filing joint returns ordinarily pay taxes at a marginal rate in excess of 50% on all income over $52,000 (see Table 1–1, page 15). Our taxpayer, therefore, has $18,000 of earned income that would be subject to a higher marginal tax rate were it not for the special tax limit on personal-service income, and $10,000 of taxable income not subject to the special limitation.

The tax on the personal-service portion of the taxpayer's income in Example 4–2 is the tax on $52,000 (from Table 1–1, page 15), plus 50% of the excess of personal-service income over $52,000. The total tax on the personal-service portion of his income is, therefore, $27,060, computed as follows:

Total personal-service income	$70,000
Less portion taxed at 50% or less (see Table 1–1, page 15)	52,000
Balance, taxed at 50%	$18,000
Tax on first $52,000 (from Table 1–1)	$18,060
Plus 50% of balance ($18,000)	9,000
Tax on earned portion of income	$27,060

The tax on the $10,000 of the taxpayer's income that is not subject to the special limitation must now be computed. This amount is based on the rate that would have applied had there been no special limitation on the personal-service portion. To figure this tax, simply determine the difference between the tax from Table 1–1 on the total taxable income of $80,000 and the tax on the first $70,000 of ordinary income:

Tax on \$80,000 of taxable income (no special limitation) from Table 1–1	\$33,340
Tax on \$70,000 of taxable income (with no special limitation) from Table 1–1	27,720
Difference (total tax on the \$10,000 that does not qualify for the special limitation)	\$ 5,620

The taxpayer's total tax bill is the sum of the tax on the personal-service portion of his income plus the tax on the unearned portion.

Tax on income subject to the special limitation	\$27,060
Tax on income not subject to the special limitation	5,620
Total tax liability	\$32,680

The net effect of the maximum tax provision is to divide the total taxable income into two segments. The lower, or bottom segment, is the portion that is considered personal-service income and thus subject to the special limitation. The upper, or top segment, is taxed as if no special rate existed. The personal-service income limitation substitutes a special, lower tax rate on the bottom segment without affecting the rate on the top segment of income. Figure 4–1 illustrates how the income is segmented for purposes of applying the special rule, and the tax that applies *before* the special rule is applied. Figure 4–2 illustrates the effect of the special rule,

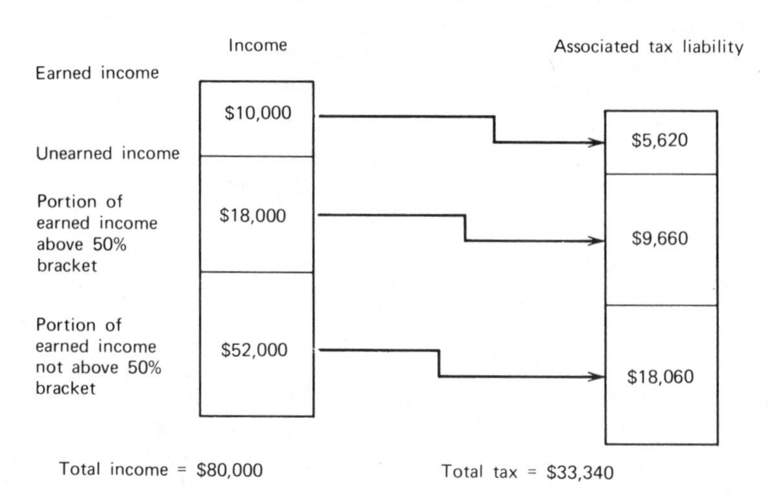

Figure 4-1. Tax liability on \$80,000 of taxable income, before applying special tax limitation on earned income (based on married taxpayer filing a joint return).

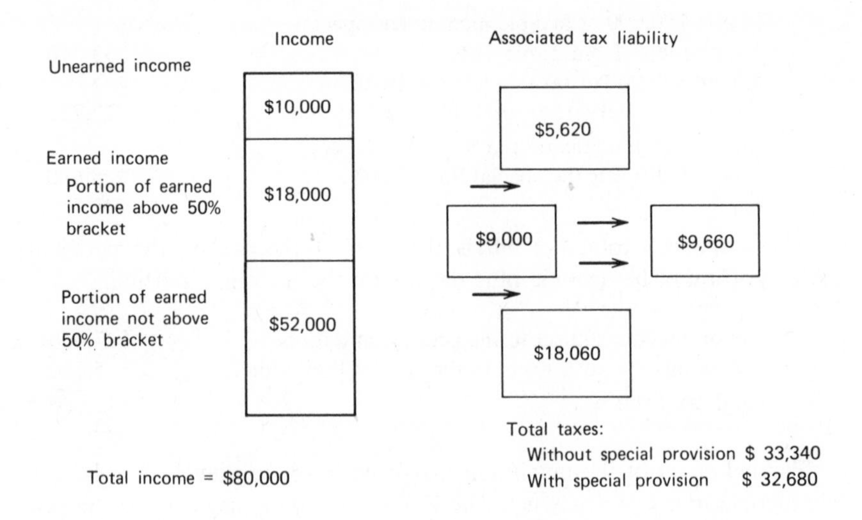

Figure 4-2. Tax liability on $80,000 of taxable income, with special tax limitation on earned income (based on married taxpayer filing a joint return).

as the regular tax on the personal-service segment of income is replaced with the smaller, limited tax on personal-service income.

Personal-Service Income Defined. Taxable income subject to the special limitation includes salaries and wages and compensation for personal services, including professional fees. It also includes pensions, annuities, and deferred compensation. If both personal services and capital are material income-producing factors in one's personal business, personal-service income constitutes a "reasonable" portion of the total income of the business but may not be more than 30% of the total.

To calculate personal-service taxable income:

1. From "personal-service income" subtract all adjustments attributable to the personal-service portion of total gross income. The resulting figure is "personal-service net income."
2. Determine the fractional portion of adjusted gross income comprised of personal-service net income by dividing the latter by the former. Multiply taxable income (adjusted gross minus deductions and exemptions) by this fraction to determine the portion of taxable income from personal services.
3. Subtract total "preference items" from this amount. The balance is the income to which the maximum tax provision applies. (Preference items are defined on page 60).

Example 4–3

A taxpayer has adjusted gross income of $100,000 and taxable income (adjusted gross minus deductions and exemptions) of $80,000. Included in the calculations resulting in gross income are $6000 of preference items and $95,000 of personal-service net income. His earned taxable income for the year is $70,000, determined as follows:

Personal-service	$ X,XXX
Less adjustments attributable to personal-service income	XXX
Personal-service net income	$ 95,000
Total taxable income	$ 80,000
Percent of adjust gross income from personal services ($100,000/$95,000)	95%
Portion of taxable income that is from personal services	$ 76,000
Less preference items	6,000
Amount of income to which personal-service income limitation applies	$ 70,000

MINIMUM TAX ON PREFERENCE ITEMS

The complexity of our tax system has spawned legions of counselors, attorneys, and accountants whose speciality it is to exploit the peculiarities, inconsistencies, and downright stupidities incorporated into the code. That one man's tax shelter is another man's loophole is demonstrated by the extent to which the success of these specialists has raised both their fees and public indignation. A reform-minded Congress in 1969 introduced legislation designed to eliminate many of the tax avoidance techniques developed by the "shelter" specialists. There resulted a vigorous debate concerning the merits of using the tax code to effect social welfare goals.

Code Section 56 emerged from all the sound and fury. It provides for a minimum tax on certain items of income that are otherwise exempt from taxation due to provisions found elsewhere in the code. The 1969 version contained liberal exemptions and carry-over provisions making the preference tax little more than a nuisance item. The 1976 Tax Reform Act revised Section 56 to include a set of teeth capable of eviscerating most tax shelter plans. Today, tax planning that does not consider the minimum tax on preference items is a dangerous exercise in fantasy.

Definition of Tax Preferences. Certain tax deductions generally available only to the affluent are dubbed "preference items" by the language of Section 56. Preference items of particular concern to real estate investors are:

1. Depreciation in excess of straight-line. Under some circumstances, deductions for depreciation of real estate are allowed on an "accelerated" basis (see Chapter 7). The portion of this accelerated depreciation in excess of straight-line rates is subject to the minimum tax on preference items.
2. Tax-exempt portion of long-term capital gains. Capital-gains tax rules permit 50% of long-term capital gains to be excluded from taxable income in determining one's regular tax liability. The one-half the long-term gain that is not included in ordinary income is a tax preference item. The 50% rule remains invariant even if the taxpayer chooses to use the alternative method of determining his capital gains tax liability (see Chapter 8).

Other preference items not of immediate concern to real estate investors are presented here in the interests of completion. Taxpayers affected by these latter items should look elsewhere for a detailed explanation:

1. Bargain element in stock options. This is the difference between the fair market value and the exercise price of stock received under a qualified stock option plan.
2. Excess itemized deductions. The excess of itemized deductions (excluding medical expenses and casualty losses) over 60% of adjusted gross income.
3. Intangible drilling costs. Certain portions of intangible drilling costs in connection with productive oil and gas wells.
4. Accelerated depreciation on personalty under net lease. The excess of accelerated depreciation over straight-line on personalty, where the personalty is under a net lease.
5. Excess amortization. The excess of amortization over regular depreciation allowable for certain assets.
6. Depletion in excess of cost. The excess of allowable percentage depletion over the adjusted basis of property at the end of the taxable year.
7. Bad debt deductions in excess of actual losses. The addition to reserve for bad debts allowable to certain financial institutions in excess of what would have been allowed had the addition been based on actual loss experience.

Preference Tax Exemption. Individual taxpayers are allowed to exempt from the minimum tax liability an amount equal to the greater of $10,000 or one-half their regular tax liability for the year. The "regular tax" includes the total tax for the year (before adding the preference tax) minus the following items where applicable.

1. Foreign tax credit.
2. Retirement income credit.
3. The work incentive credit.
4. Credit for political contributions.
5. Personal tax credits.

Corporations are subject to the same rule as individual taxpayers, except that the corporate exemption is equal to the greater of $10,000 or the *total* of the regular tax liability for the year.

Computing the Preference Tax Liability. The tax rate on preference items in excess of the exemption is 15%. This is in addition to the regular tax liability. The rate is the same for individuals and corporations.

Example 4–4

A taxpayer incurs income-tax liability of $18,000 before accounting for the minimum tax on preference items. During the year he had long-term capital gains of $23,000 and depreciation deductions on real estate totaling $12,000. Had he used the straight-line method, his depreciation deductions would have been only $8200. His minimum tax on preference items is $795, determined as follows:

Preference items:		
One-half long-term capital gain		$11,500
Excess depreciation:		
Total depreciation deductions	$12,000	
Less straight-line depreciation	8,200	3,800
Total preference items		$15,300
Less exemptions:		
(a) One-half regular tax liability	$ 9,000	
(b) Minimum exemption	10,000	
Greater of (a) or (b)		$10,000
Amount subject to preference tax		$ 5,300
Preference tax (at 15%)		$ 795

LIFE CYCLE OF REAL ESTATE INVESTMENTS

Their pervasive nature makes it imperative that investors understand how tax factors impact on each stage of the real estate investment cycle. Tax benefits reaped early in the ownership period are often offset by later tax penalties. Careful consideration should be given to the timing and the full extent of the consequences at each step in the decision-making process. This section develops a framework for real estate investment analysis and explains how the various chapters in the remainder of the book relate to each stage in the investment cycle.

The Three Phases of the Investment Cycle. The real estate investment cycle can be conveniently divided into acquisition, operation, and divestiture phases. Each phase has distinct income-tax consequences attaching to alternative courses of action. Moreover, the tax consequences attaching to the various phases are interdependent. Decisions made during the acquisition phase, for example, have tax consequences that carry over all the way through the operations and into the divestiture phase.

Because of this interdependence of tax consequences, the prudent investor must develop a complete plan for a venture, all the way through the divestiture phase, before initiating action for acquisition. This is not to imply that he forecloses options not included in the original plan. The plan is based on his projections of market factors and personal considerations as forecast at various points in the future. The limit on human perspicacity insures that these projections will be awry. Plans must, therefore, be adjusted periodically on the basis of better information. But a comprehensive plan at the outset increases the probability of making decisions having the most favorable financial and income-tax consequences over the full cycle of the investment.

The Acquisition Phase. Acquisition of real property involves decisions regarding ownership entities, price, debt-to-equity ratios, and loan terms.

A bewildering array of alternatives faces the investor who must make an entity choice. He must decide whether to take title in his own name or jointly with his spouse or another investor, in the name of a partnership or corporation, or to have the property held by a trustee. Each alternative has distinct income-tax consequences, some of which are favorable and others unfavorable. These tax considerations must also be weighed against legal and financial issues aside from the immediate tax question.

Chapter 5 provides guidance regarding the income-tax consequences of various ownership entities. The more complex questions of limited partnership and corporate entities are discussed at length in separate chapters. Limited partnerships are covered in Chapter 11, whereas Chapter 12 considers the consequences of incorporation.

Investors seeking third-party financing have rather limited tax strategy options with respect to financing alternatives. The only field of maneuver is the question of how loan closing costs, prepaid items, and escrows are to be handled. Chapter 6 discusses how these elements should be treated for best income tax advantage to the investor.

If acquisition involves seller-financing, there is more opportunity for structuring the terms of the sale and of the financing to the mutual advantage of both buyer and seller. This involves considering the tax consequences to both parties of various arrangements, and bargaining as to how the possible tax benefits should be shared. This topic is also covered in Chapter 6.

The Operations Phase. The major tax questions faced in the operations phase are depreciation, landlord–tenant relations, and repairs and improvements.

Because depreciation deductions shelter a part of the "economic income" from current taxes, they are of crucial importance to the viability of any investment proposal. Chapter 7 explains the various allowable methods of computing depreciation and illustrates the effect of each on the after-tax cash flow from operations.

Chapter 7 also distinguishes between repairs and improvements. This is of more than passing interest, since improvements must be capitalized and charged off as an expense over the remaining useful life of the improvements, whereas repairs may be charged as a currently deductible expense. Chapter 7 discusses strategy to characterize expenditures as maintenance and repairs whenever possible and points out possible problems that might cause an otherwise deductible item to be disallowed on the grounds that it constitutes a part of a "systematic plan of improvement."

The central tax issue surrounding tenant–landlord relations is the consequence of property improvements made by the tenant. Whether such improvements are taxable immediately to the landlord, taxable to him at some later date, or have no income-tax consequences to him whatsoever depends on the circumstances of the individual case. That these circumstances are to some degree controllable by the landlord presents a tax planning opportunity that is also discussed at some length in Chapter 7.

The Disposition Phase. Gradual build-up of the investor's equity base, combined with a rapidly declining depreciation base, causes most investments to yield a declining annual rate of return on the original investment if held beyond a certain point. This point can to some extent be extended by refinancing to reduce the investor's equity base. But even so, the day will arrive when the property is best sold or otherwise disposed of, so that the funds released thereby can be employed elsewhere with a more favorable risk/return ratio. The question of disposition raises a whole new set of income tax-related problems.

The gain on disposal of real estate held for more than 1 year may, in whole or in part, be subject to favorable tax treatment as a long-term capital gain. A portion of the gain may, on the other hand, be treated as recapture of excess depreciation and so taxed as ordinary income in the year of the sale. For the high-bracket taxpayer, this question of ordinary income versus capital gains is of special importance. The basic principles, tax rules, and computational problems surrounding capital gains are presented in Chapter 8. The question of recapture of excess depreciation, and of the total income-tax consequences of a sale of real property held for business or investment purposes, is addressed in Chapter 9.

A much better deal may be negotiated when selling one's real estate, if the seller is willing to provide a portion of the needed financing. While this strategy is a powerful tool for maximizing the selling price, it does create certain cash-flow problems related to the resultant tax liability. The tax collector is not necessarily willing to wait for his portion of the gain just because the seller must wait. There are, however, provisions in the code designed to provide relief for taxpayers faced with this problem. Qualifying transactions may be reported on the "installment basis." A tax liability on the gain is then recognized only in proportion as the purchase price is actually collected.

Spreading the taxable gain over several years through installment sales reporting provides two potentially valuable benefits. First, it may enable the taxpayer to avoid being moved into a higher marginal tax bracket, which would result in a much larger total tax on the transaction. Second, if the taxpayer anticipates a significant decrease in his taxable income in future years (such as impending retirement), he may find it possible to use the installment method of reporting to defer recognition of all the gain until that time. Installment sales are discussed in Chapter 9, as they relate to "casual" sales of real property.

Another important opportunity to defer recognition of taxable gains is provided by rules applicable to "like-kind" exchanges. Trades of real estate assets may under certain special circumstances be deemed tax-free events, on which any gain may not be recognized until the newly acquired real estate is eventually disposed of in a taxable transaction.

Circumstances may often be engineered to gain this like-kind exchange treatment where doing so is advantageous. Likewise, it is often possible to deliberately avoid having a transaction characterized as a like-kind exchange where immediate tax consequences are desired. This latter case might include a capital loss, for example, or the desire to recognize a capital gain during a year in which one is in a much lower-than-customary marginal tax bracket. These issues are treated further in Chapter 10.

SUMMARY

Real estate is a particularly appropriate investment for those seeking relief from burdensome income-tax obligations. The combination of accelerated depreciation and financial leverage often enables such investments to yield an attractive net cash flow while showing a net loss for tax-computation purposes. This tax loss can be used to offset income from other sources, further increasing the after-tax benefits to the investor.

To determine the desirability of an investment, it is helpful to project all cash flows over the investment cycle, on an after-tax basis. These after-tax cash flows may then be discounted at the appropriate rate to determine the present value of the opportunity. The discounted-cash-flow approach enables a comparison of alternative investment opportunities.

Accelerated depreciation and capital gains, while having a salutary impact on the investor's ordinary income-tax obligation, may also increase his minimum tax obligation on preference items. Failure to estimate the preference-tax consequences of an investment may cause the present value of the opportunity to be grossly overstated.

SUGGESTED READINGS

1. Greer, Gaylon E., "Preference Tax Changes–The Sleeper in the 1976 Tax Reform Act," *Real Estate Issues, 2* (1), 13–21 (1977).
2. Suter, Robert C., "Tax Implications in the Ownership and Transfer of Real Estate," *The Real Estate Appraiser, 40* (6), pp. 15–18 (November–December 1974).
3. Suter, Robert C., "Tax Implications in the Ownership and Transfer of Real Estate, Part II," *The Real Estate Appraiser, 41* (1), pp. 41–49 (January–February 1975).

CHAPTER 5

OPTIONS AND OFFERS: THE ACQUISITION OF INVESTMENT PROPERTY

The investor, after careful study of the market, eventually decides upon some specific property as being most attractive in view of his particular investment objectives and personal income tax position. His efforts to acquire an interest in the property most frequently involve either an option contract or a straightforward offer to purchase. The latter alternative represents an unequivocal agreement to take title to the property under carefully stipulated conditions and is enforceable by either party in a court of law. An option, on the other hand, is binding only upon the seller. It leaves the investor the freedom to complete the transaction or to allow the contract to expire without being exercised.

These arrangements have a varying impact on the investor's legal and income tax position, depending upon the final disposition of the option or offer to purchase. The first section of this chapter explains the tax consequences under various assumptions concerning the eventual outcome of either contract.

Having acquired the right to purchase property at a satisfactory price under terms agreeable to all parties, the investor must decide upon an appropriate ownership entity. He might elect to take title in his own name, jointly with other individuals, or to have title vest in an incorporal entity such as a partnership, a trust, or a corporation. The decision has differential effects on both the investor's tax position and his personal liability for financial obligations arising from the venture. The entity choice is particularly crucial if the intent is to interest other investors in merging their resources into a joint investment venture. The latter portion of this chapter details the advantages and disadvantages of various alternative ownership entities available to the investor.

MAKING THE OFFER

The usual first step in a transaction involving real property is a contract that sets forth the details of the proposed transaction and carefully specifies the rights and obligations of all parties. From the purchaser's viewpoint, this is an essential preliminary. He does not pay the purchase price until assured that the seller has good title to the property and can deliver under the terms of the agreement. The contract, therefore, specifies the nature of the title to be conveyed, the nature of proof of good title, and the remedial steps to be taken if title defects are revealed.

The initial agreement also specifies all other terms and conditions to which the proposed transaction is to be subject. The entire agreement must be in writing. The Uniform Commercial Code, now in effect throughout the nation, provides that oral supplements are not enforceable. It is, therefore, crucial to both parties that all documents be carefully drawn. Legal counsel should be involved in all phases of documentation.

If the initial offer and acceptance is a straightforward purchase and sale contract, both parties are obligated to complete the transaction. Should either fail to fulfill his commitment, the injured party may sue for specific performance under the contract. He may also initiate a suit for damages arising from the failure to perform.

Because of the binding nature of a purchase and sale contract, the investor may prefer to acquire an option on the property. Whereas the purchase and sale contract is binding on both parties, an option agreement gives the buyer (optionee) the unilateral right to determine whether the transaction is consummated. If he exercises his option, he takes title to the property as under a purchase and sale contract. If he elects not to acquire the property, he may assign his rights to a third party, or he may simply let the option expire and have no further rights. He cannot then recover the money paid for the option, but neither can the would-be seller (optionor) proceed against him for damages or for specific performance.

The option may have a price separate and distinct from the purchase price of the property. More typically, the agreement specifies that in the event it is exercised the price of the option is to apply toward the purchase of the property. If the option is allowed to expire, the optionee simply forfeits the option right and the money paid for it.

The income tax consequences of an option contract depend upon whether it is exercised and upon the nature of the optioned property itself. The major income tax issues are the timing of recognition of losses and gains and the classification of a loss or gain as ordinary income or as a capital item.

Buyer's Income-Tax Position. If it is exercised, the consideration paid for an option is treated as a part of the purchase price of the underlying property. This rule is invariant regardless of whether the contract treats the option money as a part of the purchase price or as a separate and distinct transaction. In either instance, both the option price and the additional consideration paid when the option is exercised are treated as costs of acquiring title to the property and are included in the initial tax basis.

Example 5–1

Fred Elder sells an option on property he owns, giving Sam Younger the right to purchase the property for $20,000 at any time during the next 18 months. The price of the option itself is $2000, which is *not* to be applied to the $20,000 purchase price should Younger exercise his option. Neither Elder nor Younger are dealers.

If Younger exercises his option, his initial tax basis includes the $2000 paid for the option, the additional $20,000 paid when the option was exercised, plus any "closing" costs that are appropriately included as a cost of acquiring title.

If the optionee declines to exercise the option, he forfeits the option money. The tax treatment of the forfeited deposit depends upon the treatment that would have been accorded the real property had it been acquired on the initial option date and sold at a loss on the date the option expired (i.e., had there been a straightforward purchase and subsequent sale of the property rather than purchase and expiration of an option). The amount of the loss is the price paid for the option. It is a capital loss if the optioned property would have been a capital asset in the hands of the optionee. Assuming the loss does qualify as a capital item, it is a long-term capital loss if the period of the option is more than 12 months.

The option contract itself has no income tax consequences for the optionee during the year the contract is entered into, unless during that same year the contract is either sold, assigned, or allowed to expire. The tax consequences are effective during the year of disposition of the contract.

If an optionee who is not a dealer sells (assigns) his option contract for the same amount he paid, there are no income-tax consequences for him. If, however, he sells for more or less than his cost, he has a capital loss or gain on the transaction. The tax consequences occur in the taxable year in which the assignment occurs. Whether the capital loss or gain is long-term or short-term depends upon the length of time between entering into the contract and assigning it to a third party.

Example 5–2

Assume that the option agreement between Elder and Younger in Example 5–1 took place on November 2, 1976, and that Younger subsequently assigns his interest to Dan Trader for $2500. Younger's gain of $500 is a capital gain since he is not a dealer. Whether Younger's capital gain is long-term or short-term depends upon whether he held the option contract for *more than* 12 months before assigning it to Mr. Trader.

1. If Younger closes the assignment transaction on or before November 2, 1977, the gain is taxed as a short-term capital gain.
2. If he arranges the assignment to be completed on November 3 or later, the gain is subject only to the long-term capital-gains tax.

Of course, if in this example Mr. Younger were to sell his option rights for less than $2000, he would have a tax-deductible loss. The tax treatment of such a loss depends upon the length of time the option was held before assignment, and upon the use to which the underlying real property would have been put in the hands of Younger. If the optioned property were to be used in Younger's trade or business, the loss on assignment of the option would be treated as a reduction in his ordinary income, regardless of the period of time that elapses between the purchase of the option by Younger and its assignment to Trader. This is due to the special treatment accorded losses on such property under Section 1231 of the code. They qualify for treatment as capital assets when there is a gain on disposal but may be treated as noncapital assets when the businessman experiences a loss on their disposal. Chapter 8 deals with the special treatment of Section 1231 assets along with other categories of assets when disposed of at a gain or loss.

If the property under option in Example 5–2 were to be held for investment purposes, then it is a "capital" item, and the loss is treated as a capital loss. If the assignment were completed on or before November 2, 1977, the loss would be a short-term capital loss. If completed after November 2, 1977, the transaction is reported as a long-term capital loss. Younger would, of course, prefer that the loss be treated as short-term.

Assume now that Younger neither sells nor assigns his option but simply allows it to expire. The resulting $2000 loss is treated either as an ordinary loss or as a long- or short-term capital loss, depending once again on the intended use of the optioned realty and the length of time the option was held prior to expiration.

Seller's Income-Tax Position. Now consider Examples 5–1 and 5–2 from the perspective of Mr. Elder, the optionor. If Younger's option is exercised (either by Younger or his assignee), the $2000 originally received by Elder is simply included in his reported net selling price. Elder's loss or gain on the transaction depends upon the relationship between this net selling price and his adjusted basis, as explained in Chapter 9. Younger's assignment of the option to a third party has no effect on Elder's tax position. Elder's position with respect to the treatment of the option money is affected only by whether the option is exercised or allowed to expire.

If the option is allowed to expire, then Elder retains both title to the real estate and the $2000 option payment. The option payment in this case is treated as ordinary income to Elder, regardless of the length of the option period. Continuing the assumption that Elder is not a dealer, the income arising from Younger's forfeiture of the option deposit must be reported by Elder in the taxable year in which the option contract expires. This follows logically from the fact that the appropriate tax treatment of the deposit cannot be determined until the option either expires or is exercised.

Remember that the assumption so far has been that Mr. Elder does not have dealer status. Dropping that assumption changes the nature of the tax liability incurred by Elder. If he is a dealer and the optioned realty is properly includable in his inventory of properties held for sale, then his gain on the transaction is reported as ordinary income without regard to whether the option expires or is exercised. In this case the option money must be reported as ordinary income (to the extent that exercise of the option results in a gain on the sale of the underlying property) in the year the option contract is signed, rather than in the year it expires or is exercised.

TAKING TITLE

Investors undertaking their initial venture in commercial or investment property face a bewildering array of ownership entities. The legal and financial distinction between the alternatives may appear inconsequential. The reality is that the choice of titleholding entity is often crucial to the outcome of the venture.

A decision to involve other investors in some form of pooling-of-equity vests the entity question with particular urgency. Passive investors generally insist upon an arrangement that provides a limit on their personal liability for the financial obligations of the venture.

Asset liquidity is interrelated with the issue of financial liability and is significantly affected by the choice of ownership entity. The ability of investors to liquidate their position at their own volition is often a powerful determinant of their willingness to enter into a cooperative venture. Such ventures generally involve an entity that enables investment shares to be transferred in relatively small increments.

A continuous thread running through all deliberations concerning the entity question is the importance of maintaining decision-making control over all operational matters. Sacrificing control to induce associates to contribute additional funds to the venture is self-defeating if the associates prove to be inept managers. The entity decision should be made only after careful consideration of its impact on operational control.

In most instances, it is the income-tax advantages afforded real estate over alternative forms of investment that make it particularly attractive to those who have substantial taxable income from other sources. The financial benefits of the tax shelter provided by accelerated depreciation and capital-gains treatment, issues considered in subsequent chapters, are of limited value if they accrue directly to a taxable ownership entity rather than to the investors as individuals. Absent these advantages, and very few present real estate investment ventures would be undertaken. Yet, injudicious choice of an ownership entity can cause the investors to be denied these income tax advantages.

Title May Vest in Owners as Individuals. An investor's initial impulse is generally to have title vest solely in himself as an individual or jointly with his partners, where a pooling of financial resources is involved.

Investors pooling their resources in a joint venture often chose to hold title as individual co-tenants. The co-tenancy arrangements most commonly experienced are tenancy in common and joint tenancy. The use of these arrangements with respect to property held for personal use is described in Chapter 2. These same principles are generally applicable to property held for business or investment purposes.

When property is held as a tenancy in common, each investor's name appears on the deed, and each holds an undivided interest in the whole property. Unless there has been a specific agreement to the contrary, each common tenant has the use of the whole property. Substantial alterations or improvements would require agreement among the owners, thereby substantially reducing the operational control of any one owner. The usual arrangement is to provide that one owner operates the property under a power of attorney from the other owners.

Joint tenancy has essentially the same characteristics as tenancy in common, with one overpowering exception: In the event of death of a joint tenant, his interest in the property may go to the other joint tenants rather than to his heirs.

Co-tenancy arrangements have the attraction of ease in legal arrangements. No special provisions are required except the appropriate wording on the deed. The exact wording needed to assure creation of joint tenancy as opposed to tenancy in common differs among the states. The agreement among the co-tenants regarding operational matters can be arranged as they please but should be in writing and signed by all parties to avoid misunderstanding and to serve as a guide in case of future disputes. To insure legal enforceability and access to legal remedies, any such agreement should be made under the guidance of and drafted by legal counsel.

A co-tenancy is not a tax-paying entity. All profits and losses accrue to the investors as individual taxpayers and are reported on their personal tax returns. Profits and losses are divided among the owners in the same proportion as their ownership interest in the property bears to the total interest in the property. With respect to his personal interest in the property, therefore, the investor is in the same tax position as he would have been had he held title to a part of the property as a sole owner.

Except for estate and gift tax considerations, and ease in formation, co-tenancy arrangements have little to recommend them. The potential loss of operational control has been alluded to earlier. There is nothing inherent in the co-tenancy itself to provide any consolidation of operational authority in the hands of any particular owner, though such an arrangement is typically provided through a power of attorney granted by the other owners. The arrangements may prove extremely illiquid for any disgruntled cotenant who would like to "bail out." Though there is no inherent reason why he could not sell his interest (thus converting a joint tenancy to a tenancy in common), the interest may prove essentially unmarketable due to the peculiar characteristics of co-tenancy. Attempts to ameliorate this undesirable side effect of co-tenancy often include some sort of "buy-out" agreement among the owners designed to provide the disgruntled party the opportunity to sell his share to the others under some predetermined value formula and financial arrangement.

The investor who embarks on an investment venture without partners and who wishes to take title as an individual must decide whether to make his spouse a party to the transaction. From an income-tax perspective, there are few advantages to excluding one's spouse. Even were such an advantage to exist, it would be imperative to weigh it against the potential disadvantage in terms of the estate and inheritance tax implications. These latter considerations are discussed in Chapter 3 with respect to property held for personal use, and generally hold invariant for property held for income or investment purposes as well.

Whether or not property is held in co-tenancy with one's spouse, any subsequent purchaser generally insists that the spouse's name appear as a grantor on the deed. This is a universal precaution to extinguish any property rights the spouse may have acquired.

Individual ownership and co-tenancy arrangements have the seemingly compelling attraction of simplicity. But simplicity being one of the less significant of a myriad of considerations, further analysis is justified before making a final decision.

Title May Vest in a Corporation. We proceed under the assumption that the reader is generally familiar with the concept of a corporation. Under the laws of the various states, upon filing the appropriate documents with a state agency, there comes into existence a legal entity that is empowered to hold property in its own name, enter into contracts, sue and be sued, and be subject to the general laws governing the conduct of commerce and trade.

Corporations are taxable entities, separate and distinct from their corporate owners. They must file a separate tax return and pay income taxes on their earnings. Thus flow-through accounting treatment is not available to the corporation's shareholders.

There are two notable exceptions to the prohibition against flow-through accounting for corporations. They involve "subchapter S" corporations and "straw corporations." These exceptions are treated in the following section along with other entities enjoying the privileged position as a "tax conduit."

Any distribution of corporate earnings in the form of cash dividends is taxable to the stockholder as regular income (with the relatively minor exception of a $100 exclusion). This, in effect, results in double taxation of distributed earnings. And refusal to declare a cash dividend may result in an even higher tax on accumulated earnings in excess of the needs of the corporation. This "accumulated earnings tax" ranges from 27.5 to 38.5% of the income on which the tax is based.

For most investors, therefore, a corporation is not the best entity choice. But the corporate entity does have certain other advantages that are not to be dismissed out of hand. The one most often cited is limited liability for the shareholders. As a legal entity, the corporation is empowered to own property and contract for debt in its own name. Corporate liabilities are separate and distinct from those of the owners of the corporation. Unless they voluntarily enter into a contrary arrangement, the stockholders are not liable for any debt contracted by the corporation. Thus their personal risk exposure extends only to the extent of their investment in the corporation.

Another advantage that the corporate form of ownership may carry is added liquidity. Fractional interests in the form of one or more shares of stock can be issued as a means of transferring small portions of the ownership–a procedure that might be awkward or impossible in the case of real property held in the name of the investor himself.

An often overlooked fact is that the tax rate to which the corporation is subject may be considerably below that of the individual stockholder's. The corporate tax rate is only 22% on the first $25,000 of taxable earnings.* Individual tax rates reach this level at $8000 of taxable income for married individuals filing joint returns, and at considerably lower levels for single persons or married persons filing separate returns.

The incremental rate paid by a corporation earning in excess of $25,000 is 48% and remains invariant thereafter.* Individual tax rates reach this level at $32,000 for single individuals and at $40,000 for married persons filing joint returns, and climb rapidly above this rate as income from investments increases further. It may, therefore, be possible to effect considerable savings by shifting earning power from the individual to a corporate entity.

If an investor already controls a corporation that is profitable, or if he has other sources of income that he contemplates putting into a corporate entity, the lack of flow-through accounting may not be particularly significant. In such a case, the corporation itself can reap the benefit of the tax

* Special rates apply to corporations through 1977. They were enacted as temporary measures to stimulate economic activity. These "temporary" reductions may well become permanent. The temporary rates are 20% on the first $25,000 of taxable earnings, 22% on the next $25,000, and a rate of 48% on all corporate income in excess of $50,000.

shelter provisions that often make real estate such an attractive investment to individuals. The corporation would use the tax losses from real estate to offset corporate income from other sources, thus enhancing the after-tax cash flow available for other purposes.

Because the question of whether to use a corporate entity is complex, with both the potential benefits and the potential drawbacks too significant to ignore, a separate chapter is devoted to a more extensive exploration of the issue. Readers wishing to pursue the question are referred to Chapter 12.

Title May Be Held by a Partnership. The law permits certain organizations to pay no tax on their earnings. All earnings of the organization are, instead, taxable directly to the individuals who have an economic interest in the organization. The character of the income or deduction remains the same, moreover, in the hands of the individual as it was in the hands of the organization. The most common forms of such organizations, often termed "conduit entities," are partnerships, trusts, and straw corporations.

A partnership is created by two or more persons agreeing to place their assets and/or talents into some common income-producing activity. The economic nature of the relationship, rather than the state law under which the organization is formed, determines whether the tax rules for a partnership or those for a corporation apply. If the organization is to be treated for income-tax purposes as a partnership, then all earnings of the partnership are taxable to the individual partners, without regard to whether the income is distributed to the partners or remains in the partnership. Net operating losses, like net income, are distributed to the partners in accordance with the agreement under which the partnership was formed. The partners may use their share of any net loss to offset income from other sources.

If the organization has more corporate characteristics than noncorporate, it may be treated for income-tax purposes as "an association taxed as a corporation." Again, this determination is made without necessary reference to the state law under which the organization was formed. This distinction between a partnership and an association is crucial to the investor's search for optimum tax benefits and is treated at length in Chapter 11, which is devoted to a detailed analysis of the benefits and problems associated with participation in a limited partnership arrangement.

Assuming, for the present, that due care has been taken to assure that the partnership is not taxed as an association, there are particular benefits to be derived from holding real estate in this manner. The deductibility of interest payments and accelerated depreciation allowances often result in accounting losses during the early years of an investment, coupled with significant cash inflows. The conduit nature of the partnership entity makes it possible not only to distribute the cash to the partners with no resultant tax liability, but the partners may also use their prorata share of the accounting losses to offset income from other sources. This "tax shelter" aspect of real estate partnership arrangements can be very profitable and is often the primary motivation of those entering into the arrangement.

The benefits of the tax conduit treatment are further enhanced by the provision that the character of the individual income and loss items passed through to the partners retain their nature when reported by the partners, just as if they had been incurred without the intervention of the partnership entity.

Thus, for example, if the partnership agreement provides for a different ratio for sharing income from the one used for sharing losses, these ratios are used by the partners in determining their tax liability or tax losses to be used as an offset to income from other sources. Moreover, the partnership agreement may provide different ratios for determining the partner's share of special items, such as regular losses, capital gains and losses, and so forth. Such special provisions in the agreement usually determine each partner's allocation. The agreement is disregarded, however, if the principal purpose of the special allocation is tax avoidance. If there appears to be no economic justification other than tax considerations, the special provisions are disallowed, and the distribution ratios for regular income and losses govern.

Against the income-tax benefits of the general partnership must be weighed certain potential disadvantages. The partners may be held jointly and severally liable for any obligation contracted or incurred by any one of the partners on behalf of the partnership. This is particularly onerous for a partner who has substantial assets other than those invested in the firm. The disadvantage is compounded if one partner obviously is substantially more wealthy than the others. Because of the "joint and several" nature of the liability, any legal action would be aimed primarily at the wealthy partner.

Properly orchestrating the partnership arrangements can alleviate these disadvantages to some extent. Insurance can be employed to shift the risk of civil penalties arising from lawsuits against the partnership or against losses from events such as fire, flood, or riot. Liability for debts incurred by the partnership can be controlled by insertion of "exculpatory" clauses in all mortgage instruments. This latter strategy may, of course, create some difficulty in borrowing to the extent one might wish to obtain the benefits of favorable leverage.

A Limited Partnership May Hold Title. The limited partnership form of ownership has attained immense popularity among real estate investors in recent years. The appealing features of this entity are tax conduit treatment coupled with limited liability for the passive investors. Its popularity is probably more appropriately attributable, however, to the opportunity offered promoters to gain an equity position in real estate with no personal financial commitment and, in most cases, with little or no down-side risk to themselves.

It has been said of the limited partnership entity that it is a form of organization wherein the general partner contributes experience and takes out the cash, whereas the limited partners contribute cash and receive experience. This description proves apt with disconcerting frequency. Abuses have been so widespread that most states have begun to more closely regulate the formation of real estate limited partnerships. The sale of limited partnership shares generally receives the same treatment as does the sale of corporate securities. The Securities and Exchange Commission (SEC) is likewise exercising expanded supervision over interstate sales of limited partnership shares.

The Internal Revenue Service also has been acting to discourage the trend to ever greater use of this entity for real estate ventures. Its concern has centered primarily on the issue of whether the alleged partnership is more nearly akin to a corporation. If so, the entity is deemed an "association taxed as a corporation" and conduit treatment is denied.

The abuses of the limited partnership arrangement by unprincipled or unskilled promoters, coupled with the pitfalls resulting from the activities of the Internal Revenue Service, the SEC, and the various state securities commissions, have made the issues surrounding this entity increasingly complicated. Because the issues are so complex, and yet too important to be omitted, a separate chapter (Chapter 11) is devoted to partnerships and trusts as ownership entities.

Joint Ventures Are Variants of Partnerships. A variant of the partnership arrangement is the joint venture agreement. Joint ventures differ from partnerships primarily with regard to the extent of the partnership arrangement. The partners agree between themselves to enter into a joint venture with regard to a specific property. Title is placed in the name of the firm, just as is the case with a partnership. Flow-through accounting treatment is accorded the joint venture in the same manner as the partnership. In the case of the joint venture, however, the partnership is dissolved upon completion of the specific venture.

The Straw Corporation as an Ownership Entity. A strategy sometimes employed to gain tax conduit treatment while avoiding unlimited liability is to have title to real property vest in a straw or dummy corporation. Another reason for using a straw corporation is to circumvent state usury laws that often make it difficult to obtain financing for real estate when the market rate of interest exceeds the limits allowed by the state law. Whatever the motivation, owners of straw corporations should be particularly careful to avoid income tax problems associated with this entity.

Litigation involving the tax status of straw corporations has created a contradictory and confused picture. In some instances, the straw has been held to be a taxable entity because it engaged in business activities that caused it to be adjudged a viable corporate entity rather than a mere dummy or straw entity. The result was that the attempt to treat the corporation as a conduit entity was disallowed. This loss of conduit status would be disastrous if it were the tax shelter characteristics of the investment that made it financially desirable.

Other cases where income from property held by an ostensible straw corporation was found to be taxable to the corporation rather than to the intended beneficiaries involved a decision that the corporation itself was the beneficial owner of the property rather than merely acting in the capacity of trustee for the beneficial owners.

The legal issues surrounding the tax status of straw corporations are extensive and complex. They are unarguably beyond the scope of the present work. The objectives of limited liability with pass-through accounting for income-tax purposes can generally be obtained through alternative arrangements vested with less uncertainty. An investor contemplating the use of a straw corporation should have his legal counsel investigate the alternatives before making a final decision.

The Use of Tax Option Corporations. Shareholders of certain "small business corporations" may elect to have the income from the corporation (other than certain specified capital gains) taxable directly to the owners rather than to the corporation. Because this is a popular election among businesses in general, the first reaction of many would-be investors in real estate is to suggest the subchapter S or tax option corporation as a solution to the problem of getting flow-through accounting treatment of investment results while avoiding personal liability for the financial commitments of the entity.

Unfortunately, among the strict limitations imposed by the enabling legislation is a rule providing that no more than 20% of the corporation's gross receipts in any one taxable year may consist of "passive investment income." Rental income (other than from operation of a hotel or motel facility) and interest income are included in the definition of passive investment income. These being the primary sources of gross receipts for most real estate investment ventures, the limitation generally proves fatal to the use of the tax option corporation as an ownership entity.

It is worth noting, however, that income from disposition of real estate is not considered passive investment income. If the nature of the investment is such that the bulk of gross revenue comes from sales, then the tax option election may be practicable and advantageous. An investor in raw land, for example, might find this a convenient way to hold his investment. He would be afforded a pass-through of tax deductible losses for interest and property taxes during the holding period while enjoying the legal advantage of limited liability that is afforded by the corporate form of ownership.

The subchapter S selection is fraught with legal pitfalls. The technicalities surrounding the election can be quite complex, and its successful use requires an intimate knowledge of the mechanics of the statute and implementing regulations. Moreover, an unfavorable ruling that terminates the election could have catastrophic financial consequences for the investor. It is generally the case, therefore, that the advantages of limited-liability and flow-through accounting can best be obtained by use of an alternative ownership entity not fraught with so many constraints upon operations, and with fewer possibilities for miscalculation.

SUMMARY

Investors wishing to make an offer on a desired parcel of real property have a number of alternatives available, chief among which are the contract of purchase and sale or an option to purchase. The contract of purchase and sale should stipulate precise terms and conditions under which both buyer and seller are compelled to complete the transaction. The contract should specify the remedies and options available in the event one or more of the conditions in the contract are breached or the contingencies are not fulfilled.

The option to purchase binds the seller to convey title under the terms of the contract if the purchaser elects to exercise his option. It specifies the period within which the option must be exercised and the terms and conditions involved. The option contract usually provides for a forfeiture of the option money if the contract is not exercised by its expiration date.

If the optionee exercises his option, his initial tax basis includes the price of the option as well as the additional consideration required for its exercise. If the option is allowed to expire, its price becomes a deductible loss to the optionee and a taxable gain to the optionor.

If either party is a dealer and the optioned property is inventory, that party's loss or gain on the expired option is an ordinary income or loss rather than a capital item. If the parties are not dealers, then the loss or gain on the option has the same character as would the optioned property. The holding period for purposes of determining whether a gain or loss to the optionee is long- or short-term begins at the time the option contract is signed by the accepting party. The holding period ends when the option is assigned or expires.

The entity decision has important income-tax consequences, as well as legal implications with respect to the financial liability of an investor. The investor may elect to take title as an individual or in consort with others. In the first instance, he holds as tenant in severalty, whereas in the latter instance title may vest in the owners as tenants in common or as joint tenants. Each investor holds title to his portion of the property as an individual and is fully liable for his portion of all debts springing from ownership. He must report all income and expenses from his portion of the property on his personal income-tax return as a part of his individual income and expenses.

Parties wishing to collaborate in ownership may elect to have the property held in the name of a partnership or a corporation. If the partnership is of a general nature, each partner is fully liable for all the general obligations of the partnership, but each reports his share of partnership revenue and expenses on his personal income-tax return. The partnership itself pays no taxes. It is a tax conduit that files only an information income-tax return.

Investors seeking to limit their liability associated with a venture may elect to form a corporation that holds title to the real estate in its own name. Generally each shareholder in the corporation has liability limited to the extent of his investment in the corporation.

Offsetting the advantages of limited liability and greater liquidity are the loss of conduit status and double taxation to which a corporation is subject. The corporation is taxed as an entity in itself. And any cash distribution may be taxed to the shareholders as investment income. Investors seeking a tax shelter generally do not choose the corporate form of ownership entity.

A variation of the corporate entity is a corporation that elects subchapter S status, which enables a qualifying corporation to escape double taxation by having all its income taxed directly to the shareholders as individuals whether or not the income is actually distributed. This option may be available to investors in unimproved land but is not a viable alternative for those who expect to receive substantial rental income. The limiting factor is that the corporation's "tax option" status is automatically terminated if it receives more than 20% of its gross revenue in the form of "passive investment income," which includes rents.

Another approach sometimes used to attempt to overcome the income-tax penalties inherent in the corporate from of organization while gaining the desirable corporate feature of limited shareholder liability is to form a straw corporation, in whose name the property is held for the benefit of the equitable owners. This approach is fraught with potential tax pitfalls. It is generally possible to gain the advantages of limited liability with less risk of income-tax penalties by choosing an alternative ownership entity. Alternatives include limited partnerships and trusts. These entities are the principal topic of Chapter 11.

SUGGESTED READINGS

1. Robinson, Gerald J., "Setting Up The Real Estate Venture: An Overview," *Journal of Real Estate Taxation, 3* (1), 28–46 (1975).
2. Wasson, H. Reed, "Real Estate Investment Vehicles: A Comparison of Partnership, Affiliated Subsidiary, Subchapter S Corporation, and Ordinary Corporation as the Form of the Vehicle," *Journal of Real Estate Taxation, 4* (2), 167–205 (1976).

CHAPTER 6

TAX IMPLICATIONS OF MORTGAGE FINANCING

Mortgage financing is an almost inevitable concomitant to the acquisition of commercial or investment property. Few prospective investors have sufficient cash to buy property without the use of borrowed funds. Even those who could purchase on a "free and clear" basis are generally ill advised to do so, because financial leverage amplifies the value of the tax shelter.

The benefits of a high debt-to-equity ratio (i.e., high financial leverage) in real estate are reflected in the average relationship between debt and equity funds employed in the construction industry. Quite often the equity investment is limited to the value of the site and the "value added" by the developer. Essentially all of the actual cash involved represents debt financing.

This chapter outlines the major advantages of the use of borrowed funds. It discusses the income-tax implications of how financing is arranged and the relationship between the principal and interest components in mortgage payments. It introduces the constraint on utilizing financial leverage that results from the statutory limitation on interest expense deductions. The chapter also discusses certain creative techniques available for financing real estate deals. It concludes with a discussion of strategies enabling the alert investor to maximize the tax-shelter benefits available through imaginative financial planning.

ADVANTAGES OF FINANCIAL LEVERAGE

The practice of financing assets partly through the use of equity capital and partly with borrowed funds is referred to as the use of financial leverage. The greater the amount of borrowed funds relative to equity capital, the greater the degree of leverage employed. So long as the rate of return on the acquired asset exceeds the interest rate on borrowed funds, financial leverage increases the rate of return on equity. This is favorable leverage. If, however, the interest rate on borrowed funds exceeds the rate of return on assets, financial leverage is unfavorable, and the result is to reduce the rate of return on equity capital.

Even where the before-tax cost of borrowed funds exceeds the before-tax rate of return on assets, financial leverage may prove favorable when calculated on an after-tax basis. This is because the use of leverage amplifies the tax benefits by providing increased depreciation deductions in excess of the increased debt service requirements. Since the tax collector has a prior claim on all revenue, it is the after-tax outcome that is of interest to investors.

Amplifying the Tax Shelter. Depreciation is treated in Chapter 7. Readers who are unfamiliar with the concept may wish to refer to the introduction to that chapter before proceeding further. Briefly, depreciation is the decline in the value or useful life of one's capital investment due to wear, tear, obsolescence, and the action of the elements. Federal income-tax rules provide for a depreciation allowance to be offset against gross income each year, to account for this inevitable decline in the value or useful life of the improvements to real property.

The rules for computing the annual depreciation allowance vary with the type of property involved, but in all instances the initial basis for the calculation is that portion of the cost applicable to the improvements. The use of financial leverage enters the picture at this point to amplify the benefit of the depreciation allowance. The cost, and thus the initial basis, of the asset acquired is not limited to the equity capital invested. It includes as well any funds borrowed to finance the purchase or any debt assumed by the purchaser. The result is that the owner's tax savings from the depreciation deduction may in a matter of 3 or 4 years exceed his initial cash investment. One result is a substantial tax-deductible "loss" in the early years of the investment that serves to shelter income from the investment and, in many cases, income from other sources as well.

If Frugel makes the investment contemplated in Example 6–1, he is able to claim as a tax-deductible expense an allowance for depreciation of

$4000 for the first year. The annual depreciation allowance declines for subsequent years, since the method employed is the 125% declining balance. Note that whereas the depreciation allowance represents a tax-deductible expense it does not require a current cash outlay. In this respect, it differs from the other expenses incurred in operating the property.

Example 6–1

Fred Frugel, who is married and files a joint tax return with his wife, has taxable income (after all adjustments and deductions) of $24,000 before including the consequences of an anticipated investment in real estate. This taxable income is expected to continue for the foreseeable future. Frugel is considering the purchase of a building that generates annual gross income of $23,000 and requires an annual cash outlay for tax-deductible operating expenses of $13,000. Anticipated net cash flow before debt service and income taxes is, therefore, $23,000 minus $13,000, or $10,000.

From the $10,000 net cash flow from operations calculated in Example 6–1, Frugel must deduct the depreciation allowance to determine the impact of the investment on his taxable income from all sources. The difference between his income tax on taxable income from all sources and the income-tax liability on income from other sources (i.e., on the income he would report if this particular investment were not made) represents the income-tax consequence of the proposed investment. These calculations for the first year of the investment period are presented below:

Net cash flow from operations	$10,000
Less depreciation allowance	4,000
Increase in taxable income due to investment	6,000
Add income from other sources	24,000
Total taxable income, after all adjustments and deductions	$30,000
Income-tax liability (from tax table)	7,880
Less tax on income from other sources (from tax table)	5,660
Income-tax consequence of real estate investment	$ 2,220

The after-tax cash flow from the investment is simply the before-tax cash flow minus the income-tax consequences. The after-tax cash flow for the first year of the investment in Example 6–1 is:

Net cash flow from operations	$10,000
Less income-tax liability arising from the investment	2,220
After-tax cash flow during first year	$ 7,780

During subsequent years, the allowable depreciation deduction declines since the basis of the calculation is the 125% declining-balance method. As a consequence, the income-tax liability gradually increases, and the resulting after-tax cash flow declines. The investment decision is made based on a projection of the after-tax cash flows for the entire period of anticipated ownership. First-year calculations are sufficient, however, to illustrate the effect of financial leverage.

So far, the calculations have been made on the assumption that the real estate in Example 6–1 is purchased on a 100% equity basis, that is, that no financial leverage is employed. The initial cash investment would, therefore, be $100,000. The first year's cash flow expressed as a rate of return on the initial cash outlay would be $7780 divided by $100,000, or 7.8%. The purpose of the exercise is to see how the use of financial leverage can increase this rate of return.

Assume now that an $80,000 loan is available with interest at 8%, using the real estate in Example 6–1 as security. Assume further that the loan is to be repayed in equal monthly installments over a period of 25 years. This implies an annual debt payment of $7409, including both principal and interest. For simplicity, we assume no prepaid interest or loan fees are required in connection with the loan. Total first-year debt service is, therefore, $7409. Of this amount, approximately $6639 represents interest on the debt, with the balance representing repayment of the principal. Over the life of the loan, the portion of the payments representing interest regularly declines as the loan balance is reduced by the periodic payments.

If Frugel borrows the $80,000 his first year, net cash flow from the investment in Example 6–1 is reduced by the amount of the debt service. The cash flow before taxes is:

Gross revenue from rents		$23,000
Less: Operating expenditures	$13,000	
Debt service	7,409	20,409
Before-tax cash flow from investment		$ 2,591

The income-tax consequences of the investment is also altered by the use of borrowed funds. That portion of the debt service representing interest is tax deductible in the year paid. The income-tax consequences of the investment, if the available financial leverage is employed, are as follows:

Net cash flow from operations		$10,000
Less: Depreciation allowance	$4,000	
Interest expense	6,639	10,639
Taxable income (loss) from investments		$ (639)
Add taxable income from other sources		24,000
Total taxable income, after all adjustments and deductions		$23,361
Income-tax liability (from tax table)		$ 5,456
Less tax on income from other sources (from tax table)		5,660
Tax savings due to real estate investment		$ 204

As before, the after-tax cash flow from the investment is simply the before-tax cash flow, adjusted for the income-tax consequence. The after-tax cash flow is $2795, calculated as follows:

Net cash flow from operations	$10,000
Less debt service	7,409
Cash flow before taxes	$ 2,591
Add tax savings	204
After-tax cash flow from investment	$ 2,795

During subsequent years both the depreciation and interest expense deductions decline as the depreciable base and the loan balance are reduced.

As a result of the use of financial leverage, the after-tax cash flow in Example 6–1 has been reduced from $7780 to $2795. The initial cash outlay has also been reduced, however, from $100,000 to 20,000. The first year's cash flow expressed as a percent return on the initial cash outlay is now $2795 divided by $20,000, or 14%.

The expected results with and without the use of financial leverage are summarized on page 87.

Amplifying the Capital-Gain Potential. It has been stated (overly dramatically) that from the moment of their construction all improvements to real estate embark on an irreversible trek to the salvage yard. This inevitable consequence of physical deterioration and social and economic change is

	Without Financial Leverage	With Financial Leverage
Income tax consequences		
Gross revenue from operations	$ 23,000	$23,000
Less tax-deductible items:		
Current operating expenditures	$ 13,000	$13,000
Depreciation deduction	4,000	4,000
Interest expense	0	6,639
Total tax-deductible items	$ 17,000	$23,639
Taxable income (loss) on investment	$ 6,000	$ (639)
Add income from other sources	24,000	24,000
Total taxable income	$ 30,000	$23,361
Income-tax liability (from tax table)	$ 7,880	$ 5,456
Less tax on other income (from tax table)	5,660	5,660
Tax (tax saving) on investment	$ 2,220	$ (204)
Cash flow from investment		
Gross receipts	$ 23,000	$23,000
Add income-tax savings	0	204
Subtotal	$ 23,000	$23,204
Less cash outlay for:		
Operating expenses	$ 13,000	$13,000
Debt service	0	7,409
Income-tax on investment	2,220	0
After-tax cash flow, first year	$ 7,780	$ 2,795
Return on initial cash outlay		
Initial cash outlay	$100,000	$20,000
First-year cash flow	7,780	2,795
Cash flow/initial outlay (rate of return)	7.8%	14.0%

the basis for the depreciation allowance discussed in the preceding section, and in Chapter 7.

But other social and economic forces may cause an offsetting increase in the value of real estate. Changes in tastes and locational preferences may interact to cause an increase in the relative desirability of the site so that its value increases more than proportionally to the decline in remaining useful life of the improvements. Who has not seen evidence of this as cities spring up on what were cornfields only a generation before? A second phenomenon counteracting the forces of deterioration is inflation of the currency. As prices have continued to spiral at varying rates since World War II, the financially astute have sought opportunities to invest in assets that increase in value at least on a par with the increase in the general price level. Real estate has an enviable record in this respect. It is justifiably considered to be a generally good inflation hedge.

This combination of forces often more than offsets the physical, social, and economic factors causing a decline in value. While being allowed a current tax-deductible allowance for depreciation, the investor frequently finds his property actually increasing in value. A significant consideration on any real estate investment proposal must, therefore, be the prospect for capital appreciation.

The potential gain to the investor from an increase in the market value of his holdings can be multiplied by the use of financial leverage. Disregarding for the moment the income-tax aspects of the situation, consider the case of a parcel of undeveloped land that is increasing in value at an average rate of 15% per annum due to favorable locational characteristics, and note how an investor can multiply his expected rate of return through the use of favorable financial leverage.

Example 6–2

Igot Bigbucks intends to purchase a tract of land on the outskirts of Embrio City. The land, which is situated in the most probable path of urban growth, can be acquired for $30,000. Bigbucks expects the land to be worth approximately double that amount in 5 years (representing a compound rate of growth of approximately 15% per annum) at which point he intends to sell. During the holding period, the land can be leased to a peanut farmer for $3000 per annum on a net–net basis (i.e., the farmer pays all property taxes and maintenance costs). Bigbucks is *not* a dealer in real estate.

Bigbucks finds that he can borrow 50% of the purchase price of the land on the following terms: annual payments of interest only (at 12% per annum) payable at the end of each year during the holding period. The principal of the loan is to be repayed at the end of the fifth year, coincident with resale of the land.

If Bigbucks purchases the land in Example 6–2 with 100% equity funds (i.e., on a "free-and-clear" basis), his anticipated before-tax rate of return on equity is approximately 25% per annum over the holding period. If, however, he utilizes the available financial leverage his expected rate of return on equity is increased to about 33% per annum. The calculations are as follows:

	Unleveraged (100% Equity)	Leveraged (50% Equity)
Initial cash outlay (i.e., equity investment required)	$30,000	$15,000
Annual net cash inflow (before tax):		
Annual rent receipts	$ 3,000	$ 3,000
Less annual interest payment	0	1,800
Net inflow annually	$ 3,000	$ 1,200
Net proceeds from disposal (before tax):		
Sales price	$60,000	$60,000
Less principal balance of note	0	15,000
Net proceeds from sale	$60,000	$45,000
Rate of return on investment (before tax):		
Annual cash inflow as percent of initial investment (net annual cash flow/initial investment)	10%	8%
Add annual rate of increase in cash value of initial investment*	15%	24.7%
Anticipated rate of return on investment, over anticipated holding period	25%	32.7%

* The relationship between the initial cash expenditure, the net cash receipts on disposal, and the rate of growth in the investor's capital is expressed by the equation:

$$\text{Net proceeds from disposal/initial cash outlay} = [1 + r]^n$$

where r is the rate of increase in the cash value of the initial cash invested, and n is the number of years between purchase and subsequent resale. In the present case, the value of n is known to be 5. The unknown factor is the rate of growth, r. Solving for r is simplified by the use of precomputed tables or with the aid of a hand-held electronic calculator. There are a number of frequently employed alternative ways to measure rate of return. Most of the alternatives owe their popularity to ease of calculation and understanding. The choice of how the rate of return is measured does not affect the analysis at the present level of abstraction but could become a crucial issue in the investment decision at some other point.

When income-tax consequences are introduced into the equation, the potential benefits from such a situation become even more attractive. This is because the interest paid on borrowed funds is a tax-deductible item, whereas the gain on disposal is subject to favorable capital-gains treatment (capital gains are considered in detail in Chapter 8). Example 6–3 reconsiders the details of Example 6–2, except that now we include the tax effects of the transaction.

Example 6–3

Assume the same facts as in the previous example, but assume further that Bigbucks is in the 50% income-tax bracket.

The calculations of the previous example are adjusted below to reflect the after-tax rate of return on equity.

	Unleveraged (100% Equity)	Leveraged (50% Equity)
Initial cash outlay	$30,000	$15,000
Annual cash inflow:		
Annual rent receipts	$ 3,000	$ 3,000
Less interest payments	0	1,800
Net taxable annually	$ 3,000	$ 1,200
Less tax liability (50%)	1,500	600
After-tax cash flow	$ 1,500	$ 600
After-tax sales proceeds:		
Selling price	$60,300	$60,300
Less capital-gains tax [25(60,300 – 30,000)]	$ 7,575	$ 7,575
Loan balance	0	15,000
Net proceeds after tax	$52,725	$37,725
Rate of return on investment:		
Annual cash flow as percent of initial cash outlay	5%	4%
Anticipated after-tax proceeds from sale, as percentage rate of increase in initial outlay*	11.9%	20.25%
Anticipated rate of return on investment, over anticipated holding period	16.9%	24.25%

* After-tax proceeds = initial outlay $(1 + r)^n$, where r is the rate of increase and n is the number of years the investment is held. Solve for r.

TAX CONSEQUENCES OF INTEREST AND CLOSING COSTS

An early observation one needs to make is that the nature of financing has no direct effect on the tax basis of property. The initial basis is the amount paid for the property and the fair market value of any goods or services given in exchange. Thus if the seller takes back a purchase money mortgage in part payment, the principal amount of the mortgage is included in the purchase price. Likewise the purchase price includes any mortgage debt outstanding when the purchaser takes title. This rule holds whether the buyer assumes personal liability for the balance on an outstanding mortgage to which the property is subject after closing. The rule remains invariate even where the outstanding mortgage is payable to the purchaser himself.

The Treatment of Loan Closing Costs. Whether the problem is to minimize the down payment of a "cash rich" investor to obtain the advantages of leverage or to obtain mortgage financing to meet the needs of a buyer who is strapped for the necessary down payment, the borrower incurs substantial costs in connection with a mortgage loan. These costs can conveniently be divided into two categories.

The first category represents costs incident to the acquisition of the loan. Examples include legal fees, appraisal fees, brokers' commissions, and survey and title search fees. These are costs that may not be deducted as current expenses but may be capitalized and charged off (on a straight-line basis) over the life of the mortgage loan. Should the loan be repaid prior to maturity or the property sold subject to the balance of the loan, the unamortized portion of the loan charges may be charged off in the year of prepayment or sale.

The second category of charges represents prepayment of interest on the borrowed funds. This has been an area of great controversy and litigation in the past. The deck was decisively stacked in favor of the government by the Tax Reform Act of 1976, which states unequivocally that any charge for the use of borrowed money must be allocated ratably over the period of the loan. The act leaves undetermined the precise method to be employed in prorating any such charge. Nor, as of the date of this publication, has the Treasury issued any clarifying rules. The following example illustrates a procedure that appears to be permissible and that provides for a greater charge-off in the early years of the loan than in the later years.

Of course, if the loan is paid off before the specified period, the mortgagor can also deduct the remaining closing costs at that time. The same rule applies if the loan is rolled over (refinanced) prior to maturity, or if the property is sold subject to the balance of the loan.

Example 6–4

A taxpayer procures a $100,000 mortgage loan in connection with the purchase of investment realty. The loan is to be repaid in equal monthly installments of principal and interest over 20 years, with interest at 8% per annum on the unpaid balance of the loan. The borrower incurs $5500 of costs incident to the loan, as follows:

Survey	$ 250	
Legal fees	500	
Title insurance	750	
Mortgage broker's commission	1,500	$3,000
Loan origination fee (i.e., "points")		2,500
Total charges		$5,500

The first set of fees is incidental to the procurement of the loan, rather than representing a charge for the use of borrowed funds. These charges (totaling $3000) must be written off over the 20-year life of the loan on a straight-line basis. The amount to be charged off annually as a tax-deductible expense is 1/20 × $3000, or $150. The $2500 loan origination fee represents prepaid interest that must be charged off ratably over the life of the loan. The procedure is left indeterminate by the code, but the following is probably an acceptable method of calculating the annual amount to be charged as a tax-deductible interest expense:

Annual debt service (from standard amortization table)	$ 10,037
Times number of years	20
Total debt service over life of loan	$200,740
Less face amount of note	100,000
Total nominal interest charge over life of loan	$100,740
Deferred interest (amount of discount)	$ 2,500
Percent to be charged-off during first year:	
First-year interest (from standard amortization table as a percent of total nominal: $7923/$100,740)	0.0786
Amount of deferred interest allocatable to first year	$ 197

The rules are somewhat different for taxpayers who are treated for tax purposes as dealers in real property. For a dealer, the costs of obtaining a loan (but *not* prepaid interest) may be claimed as an ordinary and necessary business expense and so deducted in the year incurred.

Income-Tax Consequences of Interest Payments. Interest on borrowed funds is generally tax-deductible whether for the purchase of investment or income property or for any other purpose. The only exception to this rule is the restriction against deducting interest on funds borrowed to purchase tax-exempt securities, for certain insurance policies and annuities, and interest paid during construction of real property. All other interest paid on mortgage indebtedness is deductible if the taxpayer is the legal or equitable owner of the property.

There is, however, a potentially significant difference in the tax treatment of interest incurred in the production of rental income or in a trade or business and interest that is not for these purposes. Interest on a loan for personal use is deductible only if the taxpayer itemizes his deductions. But interest on a loan for business or investment purposes (with the exceptions noted earlier) is subtracted in computing adjusted gross income. This figure may then be reduced by the amount of the allowable standard deduction, or the taxpayer may proceed to itemize deductions if it is advantageous to do so.

In determining whether interest expense is an adjustment to gross income or an itemized deduction, the key factor is the use to which the funds are put. The security pledged to secure the loan is not a factor. For example, if an investor places a mortgage on his personal residence as a means of financing it, the interest is a personal expense and would be deductible only if he itemizes his deductions. But interest on a mortgage on his personal residence would be deductible in computing adjusted gross income if the funds were used as a down payment on income property.

Statutory Limitations on Interest Deductions. Section 163(d) of the Tax Reform Act of 1969 introduced limits on the amount of interest expense that is tax deductible. The limitation, which was made far more stringent with the 1976 Act, applies to interest on loans made to purchase property that is held for investment purposes. It does not apply to interest on business loans or loans for the purchase of consumer goods or amenity property. The new provision allows the deduction of interest expense on investment loans to be used only to offset investment income. However, the first $10,000 of investment interest each year is exempt from this provision ($5000 for a married taxpayer filing a separate return).* Under most cir-

* Trusts do not get the exemption.

cumstances rental property would be considered a business, and thus not subject to this limitation.

Investment interest in excess of the stipulated exemption can be used only to offset net investment income. This is total (gross) income from investment (but not business operations) and net short-term capital gains minus the expenses other than interest resulting from these investments (e.g., management fees, depreciation, and depletion).

Any investment interest that, due to this limitation provision, is not allowed as a tax-deductible expense in the year incurred can be carried over to the next taxable year. It may then be deducted to the extent of $10,000 plus one-half the net investment income for the year of the carry-over.

Example 6–5

During the year a taxpayer incurred investment interest of $12,000. His total taxable income before deducting investment interest was $28,500, all of which was from noninvestment sources. He had no investment income. His deduction for investment interest is limited to $10,000. The balance may be carried over to succeeding years.

Example 6–6

During the year a taxpayer incurred investment interest of $18,000. He had net investment income (before offsetting investment interest) of $5000. He may deduct $15,000 of the investment interest. The balance may be carried over to succeeding years.

TAX STRATEGY

The particular virtue of investing in real property with potential for appreciation in value is the favorable income-tax treatment afforded gains of this type. Likewise, depreciable real property is attractive to the tax-burdened investor because it permits significant tax-deductible losses without corresponding cash expenditures (i.e., tax shelter due to accelerated depreciation). But even these reductions in one's tax obligation leave something to be desired. There arrives the day when the tax shelter is exhausted and the investor would like to take some profit from his portfolio, which now has a market value greatly in excess of his tax basis. The dilemma is how to harvest this fortune without surrendering the major portion to the tax collector.

Potentially valuable tax avoidance strategies involving the use of borrowed funds in connection with real estate investments include the use of inflated or deflated mortgages when property is bought or sold, to maximize the benefits of both interest and depreciation deductions and to transmute interest income to long-term capital gains. A strategy for increasing the liquidity of one's portfolio by use of refinancing can enable conversion to cash or short-term assets without incurring a capital-gains tax.

Refinancing for "Tax-Free Liquidation." A major factor in the attractiveness of real estate as an investment is the possibility of leveraging the tax benefits through mortgage financing. The investor pays only a fraction of the purchase price when he takes title to property, financing the balance either through the seller or a third-party lender. Yet, the buyer may claim tax-deductible depreciation expense based on the total purchase price, both his equity investment and the amount financed.

But the tax advantages of financial leverage are even more attractive because the after-tax cost of borrowing to finance the purchase is reduced by the tax deduction the purchaser may claim on the interest he must pay for the mortgage loan. During the early years of the mortgage, this accounts for the bulk of the amount paid.

Example 6–7

The percent of the periodic mortgage payment that represents interest expense varies with the interest rate and the length of the amortization period. The following table presents the percentage of the total annual disbursement that constitute interest expense, for selected years and loan periods, with an interest rate of 8.5%.

Mortgage payable in equal monthly installments over–	Percentage of annual mortgage payment that represents interest expense (the balance applied to reduction of principal) during:			
	first year	second year	third year	fifteenth year
15 years	71.2	67.8	65.3	04.4
20 years	80.8	78.9	77.9	37.6
25 years	87.6	86.5	84.5	58.6
30 years	91.3	91.0	90.2	83.7

The longer the investor owns the property, however, the less the tax advantages of ownership. The advantage of deducting depreciation expense on an accelerated basis declines rapidly due to the smaller "undepreciated balance" upon which each succeeding year's depreciation expense is based. And as the balance due on the mortgage loan is reduced by the periodic payments on the principal, the portion of the payments that constitutes a tax-deductible interest charge gets progressively smaller.

Example 6–8

An investor acquires for $100,000 a property that yields a net operating income (cash flow before debt service payments and income taxes) of $12,000. He finances the purchase by borrowing $80,000 at 8.5% per annum, with level monthly payments over 25 years. Depreciation is calculated using the 200% declining-balance method, assuming a 30-year useful life and with 75% of the value attributable to the depreciable improvements.

During the first full year of ownership, the investor not only pays no income tax on the cash receipts from the property, but also has a small tax-deductible loss on the investment that can be offset against income from other sources. By the fifteenth year of ownership, however, the tax shelter has disappeared. A substantial portion of the debt service is now being applied against principal rather than being charged as tax-deductible interest expense. The annual depreciation deduction has also declined drastically. The net result of the erosion of the tax shelter is that the investor now incurs income-tax liability on investment income of $1096 *in excess* of the cash flow generated from the investment.

	First Year	Fifteenth Year
Income tax (tax saving)		
Net income from operations	$12,000	$12,000
Less: Interest expense (from amortization table)	7,637	4,730
Depreciation expense (from depreciation table)	5,000	1,904
Total deductions	$12,637	$ 6,634
Taxable income (loss)	$ (637)	$ 5,366
Times tax rate (assume marginal tax rate of 50%)	0.5	0.5
Income tax (tax saving)	$ (319)	$ 2,683

	First Year	Fifteenth Year
Net cash flow from investment, after taxes and debt service		
Cash flow before debt service and taxes	$12,000	$12,000
Add income tax savings	319	0
Less: Taxes	$ 0	$ 2,683
Debt service	7,730	7,730
Cash flow after debt service and taxes	$ 4,589	$ 1,587

After several years of ownership the property is, as a consequence of this erosion of the tax shelter, much less attractive in terms of after-tax cash flow. The investment reaches a "tipping point" where the taxable income from the property exceeds the cash flow. At this point, the prudent investor considers alternatives.

One such alternative is to sell the property and move the proceeds into another investment. This strategy has several serious imperfections, however. A major problem is the possibility of a sizable tax liability. Chapter 9 presents the details of depreciation recapture rules whereby any gain on disposal is taxed as ordinary income to the extent that total accumulated depreciation is greater than what it would have been had the owner used the straight-line rather than an accelerated depreciation method. The balance of any gain on disposal would be subject to taxation at the capital-gain rate.

There exists a strategy that permits one to move into another property without incurring the tax liability from recapture of excess depreciation and realized capital gains. It involves an exchange of like-kind properties on a "tax-free exchange" basis and is described fully in Chapter 10. Even here, however, the investor is likely to incur substantial transactions costs in the form of legal fees and real estate brokerage commissions.

An alternative that enables the investor to move the bulk of his equity out of an appreciated property without incurring either a tax liability or substantial transactions costs is to refinance. The proceeds from a loan are, unlike the proceeds from a sale, tax-free. And the periodic loan payment, which need not be increased as a result of the refinancing operation, is once again predominantly comprised of tax-deductible interest expense.

Example 6–9

Continuing the illustration from Example 6–8, assume that after 15 years the property has approximately maintained its market value of $100,000 and continues to yield a net operating income (cash flow before debt service and income taxes) of $12,000. As calculated in Example 6–8, the annual cash flow after taxes and debt service is only $1587 in the fifteenth year, and the investor finds that he is paying taxes on income of $1096, which does not even represent cash flow (going instead to the mortgage debt).

	First Year	Fifteenth Year
Taxable cash flow	$ 0	$5,366
Tax-free cash flow (excess taxable income)	4,270	(1,096)
Cash flow before taxes	$4,270	$4,270

Seeking ways to improve the after-tax cash flow on his equity, the investor finds he can either sell for $100,000 and reinvest the proceeds at 12% before taxes, or that he can roll over his loan by borrowing $80,000 at 8.5% repayable over 25 years. The proceeds of the loan, after paying off the balance of the old mortgage, would then be reinvested at 12%. The cash flow from the alternatives are compared below:

	Alternative Strategies	
	Sell	Refinance
Proceeds of sale or new loan	$100,000	$80,000
Less: Balance of old loan	51,920	51,920
Income-tax liability*	9,398	0
Net proceeds of transaction	$ 38,682	$28,080
× rate of return on new investment	0.12	0.12
Annual investment income (new)	$ 4,642	$ 3,370
Less income taxes (at 50%)	2,321	1,685
After-tax cash flow from new investment	$ 2,321	$ 1,685
Add after-tax proceeds from old investment†	0	2,976
Annual after-tax cash flow‡	$ 2,321	$ 4,661

* Income-tax liability results from both recapture of excess depreciation and from capital gain. For illustrative purposes, assume the excess depreciation is subject to 100% recapture (i.e., assume property was acquired after December 31, 1974). See Chapter 9 for explanation of calculation.

Gain on disposal

Sale price	$100,000
Less adjusted base (cost less accumulated depreciation)	73,356

Gain on disposal	$ 26,645	
Less recapture of excess depreciation	10,856	
Capital gain	$ 15,789	
Income-tax liability from disposal		
Taxable gain:		
Recapture of excess depreciation	$ 10,856	
Half of capital gain	7,940	
Total taxable at ordinary tax rate	$ 18,795	
Tax (at 50%)	$ 9,398	

† Calculations are for first year after refinancing. The cash flow declines each subsequent year due to the decrease in the tax-deductible portion of the mortgage payment.

Income tax from operation of old property		
Net operating income		$12,000
Less: Interest expense	$ 7,637	
Depreciation expense	1,776	9,413
Taxable income		$ 2,587
Income-tax liability (at 50%)		$ 1,294
After-tax cash flow from old investment		
Net operating income		$12,000
Less: Debt service	$ 7,730	
Income tax	1,294	9,024
Cash flow after income tax and debt service		$ 2,976

‡ For simplicity of calculations, transactions costs have been ignored. Some such costs are incurred with either strategy, reducing somewhat the after-tax cash flow. Transactions costs associated with the sell strategy would generally exceed those of the refinance strategy. We have also ignored the possibility of a preference tax liability arising from the sell strategy. This makes the refinance strategy even more advantageous.

Amplifying Tax Benefits Via "Deflated" Mortgage. The genesis of this strategy is the tax rule that allows a borrower to deduct from taxable income the portion of his mortgage payment representing interest but does not allow a deduction for principal payments. If the seller is taking back a purchase money mortgage for a part of the purchase price, the stage is set for improving the after-tax results for one or both parties by using a "deflated mortgage."

After a preliminary determination of the purchase price and purchase money mortgage terms, under this strategy the seller accepts a lower purchase price for a higher interest rate on the purchase money mortgage. The key is to use a trade-off so that the decrease in the purchase price exactly offsets the increase in the interest payments. The seller gets (and the buyer pays) approximately the same total dollar amount each month as before. But now a smaller portion of the debt service payment is principal and a larger portion is tax-deductible interest.

Example 6–10

A buyer in the 50% tax bracket is contemplating the purchase of a $90,000 property with 20% down and the seller to take back a 20-year, 6.5% mortgage for the balance. The buyer proposes that the price be reduced to $67,000 and the interest rate be increased to 12%, with the same $18,000 down payment. The buyer's after-tax outlay for debt service during the first year is now:

	Original Terms	Revised Terms
Annual payments on principal and interest	$6,444	$6,492
Less tax saving (50% tax rate times the portion of monthly payments representing interest)	2,328	2,940
Net annual expenditure before insurance and property tax	$4,116	$3,552

Assume that the seller is in the 30% income-tax bracket and has an adjusted basis of $30,000 for the land. His after-tax proceeds from debt service during the first year after the transaction will be:

	Original Deal	Revised Deal
Annual receipts (12 monthly installments)	$6,444	$6,492
Less income tax:		
On interest portion*	$1,397	$1,764
On principal portion†	179	51
After-tax proceeds from note	$3,868	$4,677

* Tax on interest portion:

	Original Deal	*Revised Deal*
Total mortgage payment	$ 6,444	$ 6,492
Less principal reduction	1,788	612
Interest payment (ordinary income)	$ 4,656	$ 5,880
Times ordinary tax rate	0.3	0.3
Tax on interest income	$ 1,397	$ 1,764

† Tax on principal portion:

	Original Deal	*Revised Deal*
Selling price	$90,000	$67,000
Less adjusted basis	30,000	30,000
Total capital gain	$60,000	$37,000

	Original Deal	*Revised Deal*
Portion of selling price subject to taxation (capital gain/contract price)	0.667	0.552
Times principal amount collected	$ 1,788	$ 612
Collections subject to capital-gains tax	$ 1,193	$ 338
Times capital-gains tax rate	0.15	0.15
Capital-gain tax liability	$ 179	$ 51

With respect to both amount and timing, the before-tax cash flows involved in the transaction in Example 6–10 are almost unchanged by the revised proposal. But the after-tax consequences are drastically altered. The buyer's initial cash outlay is the same as before, but his after-tax outlay for debt service is reduced by about 14% the first year. In subsequent years, the tax benefits decline as an ever-increasing portion of the debt service is applied to reduction in principal rather than to payment of tax-deductible interest. But at some future date, the investor can consider replenishing his leverage by refinancing the property.

But why should the seller accept the revised proposal? He may indeed be less than enthusiastic about a proposed 26% reduction in the price he is to receive for the property. But if he is an astute investor, he will recognize that what is most significant is the after-tax proceeds of the sale. In our example, the after-tax proceeds for the first year have been increased 21% by the revised proposal.

But there are other benefits for the seller as well. He gets to keep a greater portion of the down payment under the revised proposal. Here is how the disposition of the down payment works out under each alternative:

	Original Terms	Revised Terms
Sales price	$90,000	$67,000
Less adjusted basis	30,000	30,000
Gain on disposal	$60,000	$37,000
Down payment	$18,000	$18,000
Less capital-gains tax due [down payment × (gain/contract price) × capital-gain rate]	1,800	1,491
After-tax proceeds at time of sale	$16,200	$16,509

These calculations assume that there is no recapture of excess depreciation involved and that the seller reports the transaction under the installment sales method (see Chapter 9 for a description of the advantages and details of the installment sales method). If there were excess depreciation to be recaptured or if the installment sales method were not employed, the advantages to the seller would be even greater, since the tax savings would be at the ordinary income rate rather than the capital-gain rate and since the savings would be more concentrated in the year of the transaction.

There are two compelling factors limiting the extent to which this strategy can be used. The first of these is the observation that deflating the mortgage and so increasing the portion of the monthly payment comprised of interest *increases* the tax liability of the seller. It is important to note, however, that the increase in the seller's tax is usually far less than the decrease in the taxes of the buyer. The buyer's interest payment reduces his taxes at his marginal tax rate on ordinary income. Likewise, the increase in interest causes the seller's taxes to go up at his marginal tax rate on ordinary income. But at the same time the reduction in the purchase price *decreases* the seller's taxes at the capital-gain tax rate, which is about one-half the rate on ordinary income. By setting the deflated mortgage at a mutually agreed level, buyer and seller can share the net tax savings. Only the Internal Revenue Service loses. In our example, we assumed the seller to be in a lower tax bracket than the buyer. This assumption, which dramatized the potential benefit of the strategy, is not an unlikely circumstance.

The other potential problem is the reaction of the Internal Revenue Service to this depletion in its share of the action. If the nominal selling price of the property is obviously far below its market value, and the contract interest rate is obviously far above the market rate, IRS may tax the transaction on a reconstructed basis. The intended benefits are then lost. The secret of success in this strategy is not to be overly greedy.

Reduce the Size of the Monthly Payment with an "Inflated" Mortgage. This is simply a mirror image of the "deflated" mortgage strategy. It involves a technique for decreasing the portion of the seller's periodic receipts that are taxable as ordinary income. The higher the seller's tax bracket, the greater the potential benefit of the strategy.

An agreement involving an "inflated" mortgage results in the seller's getting (and the buyer's paying) a smaller total dollar amount (principal plus interest) than before. But now a smaller portion of the seller's annual proceeds is taxable as interest income and a larger portion as capital gains.

A "tax-wise" proposal might involve increasing the purchase price of the realty in Example 6–11, and reducing the interest rate on the mortgage, with no change in the down payment or the monthly mortgage payments. This would involve the following alterations in the deal:

	Market Terms	Revised Proposal
Sales price	$75,000	$86,000
Less down payment	15,000	15,000
Amount financed	$60,000	$71,500
Monthly mortgage payments	$ 793	$ 794
Interest rate	10%	6%

Example 6–11

Assume a parcel of developed property with a market value of $75,000 and an adjusted basis in the hands of the seller of $30,000. Assume the market rate of interest for an 80%, 10-year loan is 10% per annum. This time assume, however, that the seller is in the 50% income tax bracket and the buyer in the 30% bracket.

Since the down payment and the monthly payments are essentially unchanged by the revised proposal, both buyer and seller would be indifferent between the alternatives were it not for the differential impact of the income tax consequences.

Consider first the effect of the revised proposal on the after-tax cash receipts of the seller. Assuming that there is no excess depreciation subject to recapture, and that the sale is reported on the installment method, the after-tax proceeds at the time of the sale are:

	Market Terms	Revised Proposal
Sales price	$75,000	$86,000
Less adjusted basis	30,000	30,000
Capital gain	$45,000	$56,000
Down payment	$15,000	$15,000
Less capital gain tax [collections × (capital gain/contract price) × tax rate on capital gain]	2,250	2,442
After-tax proceeds at point of sale	$12,750	$12,558

What benefit does the seller receive to compensate him for the approximately $300 reduction in the after-tax proceeds received at the time of the sale? The payoff lies in the after-tax proceeds on the note. The difference for the first year alone is insignificant. It is calculated as follows:

	Market Terms	Revised Proposal
Collection	$9,516	$9,528
Less taxes:		
On interest*	$2,918	$2,583
On capital gain†	552	873
Total taxes	$3,470	$3,456
After-tax proceeds during first year	$6,046	$6,072

	Market Terms	*Revised Proposal*
* Interest on note for first 12 months (from standard amortization tables)	$5,836	$5,166
Times ordinary income-tax rate	0.5	0.5
Tax on interest income	$2,918	$2,583
† Collections on note	$9,516	$9,528
Less interest on the note (from preceding footnote)	5,836	4,166
Principal collected	$3,680	$5,363
Times ratio of capital gain to contract price	0.6	0.65
Capital gain to be reported	$2,208	$3,492
Times capital-gains rate (half of ordinary tax rate)	0.25	0.25
Capital-gains tax	$ 552	$ 873

But the benefits from the tax-wise structuring of the deal continue to accrue to the seller over the entire period of receipts from the note. The benefits would be less impressive were the gain subject to recapture of excess depreciation or were it not possible to report the transaction under the installment method.

Looking at the proposed restructuring of the market terms from the perspective of the buyer is less encouraging. The effect of deflating the mortgage is that less of the annual debt service payment is tax-deductible, so that the after-tax cash expenditure is increased. However, the inflated purchase price means the buyer has a much higher initial basis upon which to calculate his depreciation deduction.

As with the "inflated" mortgage, there is the ever-present possibility that over-inflation will cause the Internal Revenue Service to impute a higher interest rate and lower selling price in reconstructing the transaction to determine the resultant income-tax liabilities of the parties. This and all planning must be undertaken with full recognition that the government is not a disinterested bystander.

Example 6–12

Continuing Example 6–11, assume that the site value alone (i.e., the land separate from the buildings) has a value of $15,000. The parties to the transaction agree that the balance of the purchase price applies to the improvements. The Internal Revenue Service generally accepts such an agreement as the basis for apportioning the purchase price between buildings and land, if the parties are involved in an arm's-length transaction. Assume further that the property qualifies for 125% declining balance depreciation and a 20-year useful life. The tax saving from the increased depreciation deduction is $300 for the first year and declines thereafter. Here is the first-year calculation:

	Market Terms	Revised Proposal
Tax savings:		
Interest	$5,856	$4,166
Depreciation*	3,750	4,438
Total	9,606	8,604
Times tax rate	0.3	0.3
Tax savings	$2,882	$2,581

	Market Terms	*Revised Proposal*
*Purchase price	$75,000	$86,000
Less land basis	15,000	15,000
Basis of building	$60,000	$71,000
Times depreciation rate [1.25 × 1/20]	0.0625	0.0625
First year depreciation expense	$ 3,750	$ 4,438

There are numerous possibilities for improving the terms of trade by altering the relationship between the purchase price and the interest rate in a seller-financed transaction. The variations are limited primarily by the imagination of the parties to the transaction. The sharing of the tax savings is a function of the exact trade-off between purchase price and loan terms and depends upon the relative bargaining skills of the negotiators.

SUMMARY

Because mortgage financing is almost always an essential ingredient in real estate transactions, the income-tax consequences of financing arrangements are of great significance to both buyer and seller.

The most prominent aspect of the tax consequences of mortgage financing, from the buyer's perspective, is the potential it offers for leveraging the tax-shelter possibilities inherent in real estate investment. The portion of the purchase price financed with borrowed funds is, nevertheless, included in the purchaser's initial basis for purposes of calculating his depreciation deduction and capital gain or loss upon ultimate disposal. Meanwhile, the interest on the borrowed funds constitutes a currently deductible expense that does not in itself affect the tax treatment of the property.

There are often significant tax advantages to financing real estate with a purchase money mortgage rather than resorting to third-party financing. This strategy affords the opportunity to alter the tax consequences by adjusting the relationship between purchase price and interest rate to minimize the total tax liability resulting from the sale. The genesis of the opportunity is the differential tax treatment of interest income and capital gains. The portion of the seller's cash receipts that constitute interest and capital gains can be altered by use of "inflated" or "deflated" mortgages. Such adjustments in the terms of trade must be made with a careful eye on the probable reaction of the Internal Revenue Service.

The opportunity to affect the income tax liability of the investor by altering the financing arrangements is limited by Section 163(d) of the code, which limits the investment interest expense deduction to the amount of investment income before deducting interest expense, plus $10,000, in any one taxable year. This limitation is ameliorated somewhat by liberal carry-over provisions for any interest expense disallowed during the current taxable year.

SUGGESTED READINGS

1. Schwartz, Sheldon, "Mortgage in Excess of Basis–The 'Back-end' Problem in Real Estate," *Real Estate Review, 3* (3), 105–110 (1973).
2. Schwartz, Sheldon, "Tax Aspects of Real Estate in Trouble," *Real Estate Review, 5* (3), 47–55 (1975).

CHAPTER 7

DEPRECIATION AND OTHER ADJUSTMENTS TO THE BASIS

Depreciation is the reduction in value or usefulness of an asset due to wear, tear, action of the elements, or obsolescence. The code provides for a deduction from taxable income of an allowance for depreciation of income-generating assets. As a consequence, cash flow from real estate is often considerably greater than the taxable income reported. Indeed, investors often find their ventures generate a substantial income on a "cash-flow" basis while showing a net loss on the investment for income-tax purposes.

Liberal depreciation provisions associated with investments in real property, combined with special tax rates for long-term capital gains have thus traditionally made real estate an excellent investment medium for persons in relatively high tax brackets. In 1976 the code was revised to drastically reduce the special tax benefits associated with ownership of real estate for investment or business purposes, but many of the advantages and much of the allure remains. What has been altered is the way the game must be played.

The IRS views the depreciation allowance as providing an opportunity for the investor to "recover" his capital investment over the productive life of the asset. But the amount of the allowable depreciation bears no necessary relationship to the actual change in value of the asset. Rather, in a period of consistent inflation such as experienced in the United States since the Second World War, most property actually increases in market value while being "depreciated" for income-tax purposes.

Depreciation represents a tax-deductible expense that requires no current cash expenditure. This benefits the investor in two ways: (1) It permits accounting losses on the real estate venture that can be offset against income from other sources, so that the investor's total income-tax liability may be substantially less than in the absence of the investment. (2) It has the effect of shifting earnings from ordinary income to capital gains. And capital gains are taxed at a much lower rate.

Chapter 7 is devoted primarily, but not exclusively, to the allowance for depreciation and its effect on both the investor's current income-tax situation and the adjusted basis of his property when it is eventually sold. It addresses the issues of who can take depreciation deductions and determining the highest allowable deduction. This involves calculating the "useful life," the "depreciable basis," and the allowable methods of depreciation for various classes of real property.

Claiming a deduction for depreciation reduces the tax basis of the real estate being depreciated, of course. And the lower the adjusted basis when the property is ultimately sold, the greater is the taxable gain (assuming that the property is in fact sold for more than the adjusted basis). The total gain on disposal is the net selling price less the adjusted basis. There may be adjustments other than depreciation that affect the investor's income-tax liability when he disposes of the property. The more significant of these other adjustments are also explained in this chapter.

It is usually (but not always) in the best interests of the taxpayer to maximize the depreciation deduction in the early years of property ownership. Instances of when this is not the case are discussed in the section on tax strategies. The tax strategy section also provides guidance on maximizing the depreciation deduction by timely switching of depreciation methods. Included in the strategy discussion is the issue of the effect on taxes of alterations and improvements and the consequent adjustments to the owner's tax basis.

WHEN A DEPRECIATION DEDUCTION MAY BE CLAIMED

The code permits a deduction from taxable income for a "reasonable" provision for the wasting away of income-generating assets. This has been clarified by the Service and the courts to include both a provision for wear and tear and a reduction in value or usefulness due to "changes in the arts, shifting of business centers, loss of trade, inadequacy, supercession, prohibitory laws, etc."

A depreciation deduction is allowed on the improvements to all property held for the production of income. It is important to note that it is the intent to produce income that is important, not the actual realization of income. Thus the owner of rental property could take a depreciation deduction whether or not he actually realized any rent from the real estate. But he must be prepared to produce evidence that he in fact intended the property to produce income. For example, a personal residence that has been vacated and offered for sale would not qualify for a depreciation deduction simply because it suffered a loss in value due to the forces cited in the definition of depreciation. It would be considered income property, and thus eligible for a depreciation deduction, only if the owners actively sought to rent it during the period after vacating the premises.

Although a personal residence is not depreciable so long as it is being used as such, it becomes eligible for depreciation if it is converted to income-producing uses. If only a part of the residence is used for rental or business purposes, then that portion qualifies for a depreciation deduction.

HOW DEPRECIATION IS COMPUTED

The first step in calculating the allowable depreciation is to determine the taxpayer's "initial basis" for the property (usually cost). The portion of this initial basis that applies to the improvements (but not that which applies to the land itself) constitutes the depreciable base. Depending upon which of the permissible depreciation methods the taxpayer elects, this amount may be adjusted to reflect the estimated salvage value at the end of the useful life of the improvements. Subsequent adjustments to the depreciable base must be made to reflect depreciation deductions taken to date, capital improvements, and certain other changes prescribed by the code.

Determining the Initial Basis. When property is acquired by purchase, its basis to the purchaser is his cost. This includes everything of value given in exchange. It also includes all costs incurred in obtaining and defending title. Thus the cost would include such items as purchase commissions, legal fees, and title insurance that were incurred in connection with the acquisition, and not deductible as a current expense.

Example 7–1

Joe Tyro bought an apartment building on the following terms: He paid $30,000 cash, signed a note and purchase money mortgage for $20,000, and assumed a $270,000 note. He paid $150 for legal representation at the closing, $80 for an owner's title insurance policy, and $120 for a lender's title insurance policy.

He paid the following additional amounts at the closing: $340 into tax and insurance escrow, $35 for seller's prepaid water bill, $30 for registration of deed, and $70 for documentary stamps.

Tyro's basis is $320,330, computed as follows:

Purchase price:		
Cash down payment	$30,000	
Purchase money mortgage	20,000	
Note assumed	270,000	$320,000
Attorney's fee		150
Owner's title policy		80
Deed registration		30
Documentary stamps		70
Original tax basis		$320,330

The escrow funds, the mortgagee's title insurance policy fee, and the prepaid water are all incidental to ownership or obtaining financing, rather than to obtaining and defending title. Therefore, they do not form a part of the basis of the property to Tyro.

The basis might also include charges for property taxes and interest expenses if properly chargeable to the capital account, and if the charges were not previously deducted as expenses.

Example 7–2

An investor acquired vacant land and contracted for the construction of improvements to be used for income-generating purposes. The cost of construction must be charged to a capital account rather than being claimed as a currently deductible expense. The charges may then be written off as depreciation expense over the useful life of the improvements. Included in these charges are the interest expense and property taxes incurred during the construction period, where such charges were incurred after December 31, 1977. An exception exists for low-income housing, wherein interest and property taxes paid or accrued during the construction period may be deducted as a current expense until December 31, 1981.*

* Corporations have the option of charging construction period interest and taxes to current expense or to a capital account.

The original basis of property acquired by inheritance is explained in Chapter 3. Property received as a gift generally has the same basis in the hands of the recipient as in the hands of the donor, unless the donor also acquired the property as a gift. In this latter case, the value in the hands of the recipient is the same as it was in the hands of the last owner who *did not* receive the property as a gift, increased for any subsequent improvements or costs incurred in title defense and for any gift taxes paid, and decreased by any depreciation claimed by the intermediate owners. But the addition of gift taxes to the basis is allowed only if this does not increase the basis above fair market value at the time of the gift. If inclusion of the gift taxes would have this effect, then they are only included to the extent that the resultant basis in the hands of the recipient is equal to the fair market value of the property at the time of the gift.

Allocating the Basis Between Land and Improvements. Before computing the allowable depreciation deduction, the basis of the property at the time of acquisition must be allocated between the land and the improvements. Only that portion properly attributable to the improvements is included in the basis of depreciation. It is this amount (except for the effect of salvage value) that is written off as a recovery of capital over the useful life of the asset. The land itself is considered to be virtually indestructible and, therefore, not subject to depreciation. Of course, every investor knows that even though the land may be indestructible, its value as a site is created by external factors and can disappear with social and economic change in the surrounding area. Such a decline in the value of land represents a real loss to the investor, but it is not considered in the nature of depreciation and is not deductible concurrently with the decline in value. When the land is ultimately sold, the loss can be charged off as a capital item. In this manner, the loss, when actually realized (as opposed to its mere anticipation), reduces the tax liability of the investor. Capital losses are considered more fully in Chapter 8.

Perhaps the simplest approach to the allocation of the basis between land and improvements is to specify the price of each in the original contract to purchase the real estate. If the purchase is an arm's-length transaction, the Internal Revenue Service generally accepts the contractual allocation for tax computation purposes. This approach is accepted because the parties' interests are assumed to be antithetical. But this need not be the case. Knowledge of the tax position of both parties often enables the transaction to be structured in a manner advantageous to both.

A common alternative method of allocating the basis between the land and the improvements is to use the ratio employed by the tax assessor. Typically, property-tax assessors assess the land and the improvements separately. The assessed values themselves generally bear no identifiable relationship to the market value of the property. They, nevertheless, provide an acceptable basis for allocating the cost.

Example 7–3

An investor buys a property for $80,000. No mention is made in the purchase agreement regarding the portion of the purchase price that applies to the land and to the improvements. The county assesses the property for tax purposes at $8000, of which $2000 is specified by the assessor as applying to the land and the balance to the improvements. Using the assessor's ratio, the value of the property is divided between the land and the improvements as follows:

Land ($2000/$8000)	25%
Improvements ($6000/$8000)	75%
Total ($8000/$8000)	100%

The investor's initial basis for the property is, therefore:

Land (25% of $80,000)	$20,000
Improvements (75% of $80,000)	60,000
Land and improvements	$80,000

A third approach is to have an independent appraiser determine the relative value of the land and the buildings. Although the values determined by the appraiser may not be the same as the investor's basis, they provide a basis for allocation in the same manner as does the tax assessor's estimates.

Example 7–4

An investor acquires real property with an initial basis of $120,000. An independent fee appraisal fixes the fair market value at $140,000, representing an appraised value of $100,000 for the improvements and $40,000 for the land. The investor apportions his basis of $120,000 to the land and the improvements as follows:

Land [($40,000/$140,000) × $120,000]	$ 34,286
Improvements [($100,000/$140,000) × $120,000]	85,714
Total	$120,000

ESTIMATING USEFUL LIFE

Whichever allowable method of depreciation is adopted, the rate depends upon the estimated useful life of the property as well as upon the initial basis. The useful life is the period over which the property may reasonably be expected to yield economic benefit to the owner. Useful life is limited by both physical and socioeconomic factors; therefore, it is not necessarily synonymous with physical life.

Physical factors that are considered in estimating useful life include wear, tear, and the action of the elements. This recognizes the immutable fact that all man-made articles share the mortality of their makers. Any conceivable program of maintenance and repair can only retard the rate of decline, which may never be reversed.

Social, technical, and economic change can destroy the usefulness of property as surely as can physical decay. Obsolescence is accordingly given due recognition in estimating the normal useful life.

Example 7–5

A strip shopping center was built in a mixed residential and industrial area in 1969. Since then the rapid transition of the area away from residential use coincident to rezoning to all-industrial usage, combined with the drawing-power of a new regional shopping center erected a short distance away, has made it obvious the anchor tenant in the strip center will not renew his lease that expires in 1989. Without the anchor tenant the center is not economically viable and will be razed and replaced with warehouses. Though the physical life for the buildings is approximately 60 years, the economic life is only 20.

Over the years there has been a considerable degree of waffling by the Internal Revenue Service regarding the selection of useful life estimates for depreciable assets. During the early years of the code, wide latitude was given to property owners in making estimates. Doing an about-face in 1934, the Service began requiring taxpayers to provide proof of the appropriateness of the useful lives claimed.

During World War II, the government grew even more rigid. It issued a listing of minimum allowable useful lives for various types of assets on an item-by-item basis. While it is generally conceded in retrospect that the guideline lives were unrealistically long, they had to be accepted by taxpayers who could not prove that shorter lives were proper in the absence of records as supporting data.

In 1962, the government reversed its policy of requiring item-by-item proof for useful life estimates shorter than those prescribed. Taxpayers were permitted to group their depreciable assets in broad industry classes. This approach evolved into the current class life system, which features an "asset depreciation range" for broad classes of assets.

Class Life System. The rules now in effect were instituted in 1971. They provide an asset depreciation range (ADR) for assets of various classes. A useful life range is specified for each class of depreciable personal property, within which the Service does not require proof of accuracy. For depreciable real property, a specific "guideline" life is specified rather than a range. The following list is representative of the current ADR.

Description of Assets Included	Asset Guideline Period
Building services:	
Shelter, space, and related building services for manufacturing and for machinery and equipment repair activities:	
Factories	45
Garages	45
Machine shops	45
Loft buildings	50
Building services for the conduct of wholesale and retail trade, includes stores and similar structures . . .	60
Building services for residential purposes:	
Apartments	40
Dwellings	45
Building services relating to the provision of miscellaneous services to businesses and consumers:	
Office buildings	45
Storage:	
Warehouses	60
Grain elevators	60
Banks	50
Hotels	40
Theaters	40

It is important to note that the taxpayer is not bound by the guideline lives in the ADR system. These are estimated average physical lives and may differ significantly from useful life for depreciation allowance purposes. If the taxpayer can support the claim for a useful life that is less than that cited in the class life guidelines, he should adopt the shorter period, because the shorter the useful life the higher the annual depreciation deduction.

It is prudent also to keep in mind that the initial choice of useful life does not necessarily bind the taxpayer in the future. The regulations are specific in this regard:

> In any case in which the taxpayer shows that the estimated useful life previously used should be shortened by reason of obsolescence greater than had been assumed in computing such useful life, a change to a new and shorter estimated useful life computed in accordance with such showing will be permitted. [Reg. 1.167(a)-9]

Social or economic changes that presage a general neighborhood decline might, therefore, constitute proof that a building has a shorter remaining economic life than previously anticipated. Rezoning in the neighborhood, to cite an example, might suggest an existing building is no longer the appropriate site usage, and might support an expectation that the building will be demolished in the next few years to make room for a structure that will more nearly constitute "highest and best use."

Another approach that might substantially increase the allowable depreciation deduction is to use the "component" method of estimating useful life. This involves dividing the building into separate components (plumbing system, heating system, roof, etc.) and depreciating each component separately. Most of the components have useful lives significantly shorter than the building itself, so the aggregate effect may be large depreciation deductions in the earlier years than if the component method were not used.

The Service initially took the position that the component method could be used only with new property. Subsequently, it has agreed that in some cases used property may qualify for this treatment. The acquisition cost must be properly allocated to the various components based on relative values as the date of acquisition, and useful lives must be assigned to the components based on their condition at that time. The straight-line depreciation method must be applied to the components where this would have been the only allowable method had the building been depreciated as an entity rather than on a component basis. This would include all used structures except residential income property, which qualifies for the 125% declining balance method.

Example 7–6

Assume the improvements on a property cost $600,000 and have a 40-year useful life with only nominal salvage value. If depreciated on a straight-line basis the annual depreciation deduction would be 1/40 × $600,000, or $15,000. Now see how the component method might be used to increase the annual deduction.

Component	Cost	Life	Annual Depreciation
Building shell	$360,000	60	$6,000
Wiring	36,000	15	2,400
Plumbing	27,000	15	1,800
Roof	30,000	10	3,000
Mechanical systems	90,000	10	9,000
Landscaping	15,000	10	1,500
Ceilings	15,000	10	1,500
Elevators	27,000	15	1,800
Total annual deduction			$27,000

ALLOWABLE DEPRECIATION METHODS

Three methods of depreciation are specified in the code. Any other consistent method may be used so long as it does not, during the first two-thirds of the asset's useful life, result in cumulative depreciation deductions in excess of those allowable under the specified method for that class of asset. Because it is usually advantageous to claim the maximum allowable depreciation during the early years, the methods specified by the code are generally used. This section describes the allowable methods and gives examples of where each is applicable. The various alternatives are compared in subsequent sections.

Straight-Line Method. This simplest and most straightforward of all methods provides for recovery of a constant dollar amount in each year of the useful life of a depreciable asset. To calculate the amount to be recovered over the useful life, one subtracts the estimated salvage value from the portion of the initial basis that is applicable to the improvements. The annual depreciation can then be determined by dividing the amount to be recovered by the number of years in the estimated useful life.

The investor in Example 7–7 may continue to deduct depreciation of $1375 annually until the remaining undepreciated balance is equal to the salvage value. Under no circumstances may the improvements be depreciated below their estimated salvage value (although the salvage value estimate may change over the holding period). To determine salvage value, estimate the market value of the salvaged materials and deduct the estimated cost of demolition and removal. In most cases, the estimated salvage value is zero.

Example 7–7

A property is purchased for $80,000, of which $20,000 represents the value of the land, and $60,000 represents the value of improvements that have an estimated useful life of 40 years and estimated net salvage value of $5000. The annual depreciation deduction, using the straight-line method, is determined as follows:

Depreciable base:	
Improvements	$60,000
Less salvage value	5,000
Depreciable base	$55,000
Annual depreciation deduction:	
Depreciable base	$55,000
Times 1/40 (1/useful life)	0.025
Annual deduction	$ 1,375

The straight-line method may be used with all depreciable real property, since it does not result in a depreciation deduction in excess of the other allowable methods during the early years of the asset's useful life. Moreover, this is the only method permitted for the depreciation of real estate used for other than residential income purposes, if the taxpayer is not a "first user" of the property.

Sum-of-the-Years'-Digits Method. This method, which may be used only with new residential income property, involves multiplying the cost of the improvements (less salvage value) by a changing fraction each year. The fraction is determined by taking as a numerator the number of years of remaining life at the beginning of the tax year for which the depreciation is being calculated, and as a denominator the sum of the numbers that represents each year of the useful life of the asset at the time it is acquired. The numerator becomes smaller each year, whereas the denominator remains constant throughout the useful life of the asset. The explanation is inevitably clumsy and somewhat confusing. The procedure is not really complicated, however, and can readily be demonstrated with a simple example.

Example 7–8

Improvements to real property have a 25-year useful life and an estimated salvage value of $5000. The property cost is $120,000, of which $20,000 represents the value of the site. The annual depreciation deduction under the sum-of-the-years'-digits method is calculated as follows:

Step 1. Compute the depreciable base.

Cost		$120,000
Less: Site value	$20,000	
Salvage value	5,000	
		25,000
Depreciable base		$ 95,000

Step 2. Compute the denominator by summing the years' digits. The digits representing the years of useful life range from one through 25. The summation of these digits $(1 + 2 + 3 + 4 + \cdots + 24 + 25)$ equals 325.

Step 3. Compute each year's depreciation allowance by multiplying the (original) depreciable base by a fraction whose numerator is the number of years remaining in the useful life estimate and whose denominator is the constant derived in *Step 2:*

Year	Fraction ×	Depreciable Base =	Annual Depreciation
1	25/325	$95,000	$ 7,308
2	24/325	95,000	7,015
3	23/325	95,000	6,725
.	.	.	.
.	.	.	.
.	.	.	.
24	2/325	95,000	585
25	1/325	95,000	292
Totals	325/325	95,000	$95,000

The work of summing the years' digits can be simplified by squaring the useful life estimate, adding the useful life estimate to the square, and dividing the sum by two. This results in a quotient equal to the sum of the years' digits. In Example 7–8, the quotient of 325 could have thus been derived as follows:

$$\frac{(25)^2 + (25)}{2} = 650/2 = 325$$

Alternatively, one can determine the sum by multiplying the useful life by (1 + useful life) and dividing the product by 2. In our previous example, this is simply:

$$\frac{(\text{useful life})\ (1 + \text{useful life})}{2} = \frac{(25)\ (1 + 25)}{2} = 325$$

Declining-Balance Method. Like the sum-of-the-years'-digits method, the declining-balance method gives the greatest allowance during the first year of the useful life. A progressively smaller allowance is afforded for each successive year. The taxpayer utilizing this method applies a constant percentage rate each year to the remaining unrecovered basis of the depreciable property. Since there is always a remaining undepreciated balance, no adjustment need be made for salvage value. But the asset may not be depreciated below its estimated salvage value.

The constant rate to be applied to the declining balance is 200, 150, or 125%, depending upon the nature of the real estate being depreciated. The 200% rate applies only to new residential income property. The 150% rate applies only to new nonresidential income property, and the 125% rate applies to used residential income property.

In the example that follows (Example 7–9), the declining-balance method is illustrated using each of the three rates. The example assumes a building which has a 20-year useful life. For a useful life of less than 20 years, only the straight-line method may be employed. In each of the illustrations, one calculates the allowable rate by multiplying the straight-line rate (in this case 1/20, or 5%) by the appropriate multiple (i.e., 200, 150, or 125%). This product is then applied against the remaining balance (cost less accumulated depreciation) for each year.

CHOOSING A DEPRECIATION METHOD

The taxpayer's choice from among the depreciation methods is constrained by restrictions in the code. It specifies the maximum allowable rate for various types of real estate and permits any consistent method that does not, during the first two-thirds of the asset's useful life, result in a greater cumulative depreciation deduction than the prescribed maximum.

Residential Income Property. New residential real estate qualifies for the greatest accelerated rate. The taxpayer may choose either the 200% declining-balance method or the sum-of-the-years'-digits method.

Example 7-9

Assuming a $60,000 cost applicable to the improvements and a useful life of 20 years, the annual depreciation allowance for the first 5 years of ownership is:

Year	Declining Balance* ×	Rate† =	Depreciation Allowance‡
Using the 200% declining-balance method			
1	$60,000	10%	$6,000
2	54,000	10%	5,400
3	48,600	10%	4,860
4	43,740	10%	4,374
5	39,366	10%	3,937
Using the 150% declining-balance method:			
1	$60,000	7.5%	$4,500
2	55,500	7.5%	4,162
3	51,338	7.5%	3,850
4	47,488	7.5%	3,562
5	43,926	7.5%	3,294
Using the 125% declining-balance method:			
1	$60,000	6.25%	$3,750
2	56,250	6.25%	3,516
3	52,734	6.25%	3,296
4	49,438	6.25%	3,090
5	46,348	6.25%	2,897

* The declining balance is simply the balance from the preceding year minus last year's depreciation allowance. The beginning depreciable balance of $60,000 is thus reduced by the first year's depreciation allowance of $6000 in the 200% declining-balance illustration, for a second-year declining balance of ($60,000 – 6000), or $54,000.

† The straight-line rate of depreciation is (1/useful life). In the present example this is 1/20, or 5% per annum. The 200% declining-balance rate then is 200% of the straight-line rate, or 10%. Likewise the 150% declining balance rate is 150% of the straight-line rate, or 7.5%, whereas the 125% declining-balance rate is 125% of 5%, or 6.25%.

‡ The depreciation allowance is calculated by multiplying the declining balance by the appropriate accelerated rate.

Used residential real property qualifies for a lesser rate of depreciation than is the case for new property, either residential or nonresidential. The owner of used residential income property may utilize the 125% declining balance method if the estimated useful life at the time of acquisition is not less than 20 years. If the used property has less than 20 years of useful life remaining when acquired by the taxpayer, special permission from the Commissioner is required to use other than the straight-line method.

Property is considered to be residential in nature if at least 80% of the gross rental income is from dwelling units. This 80% gross income test must be met each year in order for the rates applicable to residential income property to apply that year. During any year in which the 80% test is not met, the taxpayer must shift to a method allowed for nonresidential income property for that year. Should the 80% test be satisfied in later years the taxpayer may shift back to the more accelerated method. Should he fail to take the more accelerated depreciation in any year in which the property qualifies, he loses the right to do so in any succeeding year without express permission of the Commissioner.

Example 7–10

Mr. Wheelin Deal acquires property having a depreciable basis for the improvements of $350,000 and an estimated useful life of 25 years. The net salvage value is estimated to be $25,000. The property, which consists of an apartment building having offices located off the lobby, meets the 80% test for treatment as residential income property in the first 2 years of Deal's ownership. Due to a long-term vacancy in one of the residential units, the property fails to meet the 80% test in year three. The apartments are thereafter fully rented and the building does meet the 80% test during the fourth and subsequent years.

Assuming that Deal is a "first user," the allowable depreciation during the first 5 years will be as follows:

Year	Depreciable Base ×	Rate =	Depreciation Allowance
1	$350,000	8%	$28,000
2	322,000	8%	25,760
3	296,240	6%	17,774
4	278,466	8%	22,277
5	256,189	8%	20,495

Since Mr. Deal is assumed to be the first user, the property qualifies for the 200% declining-balance method or the sum-of-the-years'-digits method in each year in which it qualifies for treatment as residential income property by having not less than 80% of the gross income generated from residential rents. In any year in which it fails the 80% test, it can be reported as new nonresidential income property and, therefore, qualify for the 150% declining-balance method.

During the first and second years, the property qualifies for the 200% declining-balance method or the sum-of-the-years'-digits method. Assume here that Deal chooses the 200% declining-balance method. Since the property has a 25-year estimated life, the rate (fixed percentage) is 200% × 1/25, or 8%.

This is applied in each of the first 2 years to the declining balance of cost less accumulated depreciation.

In the third year, the property fails the 80%-of-gross-revenue test, and so must be treated as nonresidential income property.

Since Deal is the "first owner," he may use the 150% declining-balance method in year three. The rate of 6% (150% × 1/25) is applied to the declining balance for that year, resulting in a depreciation allowance of $17,774.

In the fourth and fifth years, during which the property meets the 80% test, the depreciation is computed as in the first and second years, by applying the 8% rate (200% × 1/25) to the declining balance.

Had Mr. Deal not qualified as a "first user" of the property in Example 7–10, the maximum rate of depreciation would have been based on the 125% declining-balance method during those years in which it qualified as residential income property. During any year in which the 80% test was not met, Deal would have been limited to the straight-line method of computing depreciation. Depreciation deductions for the first five years, calculated on the assumption that Deal was *not* a first user, are presented in Example 7–11.

Example 7–11

Using the data provided in Example 7–10, but assuming that Wheelin Deal does not qualify as a first user, the allowable depreciation in each of the first five years is as follows:

Year	Depreciable Base ×	Rate =	Depreciation Allowance
1	$350,000	5%	$17,500
2	332,500	5%	16,625
3	290,875	1/23	12,647
4	303,228	5%	15,161
5	288,067	5%	14,403

The depreciation for years one and two in Example 7–11 were calculated in the same manner as in Example 7–10, except that the applicable rate is 125% × 1/25 = 5%. In the third year, however, when the building fails to qualify as residential-income property, Deal must calculate the depreciation based on the straight-line rate. At this point, the property has 23 years of remaining useful life (25 less years one and two), so the appropriate factor is 1/23. The amount to be written off over the remaining

23 years is the cost less salvage and less depreciation taken in the first 2 years:

Cost	$350,000	
Less estimated salvage	25,000	
Amount to be written off over total life		$325,000
Less: First year's depreciation	17,500	
Second year's depreciation	16,625	34,125
Amount to be written off over remaining life		$290,875

Third year's depreciation = Depreciable basis/remaining life, or
($290,875) (23) = $12,647

For years four and five, Mr. Deal's property (in Example 7–11) once again qualifies as residential income property, so he may revert to the 125% declining-balance method of calculating depreciation. The base upon which the fourth-year's depreciation is computed ($303,228) is the original depreciable base from year one ($350,000) minus the sum of all depreciation taken to date:

Original cost of improvements		$350,000
Less accumulated depreciation:		
First year	$17,500	
Second year	16,625	
Third year	12,647	46,772
Depreciable base in fourth year		$303,228

The depreciable base applicable for the fifth year is that of the fourth year reduced by the fourth year's depreciation allowance. Remember that it is important for Mr. Deal to revert to the 125% declining-balance method in the fourth year. If he fails to do so, then he must get permission to revert at some future date. Such permission is not assured.

Nonresidential Property. Any property that does not meet the minimum income requirements for treatment as residential income property (i.e., at least 80% of gross rental income from residential rents) is by definition nonresidential.

The maximum allowable rate of depreciation for nonresidential income property is the 150% declining-balance method. This method is permissible only for new nonresidential property. Used nonresidential income property does not qualify for any accelerated method. Only straight-line depreciation is permissible.

SWITCHING DEPRECIATION METHODS

While the code and IRS regulations specify the maximum allowable depreciation rates, they do not require the taxpayer to claim depreciation at these rates. Moreover, the rules permit the taxpayer to switch from an allowable declining balance method to the straight-line method at any time. He need only notify the IRS of his intention to make the switch. But special permission is required to switch from the straight-line method to an allowable accelerated method or from one allowable accelerated method to another, even though the alternate method would have been allowed had it been chosen initially.

Two rules follow logically from these observations. The first is that the investor should initially choose the most advantageous allowable depreciation method, to avoid losing that option. The second is that he should carefully compare the depreciation deduction under the method chosen and the deduction that would result from a switch to the straight-line method each year. At the point where the straight-line method yields the greater annual deduction he may wish to make the election to switch.

At the time the election is made to switch to the straight-line method, the annual depreciation deduction is based on the remaining (not the original) useful life and the remaining depreciable basis, adjusted for estimated net salvage value. The procedure is illustrated in Example 7–12. The investor's initial choice of the 125% declining-balance method yields the maximum allowable depreciation during the early years of ownership. But the depreciation deduction drops off rapidly so that by the sixth year the straight-line method is more advantageous. At the time of the switch to the straight-line method, the asset has a remaining useful life of 15 years (the original estimate of 20 years, less the 5 years of ownership to date). The basis for computing straight-line depreciation in the sixth year is determined by deducting the estimated net salvage value (in this case zero) and all depreciation deductions taken to date, from the initial depreciable base.

Example 7–12

An investor acquires property that results in an initial basis for the improvements of $100,000. The property has been in existence for many years and has been owned by several previous investors. Because of its advanced age, the improvements are estimated to have a remaining useful life of only 20 years with zero salvage value. The building meets the test for classification as used residential income property, so that the maximum allowable depreciation results from use of the 125% declining-balance method. The investor intends to exercise his option to switch to the straight-line method when it becomes advantageous to do so. The annual deduction resulting from the declining-balance method and from switching to the straight-line method each year is as follows:

	Annual Depreciation Allowance	
Year	125% Declining-balance Method	If Switch to Straight-Line Method During Current Year
1	$6,250	$4,000
2	5,859	4,934
3	5,493	4,883
4	5,150	4,847
5	4,828	4,828
6	4,526	4,828

Both the annual depreciation from the 125% declining-balance method and that which would result from switching to the straight-line method decline each year. This latter effect is due to the decrease in the depreciable base upon which the straight-line depreciation is calculated when the switch is made. The schedule reveals that the investor maximizes his depreciation deduction if he switches to the straight-line method in the sixth year. His depreciation deduction for each year of the remaining economic life is $4828, determined as follows:

Balance to be recovered as depreciation:	
Original cost basis of improvements	$100,000
Less accumulated depreciation (first 5 years)	27,580
Balance to be recovered	$ 72,420
Remaining economic life:	
Original economic life (years)	20
Number of years owned to date	5
Remaining economic life	15
Annual straight-line depreciation:	
Cost to be recovered/remaining economic life = $72,420/15 = $4828	

OTHER ADJUSTMENTS DECREASING THE BASIS

A property's tax basis is decreased by deductions for depreciation and other forms of capital recovery. Examples of other capital recovery situations include sale of a portion of the property or its destruction by fire, flood, storm, or other casualty. In the case of casualty losses, the basis of the property must be reduced to reflect the amount of the allowable loss deduction in the year of the casualty. A discussion of casualty losses is included in Chapter 2. The rules described there for real property held for personal use apply generally for investment and income property as well.

ADJUSTMENTS INCREASING THE BASIS

An owner's tax basis is increased by all expenditures he is permitted or required to capitalize. Generally this includes any expenditure connected with the property that is not deductible as a current expense. Of course, a taxpayer usually prefers to deduct expenditures currently as operating expenses where permissible. This causes an immediate reduction in his tax liability, whereas capitalizing the expenditure results in a reduction of tax liabilities in future years as the capitalized expenditure is deducted as a depreciation expense over the remaining life of the improvements. Exceptions to this rule are discussed in the tax strategy section.

When Must Expenditures Be Capitalized. The distinction between capital expenditures and currently deductible repairs and maintenance is set forth in Treasury Regulation 1.162–4. It specifies that owners of income and investment property may deduct currently those expenditures for repairs that materially add to neither the value nor the life-span of the improvements, but only keep it in an ordinarily efficient operating condition. Those expenditures that arrest deterioration and appreciably prolong useful life must, according to the regulation, be capitalized and charged off over the period during which benefits are reaped.

The theoretical difference between currently deductible expenditures and those that increase the basis of the property is unequivocal. It is simple to determine the proper treatment of expenditures that fall at the polar ends of the distinction. Patching a leak in the roof is clearly a currently deductible item, whereas the cost of complete replacement of a roof is clearly a capital item. But there are literally hundreds of cases where the distinction has been the subject of extensive litigation.

In some instances, the decision as to whether an expenditure is currently deductible or must be added to the basis hinges upon how the expenditure transpired. For example, a general plan of improvement of the property often requires a series of separate repair operations. Taken individually these repairs may be currently deductible. But because they are a part of a general plan, they would probably be considered capital expenditures to be added to the owner's basis. Fractionalizing the job and spreading it among several contractors and over several years may have the salutary result of enabling the taxpayer to successfully claim that each step was a currently deductible repair.

Tenant Improvements. Often, a tenant either is required under the terms of a lease or elects to make permissible alterations and improvements to property. The landlord usually acquires the improvements on the termination of the leases. This event raises several tax questions, the first of which is whether the value of the improvement represents taxable income to the landlord. A second is whether the landlord's tax basis is affected, and if so, how.

If a tenant receives a rent concession equal to the cost of the improvements, the cost is taxable as rental income to the landlord. Whether the improvements have been made in lieu of, and so constitute, rent depends upon the agreement between the parties. Evidence of agreement might be based upon the terms of the lease or upon surrounding circumstances. The procedures for making the determination are set forth in Regulation 1.61–8(c).

The reference to "surrounding circumstances" in determining intent with respect to improvements made by the tenant gives the parties considerable control over how the expenditures are treated. Explicit provisions in the lease generally are acceptable evidence of intent. In the absence of an explicit statement of intent in the lease, the determination may hinge on the relationship between the cost of the improvements and the amount of the rent concession, or upon the degree of control exercised by the landlord as to the nature and timing of the improvements.

If the cost of an improvement made by a tenant is treated as rent, it is taxable as rental income to the landlord. The tax liability is generally incurred in the year the improvement is made. But where this results in a disproportionately high initial rent, the cost may be treated as advance rent and amortized over the life of the lease. The landlord's basis is increased accordingly, and the improvement costs are reflected in his depreciation deductions just as if the landlord himself had incurred the expenditure.

Landlords who can avoid having the cost of a tenant improvement characterized as rent are doubly blessed. So long as the tenant remains in possession under the lease, the value of the improvement is not taxable to the landlord. Moreover, even though possession of the improvement passes to the landlord upon termination of the lease, he need not recognize its value as taxable income and does not adjust his basis to reflect the increase in value due to the improvement. Under these circumstances, of course, the added value is also not reflected in his basis, and so does not affect his depreciation deductions. Proper structuring of any understanding between landlord and tenant is, therefore, vital if the landlord is to glean maximum benefit from his property.

Where leased property is being used by a tenant for commercial or investment purposes, his interests and those of the landlord are generally antagonistic. Tenant improvements characterized as rent are deductible by the tenant and taxable to the landlord in the year of the expenditure. Expenditures for leasehold improvements that are not considered a part of the rental consideration have to be capitalized by the tenant and amortized over the term of the lease. The tenant would generally prefer the first treatment, whereas the landlord would prefer the latter. Consequently, the government usually accepts the terms of the lease as satisfactory evidence of intent unless the lease is between related parties. Where there is reason to suspect that the lease does not reflect an arm's-length transaction, however, there is likely to be a much closer examination of the economic consequences of the agreement.

When property is leased solely for a tenant's personal enjoyment, it is often possible to avoid characterization of the cost of tenant improvements as income to the landlord, and yet benefit both landlord and tenant. The tenant derives no tax advantage by having expenditures characterized as rent, since he is permitted no deduction for rent, depreciation, or amortization. His interests are, therefore, best served by obtaining the lowest possible rent under the lease, without regard for the tax treatment of expenditures for improvements. It should be much easier under these circumstances to structure an agreement to avoid characterization of tenant improvements as rent to the landlord.

When tenant improvements are treated as income by the landlord, the total cost is so treated if fully offset against the rent. In other cases, the amount of the income to the landlord is the fair market value of the improvements. Generally, this means the increase in the fair market value of the property subject to the lease, rather than what the value would be were the lease not in existence. The landlord's basis is, of course, increased to reflect only the amount taxable to him as rent.

Carrying Charges on Unproductive Property. Interest on borrowed funds and real estate taxes paid or accrued on vacant or unproductive property are deductible currently, or may be capitalized at the option of the taxpayer. He generally prefers the current deduction. There may be circumstances, however, where current income is insufficient to warrant this treatment. A property owner may then wish to defer the tax benefit until he is in a much higher tax bracket. In such a case, he elects to capitalize the expenditures. This increases the tax basis of the property and is charged off against future income. Of course, to the extent the property is not depreciable, the benefit derived from capitalization is substantially reduced due to the capital-gains tax provisions.

TAX PLANNING STRATEGY

An optimum strategy for planning depreciation deductions springs from the observation that the investor prefers income sooner rather than later, and more rather than less. Since the locus of attention is properly on after-tax income, it follows that he generally would prefer a tax deduction sooner rather than later, and a larger tax deduction rather than a smaller (assuming, of course, that the tax deduction does not in itself affect expenditures other than those in satisfaction of income tax liabilities).

The taxpayer's strategy, therefore, is to take depreciation at the maximum accelerated rate permissible under the law, and to switch to another method where permissible at anytime this increases the annual depreciation deduction.

Comparison of Allowable Depreciation Methods. The one instance in which the initial choice of depreciation method is not unequivocally clear is the case of new residential income property. The taxpayer has an option of either the 200% declining-balance method or the sum-of-the-years'-digits method. Where there is little or no salvage value to consider, the sum-of-the-years'-digits method is generally preferable. The longer the anticipated holding period, the greater the advantage of the sum-of-the-years'-digits over the declining-balance method. This advantage is clearly illustrated in Example 7–13. In this example, the advantage of the sum-of-the-years'-digits is indicated for any holding period in excess of 3 years, as evidenced by the excess of the cumulative depreciation deduction taken via the sum-of-the-years'-digits over that available if the declining-balance method had been adopted.

Where there is a substantial estimated salvage value to be considered, and where the anticipated holding period is quite short, the choice is less clear. The declining-balance method yields the greatest tax savings during the early years of ownership, with the sum-of-the-years'-digits method becoming more advantageous only after a substantial period of time. The problem is demonstrated in Example 7–14, which modifies the previous calculations by including an assumption of a salvage value.

Example 7–13

An investor acquires income property that qualifies for either the 200% declining-balance or the sum-of-the-year's-digits method of computing depreciation. The improvements have a cost basis of $100,000 and an estimated 40 years useful life, with zero estimated salvage value. The depreciation deductions resulting during the first 10 years from the alternative allowable methods of accelerated depreciation are presented below:

	Depreciation Deductions			
	Current		Cumulative	
Year	Declining-Balance	Sum-of-the-Years'-Digits	Declining-Balance	Sum-of-the-Years'-Digits
1	$5,000	$4,878	$ 5,000	$ 4,878
2	4,750	4,756	9,750	9,634
3	4,513	4,634	14,263	14,268
4	4,287	4,512	18,550	18,780
5	4,073	4,390	22,623	23,170
6	3,869	4,268	26,492	27,438
7	3,675	4,146	30,176	31,584
8	3,492	4,024	33,659	35,608
9	3,317	3,902	36,967	39,510
10	3,151	3,780	40,127	43,290

Comparing the cumulative depreciation deductions in Examples 7–13 and 7–14, one sees that the effect of inclusion of an estimated salvage value is to make the use of the 200% declining-balance method more attractive. The cumulative depreciation deductions from the sum-of-the-years'-digits method exceeds those from the declining-balance method by the third year in the first of the two examples. This does not occur until the 12th year in Example 7–14. Barring unanticipated variations in income from other sources, the declining-balance method is clearly more advantageous in Example 7–14, if it is not anticipated that the property is to be held for substantially more than 12 years.

Example 7–14

Assume the same facts as in the previous example, except that the improvements are estimated to have a salvage value of $10,000 at the end of their useful life. The declining-balance depreciation is the same as in Example 7–13, but the sum-of-the-years'-digits depreciation is reduced. This is because the sum-of-the-years'-digits method requires that the estimated salvage value be subtracted before the depreciation is calculated.

This change in assumptions results in the revised annual depreciation allowances presented below:

	Depreciation Deductions			
	Current		Cumulative	
Year	Declining-Balance	Sum-of-the-Years'-Digits	Declining-Balance	Sum-of-the-Years'-Digits
1	$5,000	$4,390	$ 5,000	$ 4,390
2	4,750	4,280	9,750	8,670
3	4,513	4,171	14,263	12,841
4	4,287	4,061	18,550	16,902
5	4,073	3,951	22,623	20,853
6	3,869	3,841	26,492	24,694
7	3,675	3,732	30,167	28,426
8	3,492	3,622	33,659	32,048
9	3,317	3,512	36,976	35,560
10	3,151	3,402	40,127	38,962
11	2,994	3,293	43,121	42,255
12	2,844	3,183	45,965	45,438

The problem becomes more complex where there is no substantial salvage value to be considered (as in Example 7–13) or if the anticipated holding period extends for a number of years. The issue is further complicated by the effect the differential depreciation allowances might have on the investor's liability for the minimum tax on preference items (see Chapter 13). Remember also that the depreciation in excess of straight-line is all subject to recapture as ordinary income if there is a gain on disposal of the property.

One need not be dismayed by the number of variables that must be considered. The procedure for making a rational decision is, at least in principle, quite simple. The first step is to estimate the after-tax cash flow that results from each alternative over the anticipated holding period. This should include the anticipated after-tax receipts from sale of the property. Having projected the cash flows, the final step is to discount them to the present. The alternative that offers the greatest present value of expected cash flows is preferable, since there is no appreciable difference in associated risk.

For clarity of exposition we have omitted consideration of the preference tax. This is not a serious limitation for most investors. But if one has a substantial portfolio that includes preference items, failure to consider the preference tax consequences of one's depreciation method can have untoward consequences. In many such cases, it may prove advantageous to opt for a lesser depreciation rate than is allowable. The preference tax is explained more fully on page 59. Its possible adverse consequences on investors who claim accelerated depreciation is illustrated on page 268.

SUMMARY

The investor's adjusted basis, combined with the estimated useful life of improvements and the net salvage value, determines the amount of the annual depreciation deduction that results from use of each of the various methods for computing depreciation. Both straight-line and accelerated methods are allowed for all depreciable income and investment property except used nonresidential, where only the straight-line method is allowed.

A taxpayer is not required to choose the allowable method that yields the greatest depreciation deductions in the early years of ownership, but it is generally in his best interests to do so. Failure to make this election initially may result in loss of the opportunity at a later date. While the taxpayer may switch from a declining balance to the straight-line method at any time he wishes, special permission from the Commissioner is required to switch in the opposite direction. The most lucrative strategy is to initially opt for the allowable method that results in the greatest depreciation deductions in the early years of ownership, and to switch to the straight-line method when the declining balance is such that the switch yields a greater annual deduction for the remaining useful life of the asset.

Other adjustments also affect the depreciable base of the asset. Capital improvements increase the basis and, therefore, increase the amount of the annual depreciation deduction allowable. Capital recovery other than from depreciation deductions often decreases the basis for depreciation and consequently decreases the allowable annual depreciation deduction. Such recoveries are exemplified by sale of a portion of the property or by its destruction, which results in a reported casualty loss.

SUGGESTED READINGS

1. Feinschreiber, Robert, "Component and Composite Depreciation," *Journal of Real Estate Taxation, 2* (2), 250–258 (1974).

2. Feinschreiber, Robert, "Investment Credit for Commercial Real Estate," *Journal of Real Estate Taxation, 3* (2), 189–199 (1975).
3. Feinschreiber, Robert, "When to Switch Depreciation Methods," *Journal of Real Estate Taxation, 2* (2), 151–161 (1974).

APPENDIX B: DEPRECIATION DEDUCTIONS ON PERSONALTY

Ownership of real estate often involves an investment in items of personalty as well. Personalty includes any asset not "permanently attached" to the realty. The most common example is furniture. Ownership of personalty that is used in a business or investment venture also entails a deduction for depreciation to spread the cost over the useful life of the asset. Moreover, the rules governing depreciation deductions on personalty are in some instances distinctly different from those applicable to realty. This appendix ignores or skims lightly over the similarities and concentrates on the differences in the income tax treatment of depreciation allowances.

What Assets Qualify? As was the case for real property, the investor must have a capital interest in items of personalty before he can claim a depreciation deduction. This does not necessarily mean that he must hold legal title. It means rather that he must have an investment in the property. If a lease of personalty, for example, contains provisions implying that a sale is intended, then the leasee may be permitted to claim depreciation and be denied the right to claim the "lease" payments as a current expense.

Computing the Amount of the Depreciation Deduction. The amount to be recovered as depreciation over the life of items of personalty is, as in the case of realty, cost less net salvage. The asset must have a useful life of more than 1 year to be depreciable. If its estimated useful life is 1 year or less, the investor may be able to take a deduction for the entire purchase price as a current expense in the year of purchase.

The estimated useful life of an item of personalty is determined in the same manner as was discussed in Chapter 7 for real property. Once again, the Internal Revenue Service has published guideline asset depreciation ranges for various classes of assets. Claimed lives that fall within the asset depreciation range for that class of asset are not questioned by the government. Be prepared to defend a claim of a useful life shorter than the lower end of the asset depreciation range.

The code provides that any reasonable and consistent method of calculating depreciation may be used so long as it does not result in greater cumulative deductions during the first two-thirds of the asset's life than would have been the case with the 200% declining-balance method. Any of the methods discussed in the body of Chapter 7 with reference to real estate would, therefore, be suitable for depreciation of personalty. The desire for maximum depreciation in the early years of ownership generally dictates use of either the 200% declining-balance method or the sum-of-the-years'-digits method.

First Year "Bonus" Depreciation. A special provision that applies only to personalty (not to real estate) may be of great importance to the taxpayer whose investment includes a significant expenditure for assets that qualify. He may be able to take an *additional* depreciation deduction during the first year of ownership equal to 20% of the cost of the qualifying asset. This deduction applies only to $10,000 of such assets acquired in any one tax year ($20,000 if the taxpayer files a joint return).

To qualify, property must be tangible *personal* property used in a trade or business and must have a useful life of at least 6 years. The operation of rental property appears to qualify as a trade or business for purposes of satisfying the requirements of this rule. The property may be either new or used.

Although land and buildings are specifically excluded from this rule, many real estate investments involve numerous items that might qualify for the bonus first-year depreciation. Examples include stoves, refrigerators, washers and dryers, and individual room air conditioners. More questionable items that may nevertheless qualify under special circumstances are wall-to-wall carpeting that is removable and intended to be removed and movable partitions in office buildings and stores.

CHAPTER 8

REAL ESTATE AND THE CAPITAL GAINS TAX

That more fortunes have been accumulated in real estate than in any other activity during the second half of the twentieth century can be attributed in part to the steeply graduated income tax and the numerous special exceptions accorded gains on real estate ventures. Because the incremental tax rate rises rapidly to a confiscatory 70%, it is almost impossible to accumulate substantial amounts of capital from sources of income subject to these rates. The financially ambitious must rely instead on their ability or luck to increase the value of their capital assets, profits from disposition of which are taxed at not more than one-half the rate applicable to ordinary income.

Thus it is that the nouveau riche have tended to be builders rather than operators. The emphasis on after-tax proceeds places a premium on capital gains rather than operating profit. A favored strategy has been to seek opportunities where expenditures can be deducted as operating expenses during the development stage, when there is no net profit to be taxed. The net loses are offset against "ordinary" income from other sources. The asset that has been developed to a stage such that it begins to generate a taxable operating profit is then sold to the less sophisticated or the less venturous (or, more likely, to the tax-exempt). The profit is given favored tax treatment as a capital gain.

A whole industry has grown around this concept of tax shelter. Promoters find imaginative ways to exploit the inconsistencies in the tax code and develop tax-sheltered investment packages to sell to high tax-bracket investors. Many of these packages have little to recommend them other than the tax shelter they afford. The neglect of basic economic analysis has resulted in significant losses to many of the investors–losses only partly offset by tax benefits.

Recent legislation has foreclosed many of the more lucrative tax-shelter opportunities. Whereas real estate did not survive the legislative zeal unscathed, most opportunities in other areas were devastated. As a result, real estate remains about the only tax-shelter game in town.

Chapter 8 explains the basic income-tax provisions affecting capital gains and losses. It first distinguishes between capital items and ordinary income and expenses. The nature and significance of the distinction between long- and short-term capital items is then discussed.

After demonstrating the manner of computing the gain or loss on disposal and segregating the gains and losses in the appropriate "capital" or "ordinary" categories, the chapter moves to a detailed discussion of the rules for calculating the income-tax consequences of capital transactions. The explanation is of necessity rather lengthy and at times somewhat tedious. If the text seems repetitious at points, bear with us. Where multiple examples illustrating one issue are encountered, study all of them rather than simply the first. Their purpose will then become clear; they are designed to distinguish between slightly different taxpayer positions where a complex rule is involved. We have found these multiple examples to be the clearest method of making rather fine distinctions.

CAPITAL GAINS AND ORDINARY INCOME

Capital gains and losses arise from a sale or taxable exchange of either capital assets or certain other assets that are to be treated as capital items for purposes of computing taxable gains on disposition (Section 1231 assets). The code provides preferential tax treatment for such gains, if the property involved has been held for more than 12 months. The net effect is a ceiling on the tax liability arising from the gains, so that the tax is never more than 50% of what it would have been had the gains been taxed as ordinary income.

It is this preferential tax treatment of gains, combined with liberal depreciation provisions, that makes real estate such an attractive investment vehicle for persons in high income-tax brackets, and those desiring to build an estate via investment in real estate ventures. The advantage wrought by special tax provisions is amplified by financial leverage that is generally not available elsewhere.

WHEN CAPITAL-GAINS PROVISIONS APPLY

In general, assets held for investment purposes are deemed to be capital items if they have a life expectancy of more than 1 year. These include stocks, bonds, and both improved and unimproved real property. An exception exists for persons considered to be dealers in the type of asset under consideration. For the asset to be considered capital in nature, a dealer must be able to show that it was held as an investment rather than as part of his inventory for resale.

In addition to property held for investment purposes, long-lived assets of a personal nature are considered to be capital items when there is a gain on disposal. These include one's personal residence, furnishings, auto, and so forth. No provision is made, however, for recognition of capital losses on these "personal" assets.

A special rule applies to assets used in a trade or business, as opposed to those held for investment purposes or for personal use. Depreciable assets and land used in one's trade or business are treated as capital items for tax purposes when sold at a gain and as noncapital assets when sold at a loss. This rule applies only to such assets that are not a part of one's inventory and that have been held for more than 12 months before disposal. Reflecting the section of the code containing the special provision, these are generally referred to as Section 1231 assets. Real estate intended to generate rental income is considered a Section 1231 asset. The key provision is intent rather than the actual realization of income. Thus one might experience consistent losses (after deductions for depreciation) and still the asset might qualify for Section 1231 treatment if sold at a loss.

Depreciation Recapture and Capital-Gains Rules. When capital assets or Section 1231 property are disposed of, the difference between the net selling price and the adjusted basis is the gain or loss on the transaction. If the net selling price exceeds the adjusted basis, a portion of the gain may be treated as ordinary income through the provisions for recapture of excess depreciation. Only the balance of the gain is accorded capital-gains treatment. Recapture provisions are treated more fully in Chapter 9.

Long-Term Versus Short-Term Capital Gains. The code distinguishes between capital gains depending upon how long the taxpayer has owned the property. Gains from sale of assets held for 12 months or less are considered to be short-term and are taxed at the same rate as ordinary income. Assets held for more than 12 months are considered long-term capital items, and the gains from their disposal are accorded the more favorable long-term capital-gain treatment. Losses on disposal of capital assets are treated in the following section. Remember that Section 1231 losses are treated as reductions in ordinary income.

COMPUTING THE CAPITAL-GAINS TAX

The first step in the treatment of capital gains and losses is to separate them into long-term (more than 12 months) and short-term (12 months or less) categories. If there are both gains and losses in one category, the gains and losses must be netted (offset against each other).

Example 8–1

In a series of transactions during the year, a taxpayer experienced both gains and losses. The results are summarized below:

Transactions resulting in gains	
Gains on capital assets held more than 12 months	$24,000
Gains on capital assets held 12 months or less	$ 3,000
Gains on Section 1231 assets	1,500
Total gains on capital account transactions	$28,500
Transactions resulting in losses	
Losses on capital assets held more than 12 months	$ 6,000
Losses on capital assets held 12 months or less	5,200
Losses on Section 1231 assets	2,000
Total losses on capital account transactions	$13,200

Preliminary to computing his income-tax obligation resulting from transactions on capital accounts, the long-term transactions are netted, the short-term transactions are netted, and the Section 1231 transactions are netted. The result of this offsetting process is as follows:

Net short-term losses ($5200 loss minus $3000 gain) = $2,200
Net long-term gains ($24,000 gain minus $6000 loss) = $18,000
Net Section 1231 losses ($2000 loss minus $1500 gain) = $500

Had there been a net Section 1231 gain in Example 8–1, it would have been added to net long-term capital gains for the year. Since Section 1231 transactions resulted in a net loss, the loss is offset against ordinary income for the year. Subsequent steps in the calculation of an investor's tax liability depend upon whether there have been net short-term gains or losses, upon whether there have been net long-term gains or losses, and upon the relationship between the net results in the two categories. There are six different posible outcomes, each of which is considered in the following sections.

Net Short-Term Losses Exceed Net Long-Term Gains. If the taxpayer has net long-term gains and net short-term losses, the gains are offset against the losses to the extent of the greater of the two. Thus if the losses exceed the gains, all the net long-term gains are offset against the net short-term losses. The balance of the short-term losses is then offset against ordinary income, as long as the balance does not exceed $3000.

Example 8–2

An individual has $10,000 of adjusted gross income before consideration of his capital transactions. He has a $3000 net long-term capital gain and a $3500 net short-term capital loss during the year. The net long-term gain is offset against the net short-term loss, and the balance of the short-term loss ($500) is allowed as a deduction from ordinary income. His adjusted gross income after accounting for capital gains and losses is $9500.

If after offsetting net long-term gains against net short-term losses the balance of the net short-term losses exceeds $3000, only the first $3000 can be applied to reduce adjusted gross income for the taxable year.* Any remaining net short-term loss in excess of the $3000 is carried forward and treated as a part of net short-term capital losses in the succeeding year.

Example 8–3

An individual has $8000 of adjusted gross income before consideration of capital transactions. He has a $700 net long-term capital gain and a $4000 net short-term capital loss. The net long-term gain is offset against the net short-term loss, leaving a $3300 net capital loss. Of the net loss, $3000 is ap-

* If married couples file separate returns the limit is $1500 for each spouse.

plied against current income leaving an adjusted gross income for the year of $5000. The remaining $300 loss is carried forward and treated as a short-term capital loss next year.

Net Long-Term Losses Exceed Net Short-Term Gains. When net long-term losses exceed net short-term gains, the two are offset to the extent of the short-term gains. The balance of the net long-term losses is applied to offset up to $3000 of ordinary income. However, the capital losses in this case are offset against the ordinary income on a two-for-one basis. That is, $2 of net long-term losses reduce ordinary income by only $1. Thus up to $6000 of net long-term capital losses may be offset against ordinary income in any one taxable year, reducing the adjusted gross income by as much as $3000.

Example 8–4

An individual has $8000 of adjusted gross income before consideration of capital gains and losses. He has $3000 of net long-term losses and $1400 of net short-term gains. The short-term gains are offset against the long-term losses, leaving $1600 of net long-term losses to be applied against ordinary income on a two-for-one basis. Ordinary income is thus reduced by $800, leaving adjusted gross income of $7200 after accounting for all capital gains and losses.

If the balance of net long-term losses after offsetting against net short-term gains is more than $6000, only $6000 can be applied against ordinary income during the current year, reducing ordinary income by a maximum of $3000. If the taxpayer is married and filing a separate return, he is limited to offsetting $1500 of ordinary income against capital losses in any one year. Any remaining net long-term losses are carried forward and treated as a long-term loss in the next taxable year.

Example 8–5

An individual has a net long-term capital loss of $8000 and a net short-term gain of $500. The net short-term gain is offset against the net long-term loss, leaving a balance of $7500. Of this balance, $6000 may be applied against ordinary income during the current tax year, reducing adjusted gross income by $3000. The balance ($1500) is carried forward as a long-term capital loss to the next taxable year.

Net Short-Term Gains Exceed Net Long-Term Losses. If offsetting net short-term gains against net long-term losses results in a balance in the net short-term gains category, this balance is included in ordinary income for the taxable year.

Example 8–6

Adjusted gross income is $6000 before consideration of capital gains and losses. Net short-term gains are $1200 and net long-term losses $400 (including carry-over of losses from previous years). The net long-term losses are first offset against the net short-term gains, leaving a balance of $800, which is included in ordinary income for the taxable year. Adjusted gross income after consideration of capital gains and losses is $6800.

Net Long-Term Gains Exceed Net Short-Term Losses. Net long-term gains are reduced by the amount of net short-term losses when the gains exceed the losses. Fifty percent of the balance is included in ordinary income for the current year. The other 50% is not taxed.

Example 8–7

An individual has $12,000 of adjusted gross income before accounting for capital gains and losses. His net long-term capital gains are $2400 and his net short-term capital losses are $800. The net short-term losses are offset against net long-term gains, leaving a balance of $1600. Fifty percent of this balance is added to gross income for the year. Adjusted gross income after accounting for capital gains and losses is $12,800.

An alternative method of computing the income-tax obligation arising from long-term capital gains is included in the code. The effect of the alternative computation is to place a ceiling on the total effective tax rate applied to capital gains. The alternative tax is explained on page 143.

Net Short-Term Gains and Net Long-Term Gains. After offsetting short-term losses against short-term gains, and long-term losses against long-term gains, there often remains a balance of gains in each category. We would, of course, like this to be the case. A fortunate investor faced with this situation includes all the net short-term gains and one-half the net long-term gains in his gross income.

Example 8–8

Adjusted gross income is $12,000 before accounting for capital gains and losses. Also, there are $5000 of net long-term gains and $2000 of net short-term gains. Adjusted gross income after accounting for capital gains and losses is $16,500, arrived at in the following manner:

Adjusted gross before capital items		$12,000
Add capital gains:		
Net short-term gains	$2,000	
Net long-term gains	5,000	
Total capital gains	$7,000	
Less 50% of long-term gain	$2,500	$ 4,500
Adjusted gross after capital items		$16,500

Net Short-Term Losses and Net Long-Term Losses. Because this is an imperfect world, an investor may find himself encountering net capital losses in both the long- and short-term categories. A maximum of $3000 of ordinary income can be offset against these losses in any one year. Any losses not offset against ordinary income in the current year may be carried forward to be included in capital gain and loss computations in the next year. There is no limit to the number of years losses may continue to be carried, or to the amount of the losses that can be carried forward.* But the losses must be offset against ordinary income in any year where an offset is allowable.

The net short-term losses must be offset against ordinary income first. The offset is on a $1-for-$1 basis, as illustrated in Example 8–2. If there is more than $3000 of short-term losses, the excess over the $3000 offset limit is carried forward to the next year, as are all the long-term losses.

Example 8–9

A taxpayer has $3500 of net short-term losses and $800 of net long-term losses. Of the net short-term losses $3000 is offset against ordinary income on a $1-for-$1 basis, reducing ordinary income by $3000. The balance of the short-term losses ($500) and all the long-term losses must be carried forward to the next taxable year, since not more than $3000 of ordinary income can be offset against capital losses in any one taxable year. The rest of the short-term losses

* The carry-over rules differ for corporations. They are treated in Chapter 12.

are combined with next year's short-term losses, and the carried-forward long-term losses are combined with next year's long-term losses.

If after offsetting all net short-term losses against ordinary income the $3000 offset limit has not been reached, net long-term losses are then offset on a two-for-one basis as illustrated in Example 8–3. Any net long-term losses beyond those which result in a $3000 reduction in ordinary income may not be offset, but must be carried forward and added to long-term gains and losses in the next taxable year.

Example 8–10

An individual has $500 of net short-term losses and $12,000 of net long-term losses. The short-term losses are offset against ordinary income on $1-for-$1 basis, reducing ordinary income by $500. Long-term losses must then be offset against ordinary income on a two-for-one basis until ordinary income has been reduced by a total of $3000, or until the long-term losses have been completely offset. Therefore, $5000 of long-term losses are offset, reducing ordinary income an additional $2500. The balance of the long-term losses is carried forward and included with long-term gains and losses in the next taxable year.

THE ALTERNATIVE CAPITAL-GAINS TAX

The code provides an alternative method of computation that has the effect of limiting the maximum tax on the excess of long-term capital gains over short-term capital losses. The alternative method may be used where there are both long- and short-term gains and losses, or where there are long-term gains only.

The alternative tax rate is 25% on the first $50,000 of net long-term gains. This $50,000 limit applies either to single individuals or to married couples filing a joint return. For married taxpayers filing separate returns, the limit is $25,000. Long-term gains in excess of these limits are taxed at a higher rate. Since the ordinary method of computing the capital-gains tax has the practical effect of taxing them at approximately one-half the ordinary income-tax rate, the alternative method is obviously advantageous to taxpayers having no more than $50,000 of such gains, and who would be in the 50% incremental tax bracket before including their long-term capital gains. Example 8–11 illustrates the difference in the total tax liability under these circumstances, using both the ordinary and the alternative tax computation.

Example 8–11

A married taxpayer who files a joint return has net taxable income of $50,000 (after all deductions and exemptions) before inclusion of capital items. He also has $40,000 of net long-term capital gains. Using the regular computation method, his tax liability follows:

Net taxable income before capital items	$50,000
Add one-half long term capital gains	20,000
Taxable income including capital items	$70,000
Tax liability (from tax table)	$27,720
Less tax liability on $50,000	17,060
Tax consequences of capital gains	$10,660

The inclusion of $40,000 of long-term capital gains increased the tax liability by $10,660. The average tax on the capital gains is, therefore, $10,660/ $40,000, or 26.7%. Since the maximum tax rate on the first $50,000 of capital gains under the alternative method is 25%, the alternative method is clearly more advantageous.

When a taxpayer's ordinary income is such that the tax rate is substantially below 50% on the last dollar of income, and adding one-half of the long-term gains to the ordinary income still results in a tax rate of less than 50% on the last dollar of income taxed, the ordinary method should be used. This is illustrated in Example 8–12.

In all the examples used so far, there is an obvious advantage in use of one method of computation over the other. Where the tax on ordinary income is less than 50% before adding one-half the net long-term gains, and more than 50% after doing so, the advantage is less self-evident. In these situations, the only prudent course is to calculate the tax liability using both the regular and the alternative methods and to choose the method that results in the smaller tax. Such a problem is illustrated in Example 8–13.

Example 8–12

A married taxpayer who files a joint return has taxable (ordinary) income of $20,000 after all deductions and exemptions but before accounting for capital items. He has net long-term capital gains of $15,000. If he uses the regular method of calculating his capital gains tax, his tax liability is:

Net taxable income before capital items	$20,000
Add one-half net long term gains (50% of $15,000)	7,500
Total taxable after inclusion of capital items	$27,500
Tax (from Table 1–1, page 15)	6,920
Less tax on ordinary income ($20,000)	4,380
Tax consequences of capital gains	$ 2,540

Accounting for $15,000 of capital gains increased the taxpayers tax liability by $2540. The average tax rate on the capital gain is, therefore, $2540/$15,000, or 17%. Since the minimum tax on capital gains under the alternative method of computation is 25%, the regular method is unambiguously desirable.

Example 8–13

A married taxpayer who files a joint return has $50,000 of net taxable income after all deductions and exemptions, but before accounting for capital gains and losses. He also has $12,000 of net long-term capital gains and $1200 of net short-term losses.

1. Using the regular method his tax is:

Net taxable income before capital items		$50,000
Add capital items:		
Net long term gains	$12,000	
Less short term losses	1,200	
Net (Section 1201) gains	$10,800	
Less 50%	5,400	5,400
Taxable income including capital items		$55,400
Tax liability (from tax tables)		$19,862

2. Using the alternative method his tax is:

Net taxable income before capital items		$50,000
Tax on the above		$17,060
Add tax on net Section 1201 gain:		
Net long-term gains	$12,000	
Less net short-term losses	1,200	
Net Section 1201 gains	$10,800	
Times alternative tax rate	0.25	$ 2,700
Total tax liability (from tax Table 1–1, page 15)		$19,760

3. Difference:

Tax liability using regular computation	$19,862
Less liability using alternative method	19,760
Tax savings from use of alternative method	$ 102

When net long-term capital gains exceed $50,000, the alternative tax computation is somewhat more complex. This is because only the first $50,000 is subject to the alternative rate of 25%. The balance of the gain in excess of $50,000 is taxed at the same rate that would have prevailed had the regular method been used. Example 8–14 provides an illustration of the problem.

Example 8–14

A married taxpayer who files a joint return has net taxable income after all deductions and exemptions, but before accounting for capital gains, at $65,000. His net Section 1201 gains (net long-term gains minus net short-term losses) are $80,000.

The total tax liability in Example 8–14 using the regular method is $48,280. This is determined by adding one-half the net long-term gain to the ordinary income and calculating the tax from the appropriate tax table. The calculations are:

Ordinary income	$ 65,000
Add one-half the net Section 1201 gain	40,000
Total taxable income	$105,000
Tax liability (from tax table)	$ 48,280

After computing the tax liability under the regular method, the next step is to determine how much of the tax is attributable to the ordinary in-

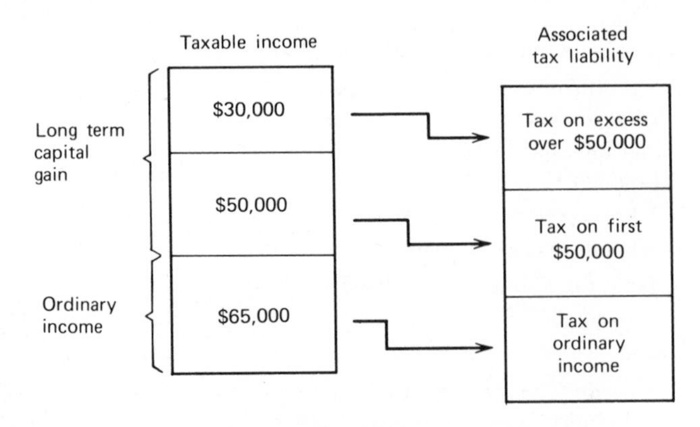

Figure 8-1. Tax liability arising from long-term capital gain.

come, how much to the first $50,000 of capital gains, and how much to capital gains in excess of $50,000. Both the income and the tax liability are thus divided into three segments as illustrated in Figure 8–1.

Continuing Example 8–14, the difference between the total income tax liability of $48,280 and the tax that would have resulted had there been only $50,000 of capital gains must logically be due to the tax consequence of the capital gain in excess of $50,000. The difference is $9100, determined as follows:

Total tax liability using regular method		$48,280
Tax liability had long-term gains been limited to $50,000:		
Ordinary income	$65,000	
Add one-half long-term gains	$25,000	
Taxable income	$90,000	
Tax on $90,000 (from tax table)		$39,180
Difference (additional tax due to last $30,000 of capital gains)		$ 9,100

Now, what is the tax liability resulting from the first $50,000 of long-term capital gains? The answer is $14,210 and is determined in much the same manner as before. First, determine the tax liability had there been no capital gain at all. The difference between this amount and the tax liability with $50,000 of capital gains (already determined) is due to the first $50,000 of such gains. The computation is as follows:

Tax liability with only $50,000 of capital gains (from previous calculation)		$39,180
Tax liability with zero capital gains:		
Total taxable income	$65,000	
Taxes (from tax table)		$24,970
Difference (tax on first $50,000 of capital gains)		$14,210

This relationship between incremental capital gains and the incremental income-tax liability which accompanies the gain is reflected in Figure 8–2. Here, each increment of gain is identified with its resultant tax liability.

The alternative method substitutes for the $14,210 of tax liability on the first $50,000 of capital gain in Figure 8–2, a tax liability of $12,500, representing 25% of the first $50,000 of the gain. The balance of the gain is taxed at the same rate it would have been had the alternative method not been used. That is all there is to it. This is pictured in Figure 8–3.

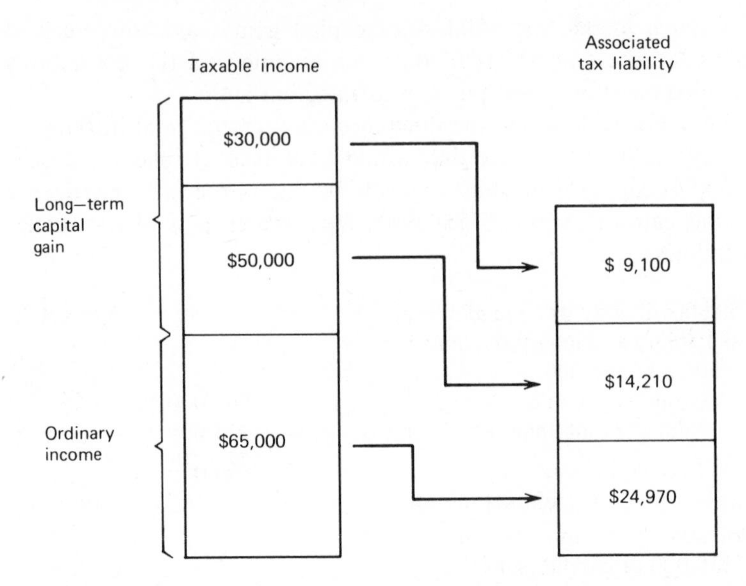

Figure 8-2. Tax liability arising from $80,000 of long-term capital gains, using regular computation method (based on married taxpayer filing a joint return).

The consequences of substituting the alternative method in Example 8–14, as pictured in Figure 8–3, is to reduce the investor's tax liability to $46,570:

Income-tax liability using regular method	$48,280
Less tax on first $50,000 of capital gains	14,210
	$34,070
Add alternative tax on first $50,000 of capital gains	12,500
Total tax liability under alternative method	$46,570

While the explanation of the alternative method has been lengthy, the actual calculations are relatively simple. The discussion has been designed to enhance understanding rather than simply to develop a "cookbook" formulation of the procedure. The cookbook approach can be used, however. The steps involved are as follows:

Step 1. Compute the total tax obligation using the regular method.

Step 2. Compute the total tax obligation under the regular method, assuming the capital gain were only $50,000.

Step 3. Subtract the tax obligation from *Step 2* from that in *Step 1.* The difference is the tax on the capital gain in excess of $50,000.

Step 4. Compute the tax obligation on ordinary income alone.

Step 5. To the tax obligation computed in *Step 4,* add:

(a) $12,500 (25% of the first $50,000 of net section 1231 gains).

(b) The tax obligation on capital gains in excess of $50,000, as calculated in *Step 3.*

The sum calculated in *Step 5* is the tax obligation under the alternative method. These calculations are demonstrated in Example 8–15.

Example 8–15

Assume the same information as in Example 8–14: a married taxpayer who files a joint return and has net taxable income after all deductions and exemptions, but before accounting for capital gains, of $65,000. He has net long-term capital gains in excess of net short-term capital losses (net Section 1201 gains) of $80,000.

1. Using the regular method, his tax liability (as computed on page 146 is $48,280.

2. His tax liability using the alternative method is $46,570, determined as follows:

Step 1.

Total tax obligation under regular method (from 1, above)	$48,280

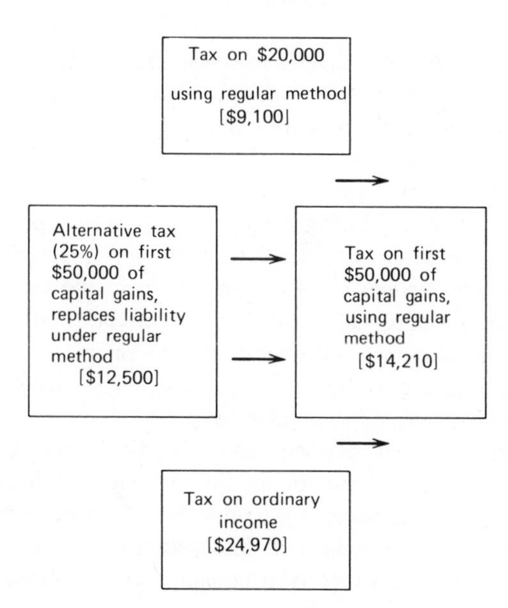

Figure 8-3. Alternative tax (at 25% rate) replaces regular tax on first $50,000 of long-term gains.

Step 2. Total tax obligation under regular method, assuming total long-term capital gain is only $50,000:

Ordinary income	$65,000	
Add one-half capital gain	25,000	
Total taxable	$90,000	
Tax on $90,000 (from Table 1–1, page 15)		$39,180

Step 3. Tax on capital gain in excess of $50,000:

Total tax from *Step 1*	$48,280
Less tax from *Step 2*	39,180
Tax on capital gain in excess of $50,000	$ 9,100

Step 4.

Tax obligation on ordinary income of $65,000 (from tax table)	$24,970
Add:	
25% of first $50,000 of long-term gains	12,500
Tax on gain in excess of $50,000 (from *Step 4*)	9,100
Total tax under alternative method	$46,570

CAPITAL-LOSS CARRY-OVERS

Time is generally kind to real estate investors. Capital gains may not always be as great as anticipated or desired, but there are seldom actual net long-term capital losses on improved real estate. This comfortable consequence of an inexorable population increase and a fixed quantity of land masks many investment errors. The general pattern of real estate prices has been a steady increase during the post-World War II period.

This does not mean, of course, that values never decline. One has only to look at inner-city property almost anywhere in the country to see this, But with the liberal depreciation rules now in effect, the decline in value of even the most injudiciously chosen improved property is seldom greatly in excess of the decrease in the investor's adjusted tax basis when the property qualifies for accelerated depreciation.

The unthinkable does happen, however. Even the most cautious investor is subject to miscalculation in his estimate of the trend of future values. When it becomes necessary to dispose of property for less than the adjusted basis, the capital-gain and -loss provisions that normally look so benign take on the appearance of a conspiracy to deprive the hapless investor of his hard won gains in other ventures. This is because the rules that are so attractive when applied to reduce one's tax liability, apply also when calculating the loss to be offset against income from other sources.

An additional unfavorable feature of the capital-loss provisions is the limitation on the amount of such a loss that can be used to offset other income in any one taxable year, even at the reduced rates.

Recall from the earlier exposition that short-term losses and gains in any one year are netted. Long-term capital gains and losses are likewise netted. If there remains a net gain in one category and a net loss in the other, these two nets are "netted" before applying the capital gain or loss tax rates.

The earlier discussion covered the eventuality that there were net short-term gains in excess of net long-term losses, and that there were net long-term gains in excess of net short-term losses. However, the situation where there are net short-term losses in excess of net long-term gains, or net long-term losses in excess of net short-term gains, was only skirted lightly. These latter situations are now analyzed in more detail.

Net Section 1231 Losses. Remember that real estate and other qualifying assets used in a trade or business (Section 1231 assets) are not actually capital assets under the provisions of the code. Rather they occupy a special, privileged position in that they are treated as capital assets when computing a net gain on disposal but are treated as noncapital assets when there is a net loss on their disposal for the taxable year.

Section 1231 assets are treated first in this section, because they are the most significant classification of assets for most real estate investors. We noted earlier that rental property generally qualifies for Section 1231 treatment. This is of overwhelming importance when there is a net loss on their disposal, since the limitations on the offsetting of capital losses against ordinary income does not apply with respect to net Section 1231 losses.

The first step in computing the effect of Section 1231 transactions is to total all such transactions for the taxable year. Having combined the gains and losses to arrive at a net gain or loss on Section 1231 transactions, the next step depends upon whether there has been a net gain or a net loss. If the net figure is a gain, it is included with long-term capital gains for the year to arrive at net Section 1201 gains. But if the net figure is a loss, it is deducted immediately from ordinary income from other sources to arrive at taxable income before provision for capital gains and losses.

Example 8–16 illustrates how net Section 1231 losses are offset directly against ordinary income from other sources before accounting for capital transactions. If, on the other hand, there are net Section 1231 gains, these

Example 8–16

A taxpayer has $12,000 of ordinary income from wages, $5,000 of Section 1231 gains, and $6500 of Section 1231 losses. He has $2500 of long-term capital gains (other than his Section 1231 transactions) and $1300 of long-term capital losses. Before figuring his tax liability from capital transactions, he must net his Section 1231 transactions to determine whether there was a net loss or a net gain on such transactions. In this instance, there was a net loss, so this is offset against ordinary income before considering the effect of capital items.

Ordinary income before capital and Section 1231 items:		$12,000
Less net Section 1231 losses:		
Section 1231 losses	$6,500	
Section 1231 gains	5,000	
Net Section 1231 losses		1,500
Taxable income before accounting for capital items		$10,500
Add one-half net long-term capital gains:		
Total long-term gains	$2,500	
Less total long-term losses	1,300	
Net long-term (Section 1201) gain	$1,200	
Less one-half long-term gains	600	600
Taxable income after accounting for long-term capital transactions		$11,100

are included in the calculation of net capital gains or losses. Example 8–17 illustrates this point.

To summarize, all Section 1231 transactions for the year are combined to determine the net Section 1231 gain or loss. If the result is a net loss, it is offset against ordinary income before accounting for capital items. A net Section 1231 gain, on the other hand, is included with net long-term capital gains before proceeding to determine the net Section 1201 gain or loss by offsetting net short-term losses against net long-term gains or net short-term gains against net long-term losses. This is of vital importance for the taxpayer experiencing substantial losses because, as we shall see, losses classified as capital in nature are treated much less charitably.

Offsetting Capital Losses Against Other Income. In an earlier section, we noted that net capital losses can be offset against ordinary income in any one taxable year only to the extent of $3000 of ordinary income. This includes all net capital losses, both short- and long-term.

Example 8–17

Assume as in the previous example that our taxpayer has $12,000 of ordinary income from wages, $2500 of long-term capital gains, and $1300 of long-term capital losses. But assume now that he has $7500 of Section 1231 *gains* and $5000 of Section 1231 *losses*. The net Section 1231 gains of $2500 are included with capital gains to determine the net long-term capital gains for the taxable year.

Section 1231 gains		$ 7,500
Less Section 1231 losses		5,000
Net Section 1231 gains (to be included in long-term capital gains)		$ 2,500
Ordinary income before accounting for capital transactions		$12,000
Add one-half net long-term capital gains (Net Section 1201 gains):		
Long-term capital gains	$2,500	
Net Section 1231 gains	2,500	
Total Section 1201 gains	$5,000	
Less one-half Section 1201 gains	2,500	
Section 1201 gains included in ordinary income		2,500
Taxable income after accounting for capital transactions		$14,500

If a taxpayer has net short-term losses in excess of net long-term gains, the excess can be used to offset up to $3000 of ordinary income, on a $1-for-$1 basis. If he has net long-term capital losses in excess of net short-term capital gains, the excess can be used to offset up to $3000 of ordinary income on a two-for-one basis. That is, $2 of net long-term capital losses can be offset against $1 of ordinary income. Any additional capital loss for the taxable year cannot be used to reduce the tax liability for the year but may be carried forward to be included in capital-gain and -loss calculations of future years.

Capital losses carried forward retain their identity in future years as short- or long-term. To make this more clear, we consider separately situations where short- and long-term capital losses are carried forward.

Carry-Over of Short-Term Capital Losses. Consider a taxpayer who has $3300 of net short-term capital losses in excess of net long-term capital gains. Of this amount, $3000 is offset against ordinary income during the current taxable year, thus reducing taxable income. The remaining $300 cannot be used to reduce taxable income during the current year, but must be carried forward to the next taxable year, where it is treated as a short-term capital loss for purposes of determining that year's net capital gains or losses. This limitation on the amount of ordinary income that can be offset against net capital losses applies each year. But unused capital losses may be carried forward for an unlimited number of years until they are used up.

Example 8–18

An unmarried taxpayer has a $300 short-term capital loss carry-over from the previous taxable year. During the current year, he has $2300 of net long-term capital gains and $200 of net short-term capital gains, before using the capital-loss carry-over from the previous year. The short-term carry-over is applied againt the short-term capital gains for the year, resulting in $100 of net short-term capital losses after accounting for the carry-over. The net short-term losses are then offset against the net long-term gains to calculate the taxpayer's capital-gain and -loss position for the current year:

Net short-term capital gains before account for short-term loss carry-over	$ 200
Less short-term loss carried over from last year	300
Net short-term gains (losses) after accounting for carry-over	($ 100)
Net long-term capital gains	$2,300
Less net short-term capital losses	100
Net Section 1201 gain	$2,200

In Example 8–18, the total short-term capital-loss carry-over is used to reduce the net Section 1201 gain for the succeeding year. But suppose the carry-over is greater than the total of long- and short-term gains in the succeeding year? In that case, the excess of the carry-over can be applied to offset up to $3000 of ordinary income, with any remaining balance being carried forward once again as a short-term loss to the next succeeding year.

Example 8–19

A married taxpayer who files a joint return has $15,000 of ordinary income before accounting for capital items. He also experiences $500 of net short-term gains and $300 of net long-term losses during the current year. Additionally, he has $4300 short-term capital losses carried forward from previous years.

The carried-over short-term losses are first offset against the current net short-term gains, then against current net long-term gains. There remain short-term losses of $3500 in excess of current capital gains. Of this amount, $3000 is used to offset ordinary income. The balance is carried forward to the next taxable year. The computations are summarized below:

Short-term losses carried over from previous year	$4,300
Less net short-term capital gains this year	500
Net short-term losses after accounting for loss carry-over from previous years	$3,800
Less net long-term gains this year	300
Excess of net short-term losses over net long-term gains, after inclusion of loss carry-overs	$3,500
Less portion of net losses to be offset against ordinary income in current year	3,000
Short-term losses carried forward to next year	$ 500

Carry-Over of Net Long-Term Capital Losses. If there are net long-term capital losses in excess of net short-term capital gains for the taxable year, the excess may be used to offset up to $3000 of ordinary income, using $2 of long-term losses to offset each $1 of ordinary income. Any remaining long-term losses may not be offset against income during the current taxable year but are carried over for an unlimited number of years to be applied against income in the future. The carried-forward long-term losses are applied first against net long-term gains on a $1-for-$1 basis until these are reduced to zero. Any remaining loss is then applied against net short-term gains on a $1-for-$1 basis. After reducing both net long-term and net short-term capital gains to zero, any remaining long-term loss carry-over may be applied against up to $3000 of ordinary income on a two-for-one basis. Any remaining loss carry-over is then carried forward to the next taxable year.

Example 8–20

A married taxpayer who files a joint return has net short-term capital gains of $400 and net long-term capital gains of $1200 during the current taxable year. He also has a long-term capital loss of $9000 carried forward from previous years. After offsetting the carry-over against current capital gains, there remains a loss carry-over of $7400. Of this amount, $6000 is used to reduce ordinary income by $3000. The balance of $1400 is carried forward to the next taxable year as a net long-term capital loss.

Carry-Over Rules with Both Long- and Short-Term Losses. So far we have assumed that the taxpayer has had either net long-term losses in excess of net short-term gains or net short-term losses in excess of net long-term gains. But suppose the taxpayer has both net short-term and net long-term losses? In this case, the net short-term losses are applied first against ordinary income, offsetting up to $3000 of ordinary income. If there were less than $3000 of net short-term losses, net long-term losses may then be used (on a two-for-one basis) to offset ordinary income to the point that a total of $3000 of ordinary income has been offset. Any remaining losses are then carried forward, maintaining their identity as long- or short-term in future years.

Example 8–21

A taxpayer has net short-term losses of $500 and net long-term losses of $6000 plus taxable ordinary income (before accounting for capital items) of $9000. He files a joint return with his spouse. First, he offsets his short-term losses against ordinary income to reduce taxable income by $500. He then offsets $5000 of his long-term losses against $250 or ordinary income, leaving a taxable income after accounting for capital items of $6000. The remaining $1000 of long-term losses is carried forward to the next year.

Example 8–22

A single taxpayer has taxable income in 1978 of $12,000 before accounting for capital items. He also has a net long-term capital gain of $600 and a net short-term capital gain of $300. But he has carried over from 1976 a long-term capital loss of $8000 and a short-term capital loss of $500. His taxable income for 1978 is computed as follows:

Capital items	
Net short-term capital loss:	
Short-term loss carry-over from 1977	$ 500
Less current short-term capital gain	300
Net short-term loss after inclusion of short-term loss carry-over	$ 200

Net long-term capital loss:		
Long-term loss carry-over from 1977		$ 8,000
Less current long-term gain		600
Net long-term loss after inclusion of long-term loss carry-over		$ 7,400
Taxable income		
Taxable income before accounting for capital items		$12,000
Less:		
Net short-term loss offset	$ 200	
Net long-term loss offset	2,800	3,000
Taxable income after accounting for capital items		$ 9,000
Capital loss carry-over to 1979		
Net short-term loss carry-over:		
Net short-term losses, from above		$ 200
Less amount offset against 1978 income		200
Amount carried forward to 1979		0
Net long-term loss carry-over:		
Net long-term losses, from above		$ 7,400
Less amount offset against 1978 income, on a two-for-one basis		5,600
Amount carried forward to 1979		$ 800

SUMMARY

Gains and losses on investment-type assets held for more than 1 year are subject to special tax provisions as long-term capital items. Gains on long-lived (more than 1 year) assets held for personal use are subject to the capital-gains tax, but losses generally have no income-tax consequences. Gains on long-lived assets held for business purposes (other than stock-in-trade) are taxed at the capital-gains rates, but losses on these items are included as reductions in ordinary income. Capital-gains rules generally do not apply to dealers in the assets under consideration.

Gains and losses on capital items and assets treated as capital items for purposes of applying Section 1250 are divided into two categories based on the length of time the assets were held. Assets held for longer than 12 months are long-term, whereas those held for 12 months or less are short-term. Where there are both gains and losses in one category during the taxable year, the gains and losses are netted. The result is the net gain or loss in that category. Where there are net gains in one category and net losses in the other, the two categories are themselves netted. The result is the net capital gain or loss for the year.

Net short-term capital losses in excess of net long-term capital gains are offset against ordinary income on a $1-for-$1 basis. Net long-term capital losses in excess of net short-term capital gains are offset against ordinary income on a two-for-one basis. Where there are both short- and long-term losses in the same year, they are both offset against ordinary income, in the ratios previously described. But the maximum amount of ordinary income that can be offset in any one taxable year is $3000. Losses in excess of those required to offset this amount of ordinary income are carried forward and included with capital transactions in the next year. Where there are losses in both the short- and long-term categories, the short-term losses are offset against ordinary income first, then long-term losses are offset (on a two-for-one basis) until either the losses are all accounted for or the $3000 maximum on total offsets is reached. In the latter case, the balance of the losses is carried forward to the next year. There is no limit on the amount of losses that can be carried forward or the number of years the losses can be carried.

Net short-term capital gains in excess of net long-term capital losses are included in ordinary income on a $1-for-$1 basis. Thus, $1 of short-term gains increases taxable income by $1. Net long-term gains in excess of net short-term losses, on the other hand, are included in taxable income on a two-for-one basis. Thus $2 of net long-term gains increases taxable income by only $1.

The maximum tax rate on the first $50,000 of long-term capital gains is 25%. Gains in excess of $50,000 are taxed as explained in the preceding paragraph, without reference to the maximum rate.

SUGGESTED READING

1. Kane, Edward R., "Capital Gains and Losses," *Journal of Real Estate Taxation, 3* (3), 234–242 (1976).

CHAPTER 9

TAX CONSEQUENCES OF PROPERTY SALES

This chapter introduces the basic income-tax factors involved in disposal of property held for business or investment purposes. The amount and nature of the gain or loss is considered first. Central to this determination is the issue of recapture of excess depreciation, which is the second major topic of the chapter. The final section describes how tax liability for gains on disposal can be deferred by using the installment-sales method of reporting transactions that are, at least in part, seller-financed.

GAINS AND LOSSES ON DISPOSAL

The longer an investor holds a judiciously chosen property, the greater the market price he might expect to receive on disposal. This does not imply, however, that the longer the property is held, the better. Both the rate of increase in market value and the income-tax consequences involved in disposal vary with the holding period. Some of the consequences suggest a longer period of ownership, whereas others engender consideration of early disposal. The investor must weigh the net effect of all the factors before making a disposal decision. The immediate issue is the amount and the tax status of the gain or loss.

Calculating the Gain or Loss. Recall from Chapter 7 that the adjusted tax basis is the cost of a property, adjusted for depreciation and improvements, plus certain other adjustments that may sometimes apply. Review Chapter 7 at this time if the concept is not clear. The gain or loss on disposal is simply the difference between the "amount realized" from the sale or exchange and the adjusted basis at the time of the transaction.

The amount realized from a sale is the fair market value of all goods and services received in exchange, plus any net debt relief, minus all costs incurred in the transaction. The balance due on a mortgage to which the property is subject is always included in the consideration, whether or not the purchaser assumes personal liability.

Example 9–1

An investor who is not a dealer sells a store building that is subject to an existing mortgage of $15,000. He receives $15,000 in cash at the closing and takes back a note and second mortgage of $20,000. He pays a real estate brokerage commission of $5000 and incurs other fees of $300. The amount realized on the sale is computed as follows:

Cash received at closing		$15,000
Add:		
Purchase money mortgage	$20,000	
Existing mortgage assumed	15,000	35,000
Selling price		$50,000
Less:		
Brokerage commission	$ 5,000	
Miscellaneous fees	300	5,300
Amount realized on sale		$44,700

If the seller receives other property or services as a part of the consideration, these items must be included in the amount realized at their fair market value.

Example 9–2

A taxpayer transfers title to a duplex (which he owns free and clear) in exchange for the following consideration: He receives $5000 in cash at the time of the transaction and a note for $10,000 due in 6 months. The purchaser transfers title to a vacant lot (market value $7000) and a pickup truck (market value $1800). The purchaser, who is an attorney, agrees to prepare the seller's income-tax return for the year and to represent him in divorce proceedings that are scheduled in the near future. The usual fee for these legal services would be $850. The total consideration involved in the transaction is $24,650, computed as follows:

Cash	$ 5,000
Note receivable	10,000
Vacant lot	7,000
Personalty (pickup truck)	1,800
Agreement to render services valued at	850
Total consideration	$24,650

At the time of execution of a real property transaction, certain "closing costs" are apportioned between buyer and seller. Of those borne by the seller, some are treated as selling costs, and some are deductible from ordinary income as operating expenses during the period of ownership. Apportionment of property taxes and water bills are examples of closing costs that are borne in part by the seller but are not treated as selling costs. Only that portion of the seller's closing costs that would have been avoided had there been no transaction are genuinely attributable to the transaction and so treated as transactions costs. Examples include broker's commission, attorney's fee, survey costs, and title insurance. These may not be deducted from ordinary income as business expenses but must instead be deducted from the consideration received to determine the amount realized from the transaction.

At times, the seller incurs loan discount points in connection with a sale. He may be required as a condition of the sale to pay the discount fee incurred by the purchaser in acquiring financing. This is almost always the case when the purchaser is obtaining government insured financing (VA or FHA). It may also be the case when conventional financing is involved. Discount points absorbed by the seller are treated as selling costs, and so deducted from the consideration in determining the amount realized from the sale.

Example 9–3

An investor sells for $100,000 an apartment complex he has owned for several years. The actual cash disbursed to the seller at the closing is $32,690, determined as follows:

Market value of property conveyed		$100,000
Less:		
Broker's commission	$ 6,000	
Attorney's fee	500	
Accrued property taxes	750	
Accrued electricity bill	60	
Balance of mortgage assumed by buyer	$60,000	$ 67,310
Cash to seller		$ 32,690

The amount realized is the selling price, minus those costs incident to the sale. This includes only the broker's commission and the attorney's fee. The accrued taxes and electricity represent operating expenses incurred but not paid during the period of ownership. They are deductible by the seller as reductions in his ordinary income. The amount of the existing mortgage assumed by the buyer represents a part of the consideration. The amount realized is, therefore, $93,500, determined as follows:

Market value of property conveyed		$100,000
Less transactions costs:		
Broker's commission	$6,000	
Attorney's fee	500	6,500
Amount realized		$ 93,500

If we assume that the property in Example 9–3 has an adjusted basis of $75,000, the gain on disposal would be the amount realized ($93,500) minus the adjusted basis ($75,000), or $18,500.

When Is the Gain Recognized? A loss or gain on a transaction must generally be recognized in the taxable year of the closing. The date of "closing" usually corresponds to the date of delivery of the deed, without regard to actual physical possession of the property. The closing might be construed as having occurred prior to delivery of the deed if the purchaser acquires possession under a contract of sale that unconditionally requires delivery of a deed at a future date, and under which the purchaser exercises all rights of ownership.

When a transaction "closes in escrow," the gain usually is not recognized until the conditions of the escrow are satisfied and funds are authorized to be released (although they need not actually have been disbursed).

Exceptions to the requirement to recognize a gain in the year of closing include transactions that qualify for treatment as installment sales and like-kind exchanges. Installment sales are treated later in this chapter. Like-kind exchanges are discussed in Chapter 10. Exceptions exist also for certain government-assisted low-income housing projects sold to the tenants, if the funds are reinvested in another qualified project within 1 year after the close of the taxable year of the initial transaction.

Another exception is an "involuntary conversion." Involuntary conversions occur when money or other property is received from property that has been destroyed, stolen, or taken for public use under the right of eminent domain. Any gain on such a conversion need not be recognized if the proceeds are reinvested in a similar or related property within a designated replacement period. The replacement period begins at the date of disposition of the property or, in the case of property taken for public use, at the earliest date of threat of requisition or condemnation. The period ends 2 years after the close of the taxable year in which any part of the gain is first realized.

RECAPTURE OF EXCESS DEPRECIATION

Having calculated the amount of the gain or loss on a taxable transaction, the next step is to determine how the gain or loss affects the seller's tax liability.

If the adjusted basis exceeds the amount realized on the transaction, the difference is a loss. The precise consequences of such a loss are explained in Chapter 8.

If the amount realized from the transaction exceeds the adjusted basis of the property, the difference represents a taxable gain. All or a portion of the gain may be treated as ordinary income, due to the rules for recapture of excess depreciation where there is a gain on the disposal of depreciable property. Any remaining gain after accounting for the recapture of excess depreciation is accorded capital-gains treatment as explained in Chapter 8. But before any capital gain can be recognized, recaptured excess depreciation must be considered.

What Is Excess Depreciation? The adjusted basis of the property sold is a major determinant of the amount of the gain on the sale. The lower the basis, the greater the amount of the gain. And the adjusted basis reflects the depreciation claimed during the period of ownership. If the amount realized on the sale is not greater than the original cost of the property plus the cost of any capital improvements, any gain on the sale will be due solely to reductions in the basis resulting from depreciation reductions.

Example 9–4

An investor acquired a new residential income property for $100,000. Eighty percent of the cost was applicable to the improvements, which had a useful life estimated at 40 years. The investment qualified for the 200% declining-balance method of calculating depreciation. After 5 years, the investor sold the property, realizing exactly the original cost ($100,000) on the transaction.

Because of the annual depreciation allowance, the investor's adjusted basis had been reduced to $78,712 by the time he sold the property. His taxable gain is the amount realized minus the adjusted basis ($100,000, less $78,712) or $21,288. In this case, the taxable gain exactly equals the cumulative depreciation. His basis at the time he sold the property would have been the original cost of $100,000 had he not taken the periodic depreciation expense deduction, and there would have been no taxable gain.

Prior to 1963, the investor in Example 9–4 would have reaped a bonanza of tax benefits from the combination of accelerated depreciation and capital-gains provisions. Claiming depreciation deductions in excess of the actual decline in value of the property would have reduced his tax liability during the period of ownership. Then when the property was sold, the gain on the sale would have reflected these excessive depreciation deductions. But the taxpayer would have benefited due to the difference between the tax savings from depreciation deductions (using the ordinary tax rate) and the tax liability from capital gains (using the reduced rate applicable to capital gains).

Recognizing this unintended windfall to investors, Congress included in the 1962 revision of the code a provision for partial recapture of the depreciation claimed in excess of the actual decline in value due to factors generally included in the definition of depreciation. These "recapture rules" were made more stringent in the 1969 and the 1976 revisions of the code. There are still tax benefits attendant to judicious planning with special attention to accelerated depreciation and capital-gains provisions, but they are much more difficult to reap.

The current recapture rules define "excess depreciation" as the difference between the cumulative-depreciation deductions taken during the holding period by a taxpayer using an accelerated depreciation method, and the cumulative depreciation deductions he would have been entitled to had he used the straight-line method of depreciation. Any gain on disposal is attributed to the taxpayer's having taken excess depreciation to the extent the gain does not exceed this difference.

Example 9–5

The investor in Example 9–4 took cumulative depreciation during his period of ownership of $21,288. Had he used the straight-line method, cumulative depreciation would have been only $10,000 (assuming as before that the useful life of the improvements is estimated at 40 years and assuming no salvage value). The cumulative depreciation actually claimed in excess of the cumulative straight-line depreciation ($21,288 less $10,000, or $11,288) is "excess depreciation."

If the sale of property results in a gain, part of which is attributed to excess depreciation, then all or a portion of the excess depreciation may be subject to recapture. To the extent that the gain is attributed to recapture of excess depreciation, it is taxed as ordinary income. Any remaining gain after accounting for recapture of excess depreciation is accorded capital-gains treatment and taxed at a much lower rate.

Example 9–6

Continuing the illustration from Examples 9–4 and 9–5, of the total gain on disposal of $21,288 (from Example 9–4), the amount attributable to recapture of excess depreciation is $11,288 (from Example 9–5) and is taxed as ordinary income. The balance of the gain ($10,000) is treated as a long-term capital gain.

Excess Depreciation Recapture Rate. If depreciable property is held for less than 1 full year, all the depreciation (not just the excess) is subject to recapture. The total gain is therefore treated as ordinary income to the extent that the taxpayer has taken a depreciation deduction. The excess of the gain over total depreciation taken is treated as short-term capital gain.

When property is held for 1 or more years all or a portion of the excess depreciation may be subject to the recapture provisions of Section 1250, depending upon when the property was acquired, how long it was held, and the type of real property involved. The first step is to divide the cumulative depreciation into four subperiods during which different recapture provisions were in effect. The rules for each subperiod must then be applied to the excess depreciation taken during that time span. The subperiods are:

1. From the time the property is acquired through December 31, 1963. None of this depreciation is subject to recapture, since the recapture rules did not become effective until January 1, 1964.
2. From January 1, 1964 through December 31, 1969.
3. From January 1, 1970 through December 31, 1975.
4. From January 1, 1976, until the property is sold.

Having determined the portion of cumulative depreciation claimed in each of these subperiods, the next step is to calculate the depreciation for each subperiod using the straight-line method. The difference is excess depreciation, which is subject to the recapture rules that were in effect during the applicable subperiod.

Example 9–7

An income property is acquired on January 1, 1969, and sold on December 31, 1977. Under the rules in effect in 1963, the property qualified for accelerated depreciation, which was taken. As a consequence, the total depreciation claimed in each year of ownership was significantly in excess of what would have been allowed under the straight-line method. The actual depreciation claimed and the amount that would have been claimed under the straight-line method, is calculated for each subperiod:

	Depreciation Allowance		
Year	Amount Claimed (Accelerated)	Straight-Line Amount	Excess of Accelerated over Straight-Line
1969	$ 5,000	$ 2,500	$ 2,500
Subtotal	$ 5,000	2,500	2,500
1970	4,750	2,500	2,250
1971	4,513	2,500	2,013
1972	4,287	2,500	1,787
1973	4,073	2,500	1,573
1974	3,869	2,500	1,369
1975	3,674	2,500	1,174
Subtotal	$25,166	$15,000	$10,166
1976	3,492	2,500	992
1977	3,317	2,500	817
Subtotal	$ 6,809	$ 5,000	$ 1,809
Totals	$36,975	$22,500	$14,475

For excess depreciation taken before 1976, the recapture rules differ with the length of time the property was held, depending upon whether the property was residential or nonresidential in character. All excess depreciation taken since 1976 is subject to 100% recapture without regard to the character of the property or the length of time it has been held, with the exception of certain rental housing intended for low-income tenants. Since, for each subperiod prior to 1976, the rules differ for residential and nonresidential property held for the same period of time, the most convenient approach is to deal with these two property classifications separately.

Nonresidential Income Property. Property is considered to be residential if not less than 80% of the gross rental income is derived from residential dwelling units. The fair market value of space occupied by an owner–occupant is included as residential rent for purposes of applying the 80% test. All other depreciable real estate must be considered nonresidential in determining the applicable recapture rules.

The rules for nonresidential-income property were not changed by the Tax Reform Act of 1976. Consequently, all excess depreciation taken after 1969 may be considered as having occurred in the same subperiod. The recapture rate on nonresidential property, applicable for each subperiod, follows:

1. For excess depreciation taken after 1969: 100%.
2. For excess depreciation taken after 1963 but before 1970: 100% minus 1% for each month the property was held in excess of 20 months.
3. For excess depreciation taken prior to 1964: Recapture rules do not apply.

In computing the holding period for purposes of determining the recapture rate, compute the number of full months the property is held. For example, property acquired on September 12th has been held one full month on October 12th, two full months on November 12th, and so on. Count *all* the time the property is held without regard to whether the holding period falls within the applicable dates for determining the excess depreciation. To determine the amount of recaptured depreciation, consider the most recent subperiod first. Thus the recapture of excess depreciation taken since 1969 is the lesser of the amount of excess depreciation claimed in that period or the gain on disposal. If the total gain exceeds the post-1969 excess depreciation, calculate the recapture for the period from 1964 through 1969. The recapture of excess depreciation taken in the earlier period is the lesser of the remaining gain on disposal or the recapture resulting from application of rule 2.

Example 9–8

Assume that the property described in Example 9–7 is nonresidential in nature and is sold on December 31, 1977 for $20,000 more than the adjusted basis. This gain on disposal is partly ordinary income resulting from recapture of excess depreciation and partly a capital gain. The recapture calculation (using data from Example 9–7) follows:

Post-1969 excess depreciation (100% recaptured)		$11,975
Excess depreciation post-1963 but before 1970	$2,500	
Recapture rate (100% minus 88% for 88 full months held over 20 months)	12%	
Pre-1970 recapture (12% of $2500)		300
Total recapture		$12,275

Residential Income Property. The recapture rules applicable to residential property are somewhat more permissive, as are the accelerated-depreciation rules. One consequence is that investment in residential property offers a much more valuable tax shelter than does nonresidential property. Perhaps this reflects the recognition among lawmakers that more voters pay residential rents than pay nonresidential rents.

As noted earlier, a property is considered residential if for the taxable year under consideration the gross rental income is comprised of at least 80% residential rents. The applicable recapture rate for each of the subperiods affected by periodic revisions of the tax code is:

1. Excess depreciation taken after 1975: 100%.
2. Excess depreciation taken before 1976 but after 1969: 100% minus 1% for each month the property was held over 100 months.
3. Excess depreciation taken before 1970 but after 1963: 100% minus 1% for each month the property was held over 20 months.
4. For excess depreciation taken before 1964, there are no recapture provisions.

Calculation of the holding period is the same as for nonresidential property. Count all the time the property was held without regard to the subperiods already outlined. This total holding period is then applied to determine the recapture rate applicable to excess depreciation taken in each of the subperiods.

Recapture is determined on a "last-in, first-out" basis. Excess depreciation taken since 1975 is recaptured first. If there remains any gain on disposal after subtracting the post-1975 recapture, proceed to calculate the recapture applicable to the period after 1969 but before 1976. If there remains any gain not accounted for by this recapture, proceed to the next earlier subperiod, and so on. Of course, the total recapture cannot be greater than the total gain on disposal. If the gain exceeds the total amount of excess depreciation subject to recapture, the balance is taxed as a capital gain.

Example 9–9

Assume the property described in Example 9–7 is residential income property and is sold on December 31, 1977 for $20,000 more than the adjusted basis. Of this $20,000 gain on disposal, $11,462 is attributed to recapture of excess depreciation. The balance of the gain ($8538) is taxed as a long-term capital gain. The calculations follow:

Post-1975 excess (100% recaptured)		$ 1,809
Post-1969 but pre-1976 excess	$10,166	
Recapture rate (100% minus 8% for 8 full months held over 100 months)	92%	
Amount recaptured (92% of $10,166)		9,353
Pre-1970 excess	$ 2,500	
Recapture rate (100% minus 88% for 88 full months held over 20 months)	12%	
Amount recaptured (12% of $2,500)		300
Total excess subject to recapture		$11,462

THE INSTALLMENT-SALES METHOD

When a seller receives only part payment for his property during the year of the transaction, it is sometimes possible to postpone payment of a portion of his income-tax liability until the balance of the cash is collected, by reporting the transaction under the installment-sales method. The tax liability is incurred only on a prorata basis with the portion of the sales proceeds collected each year.

Advantages of Installment-Sales Reporting. There are several circumstances under which the installment-sales option is advantageous. Where third-party financing is expensive or difficult to obtain, the seller can often realize a much greater price for his property by providing a substantial portion of the financing himself, through a purchase money mortgage, an installment-sales contract, or by taking back a subordinated mortgage to supplement the available third-party loan. Each of these options involves deferring receipt of a portion of the proceeds. While potentially lucrative, they may result in a substantial net cash outflow if the total gain is taxed in the year of the transaction. This unfortunate side effect of a seller-financed deal can be eliminated by using the installment-sales method of reporting the transaction.

A second potential benefit of the installment method is that taxes may be deferred until the investor is in a much lower tax bracket than at the time of the transaction. A property sale might be arranged during the investor's peak income earning years, for example, with the payment to be spread over his retirement years. The amount of the taxable gain and the nature of the gain (ordinary income and/or capital gain) are determined at the time of the transaction. But the applicable tax rate is that in effect when the taxes become due.

Example 9–10

An investor realizes a $100,000 gain on the sale of an apartment building. Assume that $80,000 of the gain represents recapture of excess depreciation and is thus taxable as ordinary income. The balance is a long-term capital gain. During the year of the sale, the investor has net taxable income (after all deductions and exemptions) from other sources of $45,000. This, however, is his last year of employment, and in future years his net taxable income is anticipated to be only $20,000, comprised of a retirement annuity and investment or interest income. The investor is married and files a joint return.

The investor has a choice of receiving cash for his property in the year of the sale or of receiving a substantial down payment, the balance to be received over a period of 5 years. If he accepts the cash alternative he invests the proceeds in corporate bonds. If he accepts the second alternative the terms are arranged so that he is taxed on $10,000 of the gain this year and $18,000 of the gain in each of the next 5 years. The interest rate on the installment note is set so that his investment and interest income are the same amount with either alternative. This amount is included in his anticipated income from other sources during the retirement years.

The income-tax consequences if the investor in Example 9–10 opts for a cash sale are calculated as follows:

Taxable income:	
Income from other sources	$ 45,000
Recapture of excess depreciation	80,000
Amount taxable as ordinary income	$125,000
Income-tax liability:	
Tax on ordinary income (using 1976 tax tables)	60,780
Capital gains tax (25% of $20,000)	5,000
Total tax liability	$ 65,780
Less tax on "other income" ($45,000)	14,560
Tax consequences of cash sale	$ 51,220

If our investor accepts the deferred-payment alternative and reports the sale under the installment method, the total income-tax consequences, spread over the period of the note, are:

Taxable Income

	Income from Other Sources	Recapture of Excess Depreciation	One-half Capital Gain*	Total Taxable Income
Year of sale	$45,000	$10,000	0	$55,000
First year after	20,000	18,000	0	38,000
Second year after	20,000	18,000	0	38,000
Third year after	20,000	18,000	0	38,000
Fourth year after	20,000	16,000	1,000	37,000
Fifth year after	20,000		9,000	29,000

Income-Tax Liability

	Tax on Total Taxable Income	Tax on Other Income	Tax Consequences of Sale
Year of sale	$19,650	$14,560	$ 5,090
First year after	11,240	4,380	6,860
Second year after	11,240	4,380	6,860
Third year after	11,240	4,380	6,860
Fourth year after	14,840	4,380	10,460
Firth year after	11,000	4,380	6,620
Totals	$79,210	$36,460	$42,750

* In the cash sale example, it was advantageous to use the alternative capital-gain method. But the regular method of simply including one-half the long-term gain in ordinary income results in a lower tax liability when the installment sale alternative is used. See Chapter 8 for details.

The tax savings from the use of the installment method are $8,470, determined as follows:

Tax consequences of cash sale	$51,220
Less tax consequences of installment sale	42,750
Advantage of installment over cash sale	$ 8,470

Even if the taxpayer's income from other sources does not decline during the period over which he incurs the tax obligation under the installment method, additional tax savings are possible. If he used the ordinary method (as opposed to the alternative method) of reporting capital gains, then one-half the capital gain to be recognized each year is added to the ordinary income for the year. Due to the graduated nature of the tax rates, spreading the gain over a number of years can avoid adding enough to the ordinary income in any one year to move the taxpayer into a higher bracket. The savings can be substantial.

If the gain on a transaction is sufficient to make total long-term capital gains exceed $50,000, the potential benefits of the installment method are even more dramatic for the taxpayer who would use the alternative method of computing his capital-gains tax. This is because long-term capital gains in excess of $50,000 are not eligible for the maximum tax rate of 25% applicable to the alternative method. The maximum tax on capital gains in excess of $50,000 can go as high as 35% (for taxpayers who would be in the 70% tax bracket for ordinary income had they not opted for the alternative capital-gains tax). If the total capital gain exceeds $50,000, it may be profitable to arrange an installment sale that spreads the gain over a number of years so that the amount recognized in any one year does not exceed the $50,000 limit.

Another potential advantage of the installment method involves avoidance of the special tax imposed on items of "tax preference." Certain sources of income are labeled tax preference items due to the preferential treatment they receive in calculating one's tax liability. There is a 15% tax on "tax preference income" in addition to the other income tax paid by the investor. The 15% rate applies to the total of the tax preference income in excess of the lesser of one-half the regular income-tax obligation or $10,000. This creates a substantial tax savings opportunity if the total of tax preference items can be held to a level that does not exceed the lesser of one-half the regular income-tax obligation or $10,000 in any one taxable year.

Among the items to be included in the tax preference calculation is one-half the taxpayer's net long-term capital gain for the year. By spreading the capital gain over a number of years through the mechanism of the

Example 9–11

Assume the same facts as in Example 9–10 except that, rather than retire, the seller expects to continue receiving $45,000 per year from "other sources" during the next 5 years. His total taxable income in the year of the transaction is not affected by this change in assumptions. But the total taxable income in each succeeding year is increased by $25,000. The tax consequences of an installment sale under these revised assumptions is $46,440 over 6 years, determined as follows:

Income-Tax Consequences of Installment Sale

	Total Taxable Income*	Tax on Total Income†	Tax on Other Income‡	Tax Consequences of Sale§
Year of sale	$55,000	$ 19,650	$14,560	$ 5,090
First year after	63,000	23,890	14,560	9,330
Second year after	63,000	23,890	14,560	9,330
Third year after	63,000	23,890	14,560	9,330
Fourth year after	62,000	23,360	14,560	8,800
Fifth year after	54,000	19,120	14,560	4,560
Totals		$133,800	$87,360	$46,440

* "Total taxable income" from Example 9–10, plus an additional $25,000 per year for the first through the fifth year after sale.
† Using 1976 tax tables.
‡ Tax on $45,000 of ordinary income.
§ Tax on total income minus tax on other income.

Tax savings from use of the installment method is $20,680:
Tax savings from use of the installment method is $4,780:

Less tax on installment sale	46,440
Tax saving from installment sale	$ 4,780

Example 9–12

An investor sells real estate for a $200,000 long-term capital gain. He has the option of a cash sale or an installment sale that would enable him to report $20,000 of the gain each year for the next 10 years. He expects to incur an income-tax obligation on income from other sources of $12,140 during each of the next 10 years. He has no other items of tax preference income. He is married and files a joint return.

installment method of reporting, the tax obligation from items of tax preference may be reduced or perhaps eliminated altogether.

If the investor in Example 9–12 accepts the cash sale proposal, his taxes on the transaction are:

Capital-gains tax (alternative method)		$57,910
Add minimum tax on tax preference items:		
Preference income (half of capital gain)	$100,000	
Less exemption (half of regular taxes) *	35,025	
Income subject to preference tax	$ 64,975	
Preference tax (15% of $64,975)		9,746
Total tax on sale		$67,656

* Regular income-tax obligation is comprised of the $12,140 tax on income from other sources plus the $57,910 of long-term capital-gains tax.

But if our investor exercises the option of receiving the proceeds in installments over 10 years, he avoids liability for the minimum tax on preference income. His annual preference income is one-half the capital gains reported, or $10,000. Since $10,000 of preference items is excluded from the tax calculation, the investor incurs no tax obligation on tax preference items. His capital-gains tax is calculated by including one-half the recognized gain ($10,000) in regular income. This increases his tax liability by $2770 each year. His total tax obligation resulting from the sale in Example 9–12, if reported on the installment basis, is, therefore, $2770 each year for 10 years, or $27,700. In this instance, the installment method results in a tax savings of $39,956 ($67,656 minus $27,700).

Requirements for Installment-Method Reporting. The basic requirement for using the installment method is that not more than 30% of the sales price be received during the year of the sale. The sales price includes the entire cost of the property to the purchaser, including all cash given in exchange, all debt assumed or paid, and the fair market value of all other assets conveyed or services rendered in exchange.

In tax parlance, the payments received during the year of the sale are called the "initial payments." They include the down payment (whether cash, services, or other assets conveyed) and all subsequent payments made to the seller during the taxable year of the transaction. Note that the initial payments include all principal payments on the installment note during the year, but not payments of interest. Note also that if the purchaser takes responsibility for payments on an outstanding mortgage, the balance of which exceeds the seller's adjusted basis, the excess of the mortgage over the adjusted basis is included in the initial payments.

An important exception to the rule regarding an existing mortgage in excess of the seller's basis relates to property sold on a contract for deed. Under this circumstance, if the *seller* continues to make the mortgage payments, the excess may not be considered a part of the initial basis.

Any charges such as back taxes or assessments or accrued mortgage interest that are assumed by the buyer are not included as a part of the initial payment (to the extent total debt assumed does not exceed the seller's adjusted basis) unless the terms of the sale provide they are to be paid out of the original purchase price. In any event, however, they are considered a part of the total selling price.

Selling expenses incurred by the seller do not affect either the initial payments or the total selling price for purposes of applying the 30% test. They do, of course, affect the gain on the transaction for purposes of determining the amount of profit to be spread over the period of the installment payments.

How the Gain Is Reported. Assuming the transaction has been structured to qualify for reporting under the installment method, the question arises as to how the gain is reported. The first step is to determine the total amount of the gain, which must then be divided between ordinary income and long-term capital gains as discussed earlier. A portion of the gain may be ordinary income due to the recapture rules for excess depreciation. The balance of the gain is a long-term capital gain if the property is owned for more than 12 months prior to the sale.

Note that reference is made only to the reporting of gains on the transaction. Losses may not be reported on the installment basis.

Having computed the total gain on the sale and divided it into ordinary income and capital gains, the next step is to determine the "contract price." The contract price is the total selling price less any mortgage on the property payable by the purchaser to a third party. Commission and other selling expenses reduce the profit on the sale, but they are not deducted in determining the selling price, the contract price, or the initial payments.

Example 9–13

Residential income property having an adjusted basis of $40,000 is sold for $100,000. The buyer assumes and agrees to pay the balance of an existing mortgage of $50,000, pays $5000 in cash at the closing and agrees to pay the balance of the purchase price ($45,000) in 10 equal annual installments payable at the end of each succeeding year, with interest at 8% on the unpaid balance. The seller pays a broker's commission of $4000 and incurs other closing costs of $500.

Having elected the installment method of reporting the transaction, the seller's total gain on the sale and the total contract price are determined as follows:

Selling price		$100,000
Less:		
Adjusted basis	$40,000	
Broker's commission	4,000	
Other transactions costs	$ 500	$ 44,500
Gain on transaction		$ 55,500
Selling price		$100,000
Less existing mortgage assumed by buyer		50,000
Subtotal		$ 50,000
Add excess of mortgage assumed over seller's adjusted basis ($50,000 minus $40,000)		10,000
Total contract price		$ 60,000

If the property is sold on a contract for deed and is subject to an existing encumbrance that the *seller* pays off on a periodic basis after the time of the transaction, the balance of that encumbrance is included in the contract price.

The relationship between the total gain and the contract price determines the portion of each year's collections on the contract that must be reported as a taxable gain. Divide the total gain by the contract price to arrive at this percentage figure. Then multiply the year's collections on the principal amount of the contract by this ratio; the product is the currently taxable portion of the gain. The balance of the year's collections represents a return of the taxpayer's principal and, therefore, is nontaxable.

To reiterate, the computation of the annual amount of collections that are subject to taxation as a gain on the sale involves five steps:

Step 1. Compute the total gain just as if the installment method were not to be employed.

Step 2. Compute the contract price by subtracting from the total selling price any mortgage that calls for payments by the purchaser to a third party, and adding back any amount by which the assumed mortgage exceeds the seller's basis.

Step 3. Divide the total gain (from *Step 1*) by the contract price (from *Step 2*) to determine the portion of annual collections on the principal amount of the contract that represents collection of the gain.

Step 4. Determine the amount of the principal collected during the year. Be careful to exclude from this calculation any amount collected that represents payment by the purchaser of interest on the indebtedness. Only the principal portion is included.

Step 5. Multiply the collections (from *Step 4*) by the percentage representing the gain (from *Step 3*). This is the amount of the collections that is to be reported as a recognized gain for the year. The balance of the (principal) collection represents a return of the taxpayer's investment and is not taxable.

Example 9–14

Continuing the calculations from Example 9–13, the seller's taxable profit in the year of the sale would be as follows:

Cash received in year of transaction	$ 5,000
Add amount of mortgage assumed by buyer in excess of seller's adjusted basis ($50,000 minus $40,000)	10,000
Initial payments	$15,000
Gross profit ratio:	
Gross profit (from Example 9–13)	$55,500
Total contract price (from Example 9–13)	60,000
Ratio ($55,500/$60,000)	0.925
Profit to be reported in year of sale (0.925 × $15,000)	$13,875

Recognize Ordinary Income Before Capital Gains. Because of the rules regarding recapture of excess depreciation, a substantial portion of the gain on disposal of depreciable property is often taxable as ordinary income. The balance is taxable as a long-term capital gain if the property was held for more than 12 months, and if the seller is not a dealer. Sellers reporting on the installment basis must recognize the ordinary income portion of their gain before recognition of the capital-gains portion.

Example 9-15

Continuing the illustration from Examples 9–13 and 9–14, assume that $10,000 of the gross profit represents recapture of excess depreciation, and the balance of $45,500 represents a long-term capital gain. Since $13,875 of the profit must be recognized in the year of the sale, it is comprised first of the $10,000 of recaptured depreciation. This represents an addition to the seller's ordinary income for the year. The balance of the gain ($3875) to be recognized in the year of the sale represents a capital gain.

The Problem of Imputed Interest. One particular issue with respect to determining the total selling price merits special notice. Its importance springs from the frequency with which it causes installment-method reporting to be disallowed and the potentially serious financial consequences.

The buyer usually signs a note as evidence of his obligation for the unpaid portion of the purchase price. The terms of the note ordinarily provide for periodic payments to retire the balance of the note plus interest payments on the unpaid balance. The principal portion of the payments is considered a part of the purchase price and is used to determine the portion of the gain to be reported each year. The interest payments, on the other hand, are simply additional income taxable to the seller and generally have no impact on the recognition of the gain on the sale.

Since the interest is taxable as ordinary income, whereas at least a portion of the gain is taxed at the more favorable capital-gains rate, the seller is tempted to sell the property at an inflated price and call for no interest or interest clearly below the market rate. The intended effect is that the buyer pays no more for the property than he would had the contract cited a fair market price and a fair market rate of interest on the unpaid balance of the note, whereas the seller realizes a greater after-tax return by having a larger portion of the receipts taxed as long-term capital gains and a smaller portion taxed as ordinary income.

Recognizing the potential for abuse of the installment reporting rules, the Internal Revenue Service insists that any installment-sales contract (or purchase money mortgage) include a provision for a reasonable rate of interest. Without such a provision, the Service "imputes" interest by reducing the total selling price to an amount representing the value of the down payment plus the present value of the obligation to make future payments, when the future payments are discounted at a reasonable rate of interest.

The imputed interest rule (embodied in Section 483 of the code) applies to all payments that are due more than 6 months after the transaction, provided that one or more payments are due as long as 1 year after the transaction. No interest is imputed under Section 483, however, unless the selling price of the property exceeds $3000.

Within these constraints, the imputed interest rule applies whenever the contract calls for no interest or for an interest rate below a minimum prescribed by the Internal Revenue Service. The current minimum is 6% per annum. If the contract rate is less than 6%, the service discounts the note at a rate of 7%, compounded semiannually. This discounted present value of the note is then added to the payment received at closing to determine the total contract price. The contract price plus any outstanding mortgage assumed by the buyer constitutes the selling price.

The danger to the seller is obvious. If the initial payments approach 30% of the total selling price before allowing for interest at 7%, the imputation of interest may reduce the total selling price so that the initial payments exceed 30%. The transaction then fails the 30% test, and all of the gain is taxable in the year of the transaction, without reference to when the seller actually collects the proceeds from the note.

Since the minimum interest rate considered "reasonable" by the Internal Revenue Service is currently 6% per annum, the problem of imputed interest can be avoided by clearly providing for interest of at least this amount. The rate that is considered reasonable may vary with market conditions. Prudence dictates a check on the current "threshold" rate before completing a transaction that one intends to report under the installment method.

SUMMARY

When a taxpayer sells real estate for more than his adjusted basis, the excess represents a gain on disposal for which he generally incurs an income-tax liability. If the property has been subject to accelerated depreciation deductions, a portion of the gain probably represents recapture of excess depreciation. This portion is taxed as ordinary income. The balance of the gain is taxed as a capital gain unless the seller is a dealer in real estate.

The entire gain on a sale is usually taxable in the year of the transaction. Important exceptions are those sales that qualify for reporting under the installment method. This permits recognition of the gain (and the consequent tax liability) only when the cash is received in a seller-financed transaction. When sales are reported on the installment basis, the first portion of the gain to be recognized is that which represents recapture of excess depreciation and is thus taxable as ordinary income. Only after all recaptured depreciation has been recognized may the taxpayer report the gain portion on his annual collections as a capital gain.

Important advantages accrue to a seller who utilizes the installment method. He may be able in this manner to defer recognition of the gain until a year or years when he is in a much lower income-tax bracket. He may also be able, by spreading the gain over several years, to avoid paying a capital-gains tax above the 25% alternative rate. An additional advantage of spreading the gain may be the avoidance of a substantial minimum tax on preference income.

Taxpayers who use the installment sales method must structure the deal carefully to gain maximum financial advantage while avoiding having the use of the installment method disallowed. The chief problems involve imputed interest and receipt of more than 30% of the sales price during the year of the transaction.

SUGGESTED READINGS

1. Feinschreiber, Robert, "The Tax-Wise Estate Installment Sale," *Real Estate Review, 4* (2), 109–114 (1974).
2. Schwartz, Sheldon, "Installment Sales of Real Estate Revisited," *Real Estate Review, 3* (1), 99–104 (1973).

CHAPTER 10

TAX-FREE EXCHANGES

A gain realized on a tax-free exchange need not be recognized in the year of the transaction. Rather, the tax liability is postponed until a future, taxable transaction occurs with respect to the newly acquired property. A series of such tax-free exchanges can pyramid one's real estate holdings by avoiding the diminution of cash flow incident to recognition of a taxable gain on each transaction. The government in effect extends an interest-free loan in the amount of the taxes so deferred.

The enabling legislation for tax-free exchanges, more accurately called "like-kind exchanges," is contained in Section 1031 of the code. From their inception, the potential benefits of the exchange rules became evident to astute real estate investors. Section 1031 became even more attractive with the tightening of the depreciation recapture rules in the 1976 Tax Reform Act.

Example 10–1

An investor has been putting all his available savings into investments in small parcels of real estate such as single-family dwellings, duplexes, and small stores. Over the years, he has built up a substantial equity in these properties and now is considering moving into a large property that can be professionally managed, will yield economies of scale, and will free him from the time-consuming chores involved in his present holdings.

Assume that his equity in his present holdings has a market value of $500,000 and an adjusted basis of $200,000. His accountant informs him that he will have $150,000 of excess depreciation if he sells, and that all the excess will be subject to recapture and taxed as ordinary income. The income-tax consequences of selling his current holdings depends upon his income-tax bracket, which we assume to be 50%. The cash available for reinvestment if he sells his equity at the indicated market value would be $373,437, calculated as follows:

Taxable gain on transaction:	
Selling price of equity	$500,000
Less adjusted basis	200,000
Taxable gain	$300,000
Federal income-tax liability:	
Recapture ($150,000 × 0.5)	$ 75,000
Capital gain ($150,000 × 0.25)	37,500
Preference tax [15% of ($150,000 − $56,250)]	14,063
Total income-tax liability	$126,563
Cash flow (available for reinvestment):	
Selling price of equity	$500,000
Less income-tax liability	126,563
Net cash flow	$373,437

In Example 10–1, the investor pays a heavy price for moving into an alternative investment opportunity: His $500,000 equity is reduced to $373,437 due to the income-tax liability he incurs. If, instead of selling his current holdings and reinvesting the net proceeds, he can involve himself in a tax-free exchange of his present assets for the desired investment opportunity, he will be able to invest his entire $500,000 equity in the new property without any reduction in his net worth due to income-tax payments. The financial advantage of this alternative is obvious.

Given the versatility and potential profitability of this tax planning tool, it is curious that it has not gained even more widespread popularity. One suspects this is primarily due to the lack of knowledge on the part of investors and the hesitancy on the part of brokers and attorneys to involve themselves in the intricate steps necessary for compliance with the strict requirements imposed by the code.

The first part of this chapter details the basic requirements for an exchange to be tax-free under Code Section 1031. The consequences of a tax-free exchange with respect to the tax liability of one or both parties and with respect to the adjusted basis of the newly acquired property is covered in the next section. This is followed by an exposition of the various benefits to be obtained and problems that may be encountered in various exchange arrangements.

REQUIREMENTS FOR A TAX-FREE EXCHANGE

Section 1031 provides that when real estate held for investment purposes or for use in a trade or business (Section 1250 assets) are exchanged solely for like-kind assets, no gain or loss may be recognized on the transaction. To the extent some of the assets involved are not like-kind, the transaction involves "boot," and one or more of the parties may incur a tax liability for all or part of their gain. The basic requirements include (1) that there be a bona fide exchange of assets, (2) that the assets be either capital assets or Section 1231 assets, and (3) that they qualify as like-kind.

Exchange Versus Sale and Purchase. To qualify under Section 1031, there must have been a bona fide exchange of the assets involved. This ordinarily creates no problem in a straightforward two-party trade. But the investor often has difficulty finding someone who has the desired property and is willing to accept the investor's property in exchange. The solution is generally a multiparty exchange. In such an event, care must be taken to avoid a sale and purchase when an exchange is intended.

It appears that the question of whether a transaction is treated as an exchange or as a sale and purchase is more a matter of form than of the intent of the parties. Thus the cautious investor ascertains that the proper steps are taken by all parties to document the transaction as a bona fide exchange. The other parties may not be in a position to have their tax liability deferred under Section 1031, regardless of the form of the transaction. They may, therefore, be considerably less motivated to structure the transaction so as to assure its tax-free nature.

The potential pitfall in the exchange versus sale-and-purchase issue is perhaps best illustrated by an example.

Example 10–2

Albert wishes to acquire property owned by Baker and offers Baker an attractive cash price. Baker, wishing to avoid recapture and capital-gains taxes, counters with an offer to exchange his present property for another parcel that he desires. The desired parcel, however, is owned by Carlton. Albert and Baker enter into a contract that states that they will exchange the two parcels, with the contract contingent upon Albert's acquisition of Carlton's property prior to the settlement date.

If Albert succeeds in purchasing Carlton's property and subsequently exchanges this for property now owned by Baker, the transaction qualifies as a bona fide exchange for Baker and is tax-free if it meets the other requirements of Section 1031. The transaction is not a tax-free exchange for either Albert or Carlton, however. Carlton has been involved in a simple sale of his property. The exchange does not qualify under Section 1031 as tax-free for Albert, because the property he traded to Baker was not held as an investment or for use in a trade or business, having been acquired simply for purposes of exchange for the desired parcel.

The deal as structured in Example 10–2 results in a tax-free transaction for Baker but not for Albert. Albert, having no particular interest in Baker's tax liability, may seek to avoid the additional cost of two closings by assigning to Baker the right to purchase Carlton's property and disburse cash to Baker in exchange for his property. If Baker accepts this arrangement, he will lose the benefit of tax-free exchange treatment for the transaction. Rather than an exchange of like-kind assets (real estate for real estate) Baker has effectively sold his property for cash and assignment of right to purchase a substitute property. Baker then is involved in a sale and purchase rather than the intended tax-free exchange.

Purpose for which Property Is Held. To qualify as a tax-free exchange, the property conveyed must have been held for productive use in a trade or business or as an investment, and must be exchanged for property of a like-kind that is also to be used in a trade or business or held as an investment. Properties may qualify for tax-free exchange treatment if they fall in either of these categories; that is, property held for use in a trade or business may be exchanged for investment property or vice versa. As a general rule, therefore, these two categories of property may be considered together in tax-free exchange transactions.

Certain types of property, however, are specifically excluded by statute. These include securities or evidence of indebtedness (stocks, bonds, notes, etc.) and inventory. For the real estate investor, this last type of property is likely to prove the most troublesome. Inventory includes one's stock in trade or other property held primarily for resale.

The motivation for excluding from Section 1031 treatment any asset held primarily for resale appears to be to bar dealers in real estate from benefiting from the tax-free exchange provision. Whatever the intent of the lawmakers, the effect is to make it crucial that the investor (whether or not he is generally engaged in "dealing" in real estate) establish that this particular parcel was not acquired primarily for resale.

In Example 10–2, Albert acquired Carlton's property specifically for the purpose of using it in a trade with Baker. The property Albert traded to Baker was, therefore, acquired primarily for resale by Albert. Albert's transaction would thus be excluded from tax-free exchange treatment, even though it were otherwise qualified, because he traded an asset that was held primarily for resale.

When Is Property of Like-Kind? Only like-kind property qualifies for tax-free exchange treatment. The like-kind concept relates to the nature of the property, but not to its quality or grade. While this distinction may be somewhat less than clear, its main implication for the real estate investor is that real estate may be exchanged for other real estate without regard for the type realty involved, so long as it is held as an investment or for use in a trade or business. Examples issued by the Treasury to amplify this point [Treasury Reg. 1.1031 (a)-1(b)] include:

1. Property held for use in trade or business, together with cash, for other property for the same use.
2. Urban real estate for a farm or ranch.
3. Improved for unimproved real estate (held for investment purposes).
4. A leasehold (with not less than 30 years to run) for a freehold.
5. Mineral interest in land (not merely an assignment of payments) for a fee title in real estate.

Previously mentioned as specifically excluded were securities or evidence of indebtedness and inventory. Treasury regulations also specifically exclude certificates of trust or beneficial interest. This latter exclusion has the effect of disqualifying from the like-kind concept real estate that has been transferred to a trust.

TAX CONSEQUENCES OF AN EXCHANGE

If all property involved in an exchange qualifies as like-kind, then no party to the exchange may recognize any gain or loss on the transaction. Note that this is mandatory rather than elective. The gain or loss that was realized in the exchange but not recognized for income-tax purposes is reflected in the tax basis of the newly acquired property.

Should some of the property involved in an exchange fail the like-kind test, then some portion of the gain (but not of a loss) must be recognized in the year of the transaction. The balance of the realized gain is deferred as before and is reflected in the adjusted basis of the acquired property.

This section elaborates on the tax consequences of receiving some unlike property in an exchange. It also illustrates the manner in which the deferred gain or loss is reflected in the basis of the property acquired in the exchange.

Not All Parties Need Qualify for Tax-Free Benefit. The test of whether a transaction qualifies as a tax-free exchange is applied separately to each party to the exchange. To qualify, an individual must not have held his property for resale or as a residence. It must have been held either as an investment or for use in a trade or business (but not as inventory). One party's motive for ownership may disqualify him from deferring his gain under Section 1031, whereas the other party to the transaction may nevertheless qualify.

Example 10–3

Axel desires to acquire Benji's property in a tax-free exchange. Benji is willing to sell his property outright, but has no interest in Axel's property. The broker involved in the deal finds a third party, who is willing to buy Axel's property. The deal is completed by a trade of property between Axel and Benji and a purchase by the third party of the property acquired by Benji from Alex. Axel has a tax-free exchange; Benji does not.

In Example 10–3, Axel may defer any gain on his transaction since he acquired like-kind property to be held as an investment. Benji, however, does not qualify under Section 1031 and so must recognize any gain he has realized on the transaction. Benji is disqualified because he held the property acquired from Axel primarily for resale.

Even if Benji had not found an immediate buyer for the property acquired from Axel in this example, it is possible that he could not have deferred recognition of gains under Section 1031. Had the property traded to Axel been listed for sale for a period of time immediately prior to the exchange, this would have established that it was held primarily for sale. But the important point here is that the tax consequences to Axel are independent of the consequences to Benji.

Effect of Receiving Unlike Property in Exchange. Receipt of property that does not meet the definition of like-kind has the effect of partially disqualifying a gain from deferral under Section 1031. The person receiving the unlike property ("boot") must recognize any gain realized on the transaction to the extent of the boot received.

Example 10-4

Blackstone trades his investment real estate (market value of $55,000) to Bluebaker, receiving Bluebaker's real property having a market value of $50,000, and $5000 in cash. Blackstone's property had an adjusted basis of $48,000. Blackstone has an indicated gain of $7000 (value received of $55,000 less adjusted basis of asset conveyed). Had Blackstone received only like-kind property in exchange the entire gain would be deferred. But his receipt of $5000 boot from Bluebaker requires Blackstone to recognize $5000 of his gain. The balance of the gain ($2000) must be deferred.

Boot, or unlike property, includes anything of economic value other than the like-kind assets involved in the transaction. Examples include cash, services rendered, or an obligation to render services, debt forgiveness, or a promise to convey something of value in the future.

Example 10-5

Franks and Smith agree to an exchange of investment real estate. Both parties own their property on a free-and-clear basis, and the properties do qualify for Section 1031 treatment. Franks, who is an attorney, agrees to handle the details of the closing for both Smith and himself. This is a service for which he customarily charges $300. Smith has received $300 boot in the form of personal service.

A special rule applies to one category of unlike property: the acceptance of the obligation to pay mortgage debt encumbering the like-kind property being conveyed by the other party, thus relieving the other party of the obligation to pay. In the case where each of the parties assumes an outstanding mortgage on the real property received in the exchange, the receipt of unlike property is computed on the basis of *net* debt relief.*

* The actual *assumption* of the debt is unnecessary. The net debt relief rule applies when properties are exchanged subject to existing mortgages, whether or not the parties assume and agree to pay the balances.

That is, the assumed mortgages are offset against each other, and unlike property is considered to have been received only to the extent the mortgage on the property conveyed exceeds that on the property received.

Example 10–6

Singleton and Doublebrace agree that their respective equities are equal in value. They agree to trade equities, each party assuming and agreeing to pay the balance of the mortgage on the property received in the exchange. Their positions before the exchange were as follows:

	Singleton	Doublebrace
Market value of property	$85,000	$150,000
Less balance of mortgage	35,000	100,000
Value of equity	$50,000	$ 50,000

Doublebrace has received boot of $65,000 in the form of net debt relief (old debt of $100,000 minus new debt of $35,000). Doublebrace incurs an income-tax liability for any gain he realizes on the transaction, to the extent of the $65,000 of net debt relief.

An investor may receive net debt relief and yet have to pay cash to balance the market value of the assets exchanged. In that case, subtract the cash paid from the net debt relief received. Only the balance must be reported as boot received. However, *receipt* of cash or other unlike assets is not offset against net mortgage liability *assumed.*

Example 10–7

Gayblade and Dutchtreat agree to an exchange of properties. Each party is to assume the balance of the outstanding mortgage on the realty received in the exchange, and Dutchtreat agrees to pay cash to Gayblade to "balance the equities." Their positions before the exchange are as follows:

	Gayblade	Dutchtreat
Market value of realty	$110,000	$110,000
Less balance of mortgage	60,000	70,000
Market value of equity	$ 50,000	$ 40,000

Based on this analysis, Dutchtreat agrees to pay $10,000 cash boot to Gayblade. Even though he received net debt relief in the exchange, Dutchtreat has not received boot as defined in Section 1031, and he need not report a taxable gain. This is because the debt relief is offset by the payment of cash boot. The effect is the same as if the $10,000 cash had been applied instead to a reduction of the mortgage balance. Offsetting the $10,000 of net debt relief against the $10,000 cash paid by Dutchtreat results in an even trade from Dutchtreat's point of view.

Note, however, that when cash is received, it is not offset by mortgage liability assumed. Gayblade, therefore, has received $10,000 boot in the form of cash, notwithstanding the fact that he has assumed $10,000 of additional mortgage liability.

A party who receives unlike property in an exchange must recognize any gain to the extent of the value of the boot received. Note, however, that this applies *only* to gains; losses realized in the transaction may not be recognized if the exchange qualifies even partly as a like-kind exchange.

Treatment of Transactions Costs. Transactions costs include such items as brokerage commissions, recording fees, transfer taxes on realty, and attorney's fees. Transactions costs incurred in the sale of property are treated as a reduction in the net sales price. In a Section 1031 exchange they may be thought of as a reduction in the proceeds from the old property or an addition to the purchase price of the new. In either case, they reduce the indicated gain and thereby become a part of the tax basis of the newly acquired property.

If one party to a transaction pays any part of the other party's transaction costs, however, this represents receipt of unlike property and so causes a part of the gain to be taxable. The effect is the same as if cash were received and used to pay the transaction costs.

Tax Basis of Acquired Property. While we ordinarily speak of Section 1031 exchanges as tax-free, it would be more accurate to use the term "tax deferred." There may be no tax liability at the time of the transaction, but the day of reckoning is merely delayed rather than totally avoided. The basis of the new property is a "substitute basis" reflecting the deferred gain. It consists of the adjusted basis of the property conveyed, with further adjustments reflecting the circumstances of the exchange.

Example 10–8

Mr. Investor exchanges property having an adjusted basis of $90,000 for like-kind property having a market value of $150,000. He pays transactions costs of $150, but neither receives nor pays any boot. Both properties are exchanged on a free and clear basis.

Mr. Investor has an indicated gain of $59,850, computed as follows:

Market value of property received		$150,000
Less: Transactions costs	$ 150	
Adjusted basis of old property	90,000	90,150
Indicated gain on transaction		$ 59,850

Mr. Investor's basis for the new property at the time of the exchange is $90,150, computed in the following manner:

Basis of old property		$90,000
Plus: Additional consideration paid	0	
Transaction costs	$ 150	150
Less additional consideration received		0
Basis of new property		$90,150

This same result may be reached by subtracting from the fair market value of the property received the amount of any gain realized but not recognized:

Market value of new property		$150,000
Less unrecognized gain:		
Amount realized	$59,850	
Less amount recognized	0	59,850
Basis of new property		$ 90,150

Because the transaction in Example 10–8 qualifies under Section 1031 as a like-kind exchange, the indicated gain need not be recognized for income-tax purposes. Indeed, it *may not* be recognized. Remember the rules are mandatory, not elective. However, the tax on the gain is merely deferred. When Mr. Investor sells the new property, his taxable gain is computed on the difference between the net proceeds and his adjusted basis at that time. And the basis of the new property reflects the unrecognized gain on the exchange.

To see why a gain is only deferred by a tax-free exchange, imagine that Mr. Investor (in Example 10–8) decides to sell his *newly acquired* property and does so at the indicated market value of $150,000, incurring transactions costs of $100. His taxable gain is:

Sales price		$150,000
Less: Transactions costs	100	
Adjusted basis	$90,150	90,250
Taxable gain		$ 59,750

If, on the other hand, the *original* property had simply been sold at its indicated market value of $150,000 (the equivalent value it commanded in the exchange) with a transactions cost of $100, the taxable gain would have been:

Sales price		$150,000
Less: Transactions costs	$ 100	
Adjusted basis	90,000	90,100
Taxable gain		$ 59,900

The difference in the taxable gain resulting from simply selling the original property, on the one hand, or exchanging it and subsequently selling the new property, on the other, is $150, the amount of transactions costs incurred in the exchange.

The purpose of this exercise has not been to denigrate the value of Section 1031, but rather to illustrate the logic involved in computing the basis of the acquired property. For income-tax purposes, the effect of the exchange is as if the two properties were one. The new property simply takes the old basis after adjusting for additional value received or given in the exchange. In fact, the code provides that the holding periods of the two properties be counted as one continuous period when determining the nature of the taxable gain or loss, for computing the recapture of excess depreciation when there is a subsequent sale.

We have deliberately kept our examples simple to better illustrate how to compute the basis of the newly acquired property. A more complex exercise demonstrates how the same rules can carry an investor through the computational thicket.

Example 10–9

Mr. Vicker owns income property with a market value of $100,000, which is subject to a mortgage of $25,000. His adjusted basis is $40,000. He exchanges it for another income property having a market value of $150,000 that is subject to a mortgage of $60,000. Vicker pays $15,000 cash for the difference in equities, and each party takes title subject to existing mortgages. Vicker pays transactions costs of $6500.

Vicker's indicated gain is the difference between the market value and the adjusted basis of his original property minus transactions costs. But having received only like-kind property in the exchange, Vicker defers recognition of the gain. The computation of the initial basis of the new property is as follows:

Basis of old property		$ 40,000
Add: Transaction costs	$ 6,500	
Mortgage assumed	60,000	
Cash paid	15,000	81,500
		$121,500
Less old mortgage		25,000
Basis of new property		$ 96,500

Note that the basis of the new property in Example 10–9 is simply its fair market value less any unrecognized gain, adjusted for transactions costs ($150,000 less $60,000 plus $6500).

If, due to receipt of unlike property, some portion of the indicated gain is recognized at the time of the exchange, the basis of the new property is increased by the amount of the recognized gain.

Example 10–10

Dr. Blue exchanges his apartment house (market value of $152,800) for another apartment building and a 1-year-old station wagon (market value estimated to be $2800). Dr. Blue owes a mortgage balance of $80,000 on his building, which has an adjusted basis of $100,000. Each party agrees to assume the existing mortgage on the building received in exchange. The building received by Dr. Blue has an outstanding mortgage balance of $70,000 and a fair market value of $140,000. Transactions costs to Dr. Blue are $5000.

Dr. Blue has a realized gain, part of which must be recognized since he receives unlike property in exchange. The indicated (realized) gain is $47,800, computed as follows:

Market value of assets received:		
Real estate		$140,000
Personalty (station wagon)		2,800
Net debt relief		10,000
		$152,800
Less basis of property conveyed:		
Real estate	$100,000	
Transactions costs	5,000	$105,000
Indicated gain on exchange		$ 47,800

The indicated gain is currently taxable to the extent of any unlike property received in the exchange. Dr. Blue must, therefore, recognize $12,800 of the indicated gain as currently taxable. This is the lesser of the indicated gain or the market value of the unlike property received:

Mortage on old property	$80,000
Less mortgage assumed	70,000
Net debt relief	$10,000
Value of other unlike property received	2,800
Total value of unlike property received	$12,800

The basis of the new property received by Dr. Blue is the adjusted basis of his old property, increased by any additional payments made and any recognized gain, and reduced by any other value received:

Adjusted basis of old property		$100,000
Add: Transactions costs	$ 5,000	
Debt assumed	70,000	
Recognized gain	12,800	$ 87,800
Less: Old mortgage	$80,000	$187,800
Auto received	2,800	82,800
Basis of new property		$105,000

The new basis in Example 10–10 can be proved by reducing the market value of the new property by the amount of the unrecognized gain and adding the transaction costs. The results should be the same as in the example. The calculations are:

Market value of property received		$140,000
Less unrecognized gain:		
Realized gain (calculated above)	$47,800	
Less recognized gain	12,800	
Unrecognized portion of gain		35,000
Basis of new property		$105,000

Effect of Losses in Section 1031 Exchange. So far all our examples have assumed a gain on the transaction, with the discussion centering on whether a portion of the gain must be recognized, and on the resulting tax basis of the new property. But what happens if instead of realizing a gain the investor experiences a loss on the exchange?

If a transaction qualifies fully under Section 1031 as a like-kind exchange, then neither a gain nor a loss may be recognized. We have seen, however, that if the party experiencing a gain received any unlike property (including net debt relief) then a portion of his gain must be recognized. This partial recognition relates *only* to gains; receipt of some unlike property in an otherwise like-kind exchange never causes the recognition of part of a realized loss.

Example 10–11

Professor Smart trades income-producing real estate for like-kind property. The property received by Smart has a fair market value of $80,000 and is subject to a mortgage of $55,000. Smart's old property has an adjusted basis of $95,000 and is subject to a mortgage of $60,000. The parties exchange equities, each assuming the mortgage on the property received.

This exchange qualifies under Section 1031 as a like-kind exchange, but Professor Smart has received unlike property in the form of net debt relief. Had he realized a gain, it would be recognized to the extent of Smart's net debt relief ($5000). In this example, though, Professor Smart has experienced a loss rather than a gain:

Market value of property received	$80,000	
Mortgage assumed by other party	60,000	$ 140,000
Less: Mortgage assumed by Smart	$55,000	
Adjusted basis of old property	95,000	$ 150,000
Gain (loss) on the exchange		$(10,000)

Although Professor Smart may not recognize his loss in the year of the transaction, it is reflected in his basis for the new property. Thus its recognition is merely deferred until the new property is sold. Smart's basis for the new property is his old basis adjusted for the other property involved in the transaction. (In this illustration, we have simplified by omitting reference to transactions costs. Were such costs incurred, they would be added to the new basis.) Smart's new basis is:

Basis of old property	$ 95,000
Add mortgage assumed	55,000
	150,000
Less mortgage assumed by other party	60,000
Basis of new property	$ 90,000

Note that the basis of Smart's new property is simply its market value adjusted by adding any additional value given by Smart and reduced by any value received plus any unrecognized loss or less any unrecognized gain:

Market value of property received	$80,000
Add unrecognized loss	10,000
Basis of new property	$90,000

Note also that the substitute basis of Smart's new property exceeds its fair market value by the amount of the unrecognized loss. It would also include any transactions costs incurred by Smart. So if he were to subsequently sell the new property his recognized loss on the sale would reflect this substitute basis in excess of fair market value and the deferred loss would be recognized at that time. Likewise in Example 10–10, the basis of Dr. Blue's new property differs from its fair market value by the amount of the deferred gain (adjusted for transactions costs) so that in a subsequent sale the realized gain reflects the initial market value in excess of the substitute basis.

Allocating the Substitute Basis. Just as the initial basis of purchased property must be allocated between land and improvements to determine the depreciable basis of the improvements (see Chapter 7), so must the substitute basis of property acquired in a Section 1031 exchange be allocated. The basic rule governing the allocation remains invariant: Allocate on the basis of relative market values.

To keep the illustration simple, assume there are no significant transactions costs in Example 10–12. Since there is no boot involved, Mr. Investor's substitute basis is the adjusted basis of his old property, or $30,000. This basis is allocated to the acquired land and improvements in the ratio of their relative market values; 10% to the land and 90% to the improvements. His basis after the exchange is:

Land (10%)	$ 3,000
Improvements (90%)	27,000
Total basis	$30,000

In our illustration, we have taken the relative market values as given. In a real life situation, these values must be determined. This may be accomplished by agreement between the parties in an arm's-length transaction, by an independent appraisal, or by use of the relative values determined by the property-tax assessor. These do not exhaust the potential means of arriving at an estimate of relative market values, but they are all approaches that have been accepted in the past.

Example 10–12

To illustrate the procedure of allocating the substitute basis assume our by now familiar figure, Mr. Investor, owns real estate that he trades with Joe Outsider. Both parties own their property on a free and clear basis. The relative values before the exchange are agreed to be as follows:

		Market Value	
	Adjusted Basis	Dollar	Percentage of total value
Investor:			
Land	$20,000	$20,000	40
Improvements	10,000	30,000	60
	$30,000	$50,000	100
Outsider:			
Land	$ 5,000	$ 5,000	10
Improvements	20,000	45,000	90
	$25,000	$50,000	100

If more than one property is received in an exchange, the substitute basis is allocated between the acquired properties in the ratio of their relative market values as of the date of the exchange. The allocated substitute basis of each property is in turn allocated between land and improvements on the basis of their relative values. To illustrate, assume the property received from Mr. Outsider in Example 10–12 consists of a store building on one small plot of land and an adjoining vacant lot. Assume further that each of the lots is worth $2500 if unimproved, and the store building alone is worth $45,000 before considering the value of the site. The $30,000 substitute basis is first allocated to the two separate properties in the ratio of their relative values: 5% to the vacant lot and 95% to the store and site. The substitute basis of the store and site ($0.95 \times \$30{,}000 = \$28{,}500$) is then allocated to the improvements and the site based on *their* relative values. The resulting substitute basis is:

	Market Values		
	Dollars	Percentage of Total	Substitute Basis
Vacant lot	$ 2,500	5	$ 1,500
Store: Site	2,500	5	1,500
Improvements	45,000	90	27,000
Total	$50,000	100	$30,000

If there is a gain to be recognized as a result of receiving boot in an exchange where the value of property received exceeds the adjusted basis of the property exchanged, the gain is taxable as ordinary income to the extent that it represents recapture of excess depreciation. Any gain to be recognized in excess of recapture of excess depreciation is taxed as a capital gain. Whether the capital gain is long- or short-term depends upon the period the property was prior to the exchange.

Example 10–13

A and *B* exchange equities in a Section 1031 exchange, with *B* paying $10,000 cash boot to balance the equities. The position of the parties before the exchange is:

	Party *A*	Party *B*
Market value of property	$150,000	$120,000
Less mortgage balance	100,000	80,000
Market value of equity	$ 50,000	$ 40,000
Adjusted basis	$ 60,000	N/A
Excess depreciation	$ 20,000	N/A

Boot is received by party *A* in the form of cash and net debt relief. Total boot received is $30,000, computed as follows:

Cash:		
Equity conveyed	$ 50,000	
Less equity received	40,000	
Cash difference		$10,000
Net debt relief:		
Mortgage assumed by *B*	$100,000	
Less mortgage assumed by *A*	80,000	
Net reduction in *A*'s mortgage debt		$ 20,000
Total boot received by *A*		$ 30,000

A's indicated gain is the difference in the market value and the adjusted basis of the property conveyed to *B:*

Market value (i.e., value received in exchange):		
Real estate	$120,000	
Net debt relief	20,000	
Cash	10,000	
Total market value received		$150,000
Less adjusted basis of property conveyed		60,000
Gain on transaction		$ 90,000

Of the indicated gain of $90,000 in Example 10–13, *A* must recognize $30,000, due to having received unlike property of this value. The recognized gain is taxable as ordinary income to the extent that there exists excess depreciation subject to recapture. In the example, this amounts to $20,000. The balance of the recognized gain is subject to the rules governing capital gains.

If the recognized gain is less than the amount of excess depreciation subject to recapture, the entire amount of the recognized gain is taxable as ordinary income. The balance of the excess depreciation is carried over to the property received in the exchange, to the extent that there is an indicated gain that is not recognized at the time of the exchange.

Example 10–14

Assume the same facts as in Example 10–13 *except* that excess depreciation subject to recapture is now assumed to be $45,000. Since the recognized gain of $30,000 is less than the excess depreciation to be recaptured, the entire recognized gain is taxed as ordinary income. The remaining excess depreciation ($15,000) carries over to the new property since it is less than the amount of the unrecognized gain.

TAX STRATEGY

A thorough understanding of the minimum requirements for Section 1031 treatment is essential because of the dire financial consequences of discovering after the fact that what was anticipated to be a tax-free transaction has resulted in a substantial income-tax liability.

In this section, we describe some basic strategies for exploiting Code Section 1031. The first issue is how one might divest oneself of property while avoiding a tax liability for recapture of excess depreciation. We then address the question of using a like-kind exchange to substantially increase the base for depreciation deductions. Finally, we review tactics for maximizing the financial benefits of an exchange, and lead the reader through a multiple-exchange transaction.

Reducing Depreciation Recapture. The reduction in financial leverage resulting from paying down the mortgage on the original loan, and the decline in the basis for accelerated depreciation results in rapidly declining annual depreciation deductions and reduces the after-tax return after real estate has been held for a number of years. The problem of how best to releverage oneself is complicated by the depreciation recapture rules that were rather stringently tightened by the Tax Reform Acts of 1969 and 1976.

Recall from Chapter 9 that when depreciable property is sold the difference between the total depreciation claimed during the period of ownership (accumulated depreciation) and the depreciation that would have been claimed under the straight-line depreciation method is "excess depreciation." Depending upon the nature of the real estate (residential or nonresidential), upon the length of time the property was owned, and upon the date of acquisition, all or a portion of the excess depreciation might be recaptured as ordinary income during the year of the sale.

Remember that the recapture rate for excess depreciation taken after December 31, 1975 is 100%. But for residential income property, the rate of recapture applicable to excess depreciation taken between January 1, 1970 and December 31, 1975 is reduced by 1% for every month the property is held in excess of 100 months. The reduction in the recapture rate is even more favorable where the excess depreciation was taken prior to December 31, 1969. For this earlier period, there is some reduction in the recapture applicable to nonresidential property as well.

A tax-free exchange offers an opportunity to take advantage of these reductions in the recapture rate for excess depreciation taken in the earlier years, without the necessity of holding the property beyond the point where other investment considerations dictate disposal. Section 1031 provides that properties involved in a like-kind exchange be viewed as a continuation of the same investment. Thus the period of time two or more such properties are held is viewed as one continuous period in determining the recapture rate for excess depreciation taken prior to December 31, 1975.

Example 10–15

Property *A* is acquired by purchase and held for 5 years before being exchanged for parcel *B* in a Section 1031 exchange. Property *B* is then held for 6 years before being sold. The holding period for purposes of computing the recapture rate is 11 years: the sum of the periods over which all property was held.

Example 10-16

An investor buys property *D* and after 3 years exchanges it for property *E* in a like-kind exchange. Four years later property *E* is exchanged for property *Z* in another like-kind exchange. After holding property *Z* for 2 years, it is sold in a cash transaction. The holding period for purposes of computing the recapture rate is 9 years:

	Number of Years Held
Property *D*	3
Property *E*	4
Property *Z*	2
Years between taxable events	9

Increasing the Basis for Depreciation. When property is acquired through a like-kind exchange, the investor is faced with the task of allocating the substitute basis between the land and the improvements that have been newly acquired. This presents an opportunity to increase the basis for depreciation through a procedure that appears illogical on its face but that seems acceptable to the Internal Revenue Service. By way of explanation, consider first the property described in the following example.

Example 10-17

Ten years ago Mr. Investor acquired property for $100,000. Eighty percent of the purchase price applied to the improvements and 20% to the land. After 10 years he has taken $45,250 of depreciation on the improvements. The land, of course, is not subject to depreciation. The remaining basis of the property after 10 years is the original basis less accumulated depreciation or $54,750 computed as follows:

	Land	Improvements	Total
Cost	$20,000	$80,000	$100,000
Less depreciation taken	0	45,250	45,250
Adjusted basis	$20,000	$34,750	$ 54,750

Assume that the investor in Example 10--17 exchanges his property for like-kind property in which 20% of the market value is attributable to the site and 80%, to the improvements. For simplicity, assume there is no boot and that there are no transactions costs. The investor's substitute basis for the new property is the adjusted basis of the old: $54,750. But the substitute basis may be allocated between site and improvements in the ratio of their relative market values: 20% to the site and 80% to the improvements. The result is a substantially increased basis attributable to the depreciable portion of the property:

	Adjusted Basis of Old Property	Substitute Basis of New Property
Land	$20,000	$10,950
Improvements	34,750	43,800
Total basis	$54,750	$54,750

The investor has managed to increase the basis of depreciation in this manner from $34,750 to 43,800, an increase of 26%. Of course, the improvement in the basis of depreciation would be even more dramatic if the land-to-improvements ratio of the new property were larger. Assume, for example, that the investor exchanged his property for a building constructed on leased ground (with the lease having at least 30 years to run). In this case, 100% of the basis would be depreciable, and the basis for depreciation would increase from $34,750 to 54,750.

Remember, too, that if the investor pays boot, the value of the boot is added to the adjusted basis of the old property in determining the substitute basis of the new property. An investor trading-up by releveraging his position can thus obtain considerable improvement in his depreciation tax shelter through a like-kind exchange.

Our investor is now in a position to exchange his property for equity in another having a market value such that his equity in the newly acquired asset (market value less mortgage) equals the equity in his old property. If he can obtain a 75% loan on the new property, his equity of $102,400 (from Example 10–18) will be 25% of market value. Market value, therefore, will be $409,600.

Example 10–18

From Example 10–17 assume the investor initially financed 75% of value of his property over 25 years. At the end of 10 years, he exchanges his equity for a 25% equity in a new property in which 80% of the value lies in the improvements. Assume further that the old property increased in market value by an average of 5% per annum (compounded) over the 10-year holding period. Mr. Investor's equity at the time of the exchange would be:

Market value at time of exchange:		
Initial market value	$100,000	
Times compound value factor at 5% per annum for 10 years $[(1.05)^{10}]$	1.63	$163,000
Less balance outstanding on initial loan*		60,600
Market value of equity exchanged		$102,400

* Assume an initial loan of $75,000 (75% of initial value) at an interest rate of 8% per annum, amortized over 25 years. Remaining balance after 10 years is 80.8% of original loan.

The basis of the new property includes the boot paid in the form of additional debt assumed (or cash paid as proceeds from a new mortgage loan). The amount of this boot is $246,900, computed as follows:

Amount of new mortgage (75% of $409,600)	$307,200
Less balance of old mortgage	60,600
Increase in mortgage debt	$246,600

The basis of the new property is calculated as illustrated on page 189. To the adjusted basis of the old property we add the boot paid by the investor, his transactions costs, and subtract any boot received. The result is simply the market value of the new property, plus the boot paid, less any unrecognized gain:

Basis of old property	$ 54,750
Add new mortgage	307,200
	$361,950
Less old mortgage balance	60,600
Basis of new property	$301,350

or

Market value of new property		$409,600
Less unrecognized gain:		
Market value of old property	$163,000	
Less adjusted basis	54,750	$108,250
Basis of new property		$301,350

Continuing the earlier assumption that 80% of the value of the new property lies in the improvements and that it has a 25-year expected life, the depreciation allowance for the first 5 years of ownership of the new property, based on double declining-balance method, is:

Initial basis of new property	\$301,350
Times percent of value attributable to buildings	0.80
Depreciable basis	\$241,080
Annual rate of depreciation = 2 × 1/25	0.08

Year	Depreciation	Remaining Balance
1	19,286	221,794
2	17,743	204,051
3	16,324	187,727
4	15,018	172,709
5	13,817	158,892

These annual depreciation deductions represent a substantial increase over the maximum annual deduction of \$3200 that could have been obtained from the old property by switching to the straight-line method at the optimal point.

Avoiding Boot. In this example, our investor has pyramided his holdings by trading up in a like-kind exchange and so avoided having his equity diluted by a substantial income-tax liability on the increase in market value of his holdings that would have resulted in a sale and purchase of another investment. Imprudent structuring of the exchange transaction, however, might result in the investor's incurring some tax liability that could have been avoided by better planning.

The receipt of boot in connection with a like-kind exchange can have doubly bad consequences if there is some excess depreciation that would have been subject to recapture in a straightforward sale of the property. Not only is any gain subject to taxation in the year of the exchange to the extent of the boot received, but the taxable gain is also taxed as ordinary income rather than as a capital gain to the extent of recapture of excess depreciation.

Two common instances where boot results are where there is a difference in the market value of the equities and where there is a difference in the amount of the outstanding mortgages. In the first instance, the party who has the more valuable equity may receive taxable unlike property for the difference. In the latter instance, the party with the smaller mortgage may receive boot in the form of net debt relief if the properties are exchanged subject to the existing mortgages.

The investor with the more valuable equity can avoid receipt of boot by insisting that the additional assets received to balance the equities be in the form of like-kind property rather than unlike property. Instead of receiving cash to balance the equities, he might insist that the other party invest the amount of the difference in a second like-kind property to be included in the exchange. In this manner, the equities are balanced without the exchange of cash or other unlike property, and no boot is involved.

Alternatively, an investor who has the larger equity and also has the smaller mortgage may be able to balance the equities by increasing the size of his mortgage prior to the exchange. By thus reducing the market value of his equity until it equals that of the other party, he can avoid receipt of boot. To illustrate, consider Example 10–19.

Example 10–19

Fred Pherd has owned his apartment for a number of years, so that the balance of his mortgage has been reduced to $50,000 while the market value has grown to $250,000. Having exhausted the tax-shelter aspects of the existing property and used up the bulk of his financial leverage, Pherd is considering a trade for nearby property which has a market value of $800,000 and is to be transferred subject to an existing mortgage of $650,000.

The positions of the parties prior to the exchange are:

	Pherd	Other Party
Market value of property	$250,000	$800,000
Less balance of mortgage	50,000	650,000
Value of equity position	$200,000	$150,000

If Pherd receives $50,000 cash to balance the equities he incurs a substantial tax liability on his gain. To avoid this, Pherd proposes either of the following:

1. That the other party apply the $50,000 to reduction of the mortgage prior to the exchange. This reduction in the mortgage to $600,000 would increase the other party's equity to $200,000 and permit an even exchange of equities. Pherd would not receive boot, so he would incur no tax liability as a consequence of the exchange.

2. That Pherd himself borrow an additional $50,000 on his property prior to the exchange, thus reducing his equity to equal the $150,000 of the other party. The two could then exchange equities with no tax liability for Pherd. The other party could then repay the $50,000 note immediately after the exchange if he so desired.

Note that in the proposed solutions to the problem posed in Example 10–19 the other party receives substantial boot in the form of net debt relief, no matter what Mr. Pherd proposes in an effort to avoid a tax liability for himself. This is, of course, a consequence of the difference in the market value of the properties being exchanged.

SUMMARY

Code Section 1031 gives the investor an opportunity to make adjustments to his investment portfolio without incurring an income-tax liability on the accumulated gains from the property being liquidated. Gains or losses on exchanges of like-kind property may not be recognized for income-tax purposes where no unlike property is involved in the trade.

Unlike property includes anything of economic value that is not the same nature as the property being exchanged. Included in the classification of unlike property is net debt relief. Thus if one or both of the properties are being exchanged subject to an existing mortgage, the party who has his mortgage indebtedness reduced has received boot in the form of net debt relief. If he also paid cash boot, the two may be netted to determine whether he actually received boot in the exchange.

Any receipt of boot makes the recipient liable for income taxes on any gain he experienced in the exchange, to the extent of the boot received. The balance of the gain is deferred until the property is subsequently transferred.

The basis of the property received in an exchange is a "substitute basis." It is comprised of the adjusted basis of the property traded, plus any additional costs (e.g., boot and transactions costs) and any recognized gain, minus any boot received.

SUGGESTED READINGS

1. Higgens, Warren J., "Like-Kind Exchanges," *The Real Estate Appraiser, 39* (6), 54–55 (May–June 1973).
2. Richter, Ralph, "Pyramiding Your Way to Wealth With the Real Estate Exchange," *Real Estate Review, 1* (3), 89–93 (1971).
3. Richter, Ralph, "The Real Estate Exchange–A Flexible Financing Tool," *Journal of Real Estate Taxation, 1* (1), 62–81 (1973).
4. Schwartz, Sheldon, "Section 1231 Revisited," *Real Estate Review, 5* (4), 19–21 (1975).

5. Schwartz, Sheldon, "Tax-Free Exchanges of Real Estate," *Real Estate Review, 5* (1), 21–25 (1975).
6. Tucker, Stefan F., "Don't Sell Your Real Estate–Exchange It," *Real Estate Review, 6* (4), 94–101 (1976).

CHAPTER 11

LIMITED PARTNERSHIPS

The legal and income-tax complications of the entity decision are introduced in Chapter 5. But limited partnerships are mentioned only briefly there because the extensive use of this entity justifies more lengthy treatment of the issues.

Someone once defined a limited partnership as a venture where the general partner provides the experience, while the limited partners provide the cash. The venture concludes, they continued, with the general partner having the money and the limited partners having the experience. While this may overstate the case, it does make the point that the real estate syndication boom has often been a victim of its own success. Competition for properties suitable for syndication became so great in the early 1960's that promoters had to turn increasingly to speculative deals to earn the kind of return necessary to lure investors. One result was the widely publicized failure of some of the larger syndication efforts, a failure that planted the seed of legislative reform of syndication laws in several states.

But even with the increased regulation by real estate and securities commissioners in the state and federal governments, this entity remains exceedingly popular as a means for the hustler with more energy than capital to literally lift himself by his financial bootlaces. In spite of widespread abuses, the limited partnership entity continues to provide one of the best opportunities for investor and promoter to join in a symbiotic relationship. The explanation lies to a great extent in the Internal Revenue Code and the Uniform Limited Partnership Act.

The nature of the limited partnership entity is explained in this chapter. Then, after discussing the potential benefits of the arrangement to all participants, the chapter delves into the detail of the law and revenue rulings governing the tax consequences of the entity. The chapter concludes with a brief discussion of the more infamous pitfalls that beset the would-be beneficiary of this most alluring and yet treacherous attempt to squeeze the last ounce of benefit from exploitation of special provisions of the code.

TAX STATUS OF THE LIMITED PARTNERSHIP

From an income-tax viewpoint, the essential feature distinguishing a partnership from corporations or other "associations" is that it is not a taxable entity. It functions instead as a conduit for passing income and loss items directly to the tax returns of the individual partners. Moreover, the individual income and loss items maintain their character on the individual returns. What would have been a tax preference or a tax credit item had the partnership been a taxable entity, for example, is a tax preference or tax credit item when reported on the personal tax returns of the individual partners.

The partnership is required to file a tax return, but the purpose is purely informational. It must show the amount and nature of its income, expenses, and deductions and indicate how each of the individual items is allocated among the partners. The partners must in turn report these individual items on their personal income-tax returns. The tax consequences of partnership business transactions thus accrue directly to the partners rather than to the business entity itself.

The limited partnership then enables the limited partners to enjoy the limitation of personal liability that they could attain using the corporate form of organization, while avoiding the double taxation that makes the corporate form less than desirable for many purposes. This propitious merging of corporate and proprietorship characteristics alone would probably assure considerable utilization of the limited partnership entity as a form of business organization in those ventures where the so-called subchapter S corporation is not permissible (see page 78 for a discussion of subchapter S corporations).

Possibly the most important element contributing to the popularity of the limited partnership entity is that the agreement can be tailored to divide the benefits among the general and the limited partners in the most advantageous manner occasioned by the partners' particular circumstances.

It is possible, for example, to allow certain partners to enjoy most of the tax shelter benefits while other partners enjoy the bulk of the cash flow, with a different agreement concerning distribution of capital gains and losses.

It is this ability to structure the deal to appeal to specialized classes of investors that enables promoters of limited partnership deals to appeal to special interest groups. Some limited partnership shares are marketed primarily to people in high tax brackets, whereas others are designed to appeal to persons contemplating imminent retirement; some are for people for whom security of principal looms as a large factor, and so on. Likewise, a number of different arrangements are employed for forming the pool of financial resources and for determining the nature of the investment venture.

The pooling of funds to gain the advantages of economies of scale for investors of limited means and the generation of spendable cash through tax-sheltered investments for partners in high tax brackets are only the most visible advantages of the limited partnership. Several traditional problems of real estate as an investment medium are also alleviated by this arrangement. Chief among these are illiquidity, a low disaster threshold, and the need for specialized knowledge of the market and professional management of the investment.

Traditionally, any funds invested in real estate had to be considered committed for the long run. The size, immobility, and specialized use of real estate has made it difficult to find a ready, willing, and able buyer at a fair market price on short notice. Investors wishing to withdraw funds on short notice have typically had to sell at distress prices that left little room for profit after paying the relatively high transactions cost associated with small-scale real estate transactions. A partnership agreement can reduce the illiquidity problem by providing for buy-back arrangements for any partner who needs to liquidate his commitment.

Instead of committing all his resources to one venture as might be necessary in an individual investment in real estate, the participant in a limited partnership can spread his resources over several such ventures and so gain the benefits of diversification, both geographically and across types of real estate. This diversification is an important method of reducing risk—an investor need not "put all his eggs in one basket." Having misjudged the market with respect to one investment venture, he is not faced with financial disaster as would have been the case had all his available resources been committed to that one project.

Investors frequently cite as a reason for avoiding real estate ventures the time required to manage the investment. Professional management is typically so expensive for a small-scale apartment or office complex as to be impractical. Pooling funds with others enables the investment in a large enough project so that professional management is both practical and economical.

Finally, the need for specialized knowledge to avoid disaster in the localized real estate market has resulted in many investors wisely choosing to avoid the temptation to invest. Reliance on the advice of brokers (who profit only if a transaction results) is often the very worst solution to the problem. Yet, this is generally the only source of information of which the investor is aware, other than the advice of his cousin Joe who "knows someone who made a killing." The promoter who sells shares in a limited partnership generally holds himself out as being a specialist who earns his promoter's share by making his knowledge available to assure the success of the venture.

THE PLAYERS AND THE PROPERTY

A limited partnership brings together three interacting elements that make the real estate business so vital: people with energy, ideas, and dreams; people with investment funds and dreams; and real estate that promises to fulfill the dreams of both groups. Those with ideas can use their energy to sell their ideas to those with money. The idea men become the general partners, whereas the monied members become the limited partners. The object is to package (or repackage) the real estate to fulfill the needs of all participants.

The Limited Partners. Partners who supply the bulk of the investment capital are usually passive investors. They are attracted to a limited partnership for the same reasons they might be attracted to any other investment opportunity; the prospect of a substantial after-tax rate of return on the funds placed at risk. But the limited partnership offers an additional attraction not always available in other opportunities. By remaining passive with respect to the operation of the venture, the money partners can usually limit their liability for partnership debt to the amount of funds actually invested in the venture, plus any additional assessments to which they may have committed themselves. Thus claims against the partnership in excess of partnership assets may be collected only from the general partners.

This protection from liability for general partnership debts is not different from the limited liability of shareholders in a corporation. What, therefore, is the special attraction of the limited partnership to the passive investor? The answer lies in the special tax status of the partnership itself and of the partners. The tax benefits that make real estate investment so attractive to persons holding their property in their individual names (and which we have been recounting in past chapters) are not generally available to shareholders when real estate is owned by a corporation. But property owned by a limited partnership is treated as if it were owned directly by the individual partners.

This special blending of the limited liability of the corporate form of organization with the tax benefits of the sole proprietorship explains why limited partnership shares are especially enticing to investors who earn substantial amounts of ordinary income from other sources, but who are not particularly knowledgeable in the specialized field of real estate. The tax shelter reduces taxes on the other income. And the limitation of personal liability reduces the fear of the unknown.

But not all passive investors in limited partnership ventures are wealthy or in high tax brackets. The middle class has been a major contributor of funds to such ventures in recent years. While the tax benefits are not so alluring for persons in lower tax brackets, they are by no means inconsequential. Of particular benefit to the investor of modest means are ventures designed for capital appreciation. Given the tax liability faced by the family head who is trying to build an estate by saving out of his regular income, real estate suggests itself as one of the few opportunities to accrue assets for the future.

The more inviting real estate investment opportunities are generally beyond the means of such would-be investors. The initial cash investment is simply greater than they can personally generate during the early years of their working life. Limited partnership arrangements can be tailored to solve this dilemma. They provide the means for a group of investors of limited means to pool their financial resources with experienced and skilful management to benefit from large projects that would otherwise be available only to the wealthy or to institutional investors.

The General Partners. Every limited partnership arrangement must have at least one general partner. It is he who usually conducts the affairs of the partnership. And since the liability of the limited partners is limited to the amount of their contribution, any claims against the partnership that exceed the assets of the entity can be collected only from the general partner or partners. The dual functions of the active partner are to exercise decision-making control (within the parameters of the partnership agreement) and to assume unlimited liability for general obligations of the partnership.

Who would assume the seemingly onerous position of a general partner, and what is the motivation? The answer to the second question suggests the answer to the first. An understanding of the potential benefits accruing to the general partner leads to an understanding of who would be in the best position to exploit these advantages.

As a start, one might note that a general partner enjoys the same potential profit and tax benefits that are available to the limited partners. Because there is generally no reason why the general partner cannot, if he wishes, invest also as a limited partner. He can purchase limited partnership shares on the same basis as can passive investors.

But there are additional benefits accruing to a general partner over and above those available to passive partners. It is these other benefits that motivate promoters to form partnerships and shoulder the unlimited liability that is characteristic of the general partner (though we shall see that this unlimited liability, in a properly structured venture, is not nearly so onerous as it sounds to the uninitiated). Any attempt to catalog the benefits to the general partner is hampered by the almost unlimited number of variations these benefits can take. They are limited only by the ingenuity of the promoter. And promoters are known more for ingenuity than for any trait other than (perhaps) their ability to insulate themselves from the consequences of an investment gone wrong.

Perhaps the most frequent promoters of limited-partnership deals are real estate brokers. Their place in the center of real estate activity uniquely positions them for this role. They know the properties that are ripe for development, the sources of loanable funds, the condition of the market, and the telephone numbers of persons interested in real estate investment opportunities. And, depending upon the laws of the state in which they are licensed, they are in a position to collect a commission or fee at every step in the process of forming the partnership and carrying out its intended purpose.

The opportunity to form a limited partnership often occurs to a broker who finds he has an exclusive listing on a property that requires a larger commitment of funds than most of his potential buyers can raise. To sell the property and collect the sales commission, he might form a limited partnership to pool the funds of enough investors to swing the financing. Or he might simply have contacted enough investors of limited means that he sees an opportunity to turn a commission by forming an investment group, even though he might not have a particular property in mind at the time.

In addition to collecting a commission when he sells a property to the partnership, and another commission when he sells the property at the conclusion of the venture, a broker may hire himself to manage the property during the ownership period—another substantial fee. If he is properly licensed, he might also collect a commission from the partnership when he sells shares to the investors. He is likely to collect a leasing fee by hiring himself to do the leasing of space on behalf of the group. If he is also an attorney (a not unusual event), he may collect legal fees for the work involved in preparing the documents and filing them with the proper county and state authorities.

Lawyers and accountants are probably the next two most active groups of limited partnership promoters after real estate brokers. They are in a position to know investors who need tax-sheltered investments, they are frequently asked for advice concerning such matters, and they are often knowledgeable in the legal and tax intricacies of the formation and operation of the partnership.

The Properties. So much for the players; now what about the game itself? What properties are of interest to limited partnership groups? The answer is as multifaceted as the reasons for forming partnerships. The range is from residential and shopping center developments through high-rise apartments and office buildings to rehabilitation projects and speculative land holdings. Of special interest to high tax bracket investors in recent years have been government financed projects to house low-income residents. This type of project offers low risk combined with a rather severe limitation on the permissible rate of return. But the permissible before-tax rate of return on the investment translates into a tidy after-tax cash flow because of liberal accelerated depreciation methods allowed on the projects.

FORMATION OF THE PARTNERSHIP

The fact that a limited partnership conforms to the laws of the state in which it operates does not assure that it will be treated as a partnership by the Internal Revenue Service. An organization formed under the laws applicable to a partnership may none the less be deemed an "association" and be taxed as a corporation. This is the case if the organization more nearly resembles a corporation than a partnership, from an income-tax perspective. The code establishes specific tests that determine whether the organization is treated as a partnership or an association taxable as a corporation. State law only governs whether the necessary legal relationships have been established to meet these tests.

The Partnership Agreement. The agreement specifies the contributions of capital to be made by each partner and how the partnership profits and losses are distributed. It should also specify how the assets are to be distributed upon dissolution of the partnership. The agreement forms the first step in determining the basis of the partners' interests and thus the extent of the flow-through of losses to the partner's individual income-tax return.

It is imperative that the initial partnership agreement incorporate the necessary provisions to assure the partnership receives "conduit" treatment under the code. Failure is disastrous for partners who rely on the tax-shelter aspects of the venture to make the investment financially viable.

But even if a partnership passes the initial test, there are other dangerous tax problems that can befall the unwary or unfortunate investor. Every step in the operation of the partnership must be taken with one eye on the Internal Revenue Code and the rulings of the Treasury Department. This section concentrates on essential elements in the initial agreement. The final section points out common pitfalls of which partners must be exceedingly wary.

Assuring Conduit Treatment. The essential income-tax advantage of the partnership form of organization is its conduit status. The revenue and expense items of the partnership are passed through to the individual tax returns of the partners without losing their identity. This being such a valuable characteristic, it is imperative that the partnership agreement be structured to avoid loss of conduit status.

An organization is treated as a partnership rather than an association taxable as a corporation only if it does not have more corporate than partnership characteristics. The regulations spell out six such characteristics, two of which are common to both partnerships and corporations.* The remaining four, therefore, determine whether the entity is treated as an association or a partnership. The four critical corporate characteristics are:

1. Continuity of life.
2. Centralized management.
3. Limited liability for all partners.
4. Free transferability of interests.

Treasury Regulation 301.7701-2 contains rules for determining whether these corporate characteristics exist. It states that continuity of life does not exist if an organization is not continued in the event of death,

* The common characteristics are the existence of associates and the objective to carry on a business and divide the profits.

insanity, bankruptcy, retirement, resignation, or expulsion of any member, without the express agreement of all the remaining members. Since such a provision is included in the Uniform Limited Partnership Act, it appears that continuity of life does not exist in states having statutes corresponding to the Uniform Limited Partnership Act. In other states, an article in the partnership agreement to the effect that unanimous agreement is required to continue the partnership under these circumstances would appear to assure that the partnership lacks continuity of life.

Centralized management is deemed to exist under Regulation 301.7701-2 when the authority of the general partner resembles "in powers and functions the directors of a statutory corporation." This implies management is empowered to make independent business decisions on behalf of the organization without the need for ratification. The regulation goes on to state that limited partnerships generally do not have centralized management unless ". . . substantially all the interests in the partnership are owned by the limited partners."

The corporate characteristic of limited liability exists if the creditors of the partnership may look only to the assets of the organization for satisfaction. This is the case if under local law no member is personally liable for debts or claims against the partnership. In a limited partnership, of course, the debtors may look to the general partner or partners for satisfaction when debts exceed the assets of the partnership. If general partners are not possessed of "substantial assets" from which to satisfy such claims, however, their personal liability may be ruled a sham by the Internal Revenue Service. The partnership would then be considered to have the characteristic of limited liability of all partners. Just what constitutes substantial assets in the eyes of the Internal Revenue Service is suggested by the net worth requirements for the general partner before the service provides an "advance ruling." This is discussed on page 217.

Free transferability of interests is the final corporate characteristic not always present. This characteristic is present only if a member can transfer his interest to an outsider without the consent of the other members, conferring on the outsider all the rights and privileges of his own interest in the partnership. A mere assignment of rights to share in profits does not constitute free transferability of interests as contemplated by the regulation. It is generally relatively simple to avoid the free transferability of interests characteristic by making the transfer to outsiders subject to a consent requirement.

Remember that to be treated as a taxable association the partnership must have *more* corporate than partnership characteristics. This means that three of the four characteristics must be present. A carefully drawn agreement should circumvent this eventuality without sacrificing the flexibility needed by the general partners to assure successful pursuit of their investment goals. Treasury Regulation 301.7701-3(b)(2) contains two examples of real estate transactions that qualify for treatment as partnerships. These examples are copied verbatim as Examples 11–1 and 11–2.

Example 11–1

Three individuals form an organization which qualifies as a limited partnership under the laws of the State in which the organization was formed. The purpose of the organization is to acquire and operate various pieces of commercial and other investment property for profit. Each of the three individuals who are general partners invests $100,000 in the enterprise. Five million dollars of additional capital is raised through contributions of $100,000 or more by each of thirty limited partners. The three general partners are personally capable of assuming a substantial part of the obligations to be incurred by the organization. While a limited partner may assign his right to receive a share of the profits and a return of his contribution, his assignee does not become a substituted limited partner except with the unanimous consent of the general partners. The life of the organization as stated in the certificate is 20 years, but the death, insanity, or retirement of a general partner prior to the expiration of the 20-year period will dissolve the organization. The general partners have exclusive authority to manage the affairs of the organization but can act only upon the unanimous consent of all of them. The organization has associates and an objective to carry on business and divide the gains therefrom, which characterize both partnerships and corporations. While the organization has the corporate characteristic of centralized management since substantially all of the interests in the organization are owned by the limited partners, it does not have the characteristics of continuity of life, free transferability of interests, or limited liability. The organization will be classified as a partnership for all purposes of the Internal Revenue Code.

Example 11–2

Three individuals form an organization which qualifies as a limited partnership under the laws of the State in which the organization was formed. The purpose of the organization is to acquire and operate various pieces of commercial and other investment property for profit. The certificate provides that the life of the organization is to be 40 years, unless a general partner dies, becomes insane, or retires during such period. On the occurrence of such death, insanity, or retirement, the remaining general partners may continue the business of the partnership for the balance of the 40-year period under a right so to do stated in the certificate. Each of the three individuals who is a general partner invests $50,000 in the enterprise and has means to satisfy the business obligations of the organization to a substantial extent. Five million dollars of additional capital is raised through the sale of freely transferable interests in amounts of $10,000 or less to limited partners. Nine hundred such interests are sold. The interests of the 900 limited partners are fully transferable, that is, a transferee acquires all the attributes of the transferor's interest in the organization. The general partners have exclusive control over management of the business, their interests are not transferable, and their liability for debts of the organization is not limited to their capital contributions. The organization has associates and an objective to carry on business and divide the gains therefrom. It does not have the corporate characteristics of limited liability and continuity of life. It has centralized management, however, since the three general partners exercise exclusive control over the management of the business, and since substantially all of the interests in the organization are owned by the limited partners. While the interests of the general partners are not transferable, the transferability test of an association is met since substantially all of the interests in the organization are represented by transferable interests. The organization will be classified as a partnership for all purposes of the Internal Revenue Code.

"Safe Harbor" Rules. It is not enough, of course, for the general partner or partners to be confident they can avoid loss of conduit status for the limited partnership. Passive partners, with little control over the activities of the organization, and with little knowledge of relevant tax law, rely on the advice of their own legal counsel concerning the probability that they will reap the contemplated tax benefits. Prudent counsel so queried advises insistence upon an advance ruling from the Internal Revenue Service that the organization will be treated as a partnership rather than as a taxable association. Such a ruling is, therefore, almost a "must" item from a marketing perspective.

Faced with an almost overwhelming wave of requests, the Internal Revenue Service published guidelines setting forth certain minimum requirements for advance rulings. These guidelines came generally to be called the "safe harbor" rules. They relate primarily to the control exercised by limited partners and the ability of the general partner to bear his alleged unlimited liability.

If the general partner is a corporation, no favorable advance ruling is made if the limited partners own an aggregate of more than 20% of the stock of the corporate general partner. This includes either direct or indirect ownership. Ownership by relatives of a limited partner may be construed as constructive ownership by the partner himself.

A second requirement for a favorable advance ruling where a corporate general partner is involved relates to the net worth of the corporation. Where total partnership contributions exceed $2,500,000 the net worth of the corporation must be at least 10% of the total partnership contributions. Where total partnership contributions are less than $2,500,000, the minimum net worth requirement is the lesser of $250,000 or 15% of the total partnership contributions.

Other requirements for advance rulings where the general partner is a corporation include a provision for compliance with applicable state statutes and a provision that limited partners be under no obligation to purchase any security of the general partner or its affiliates. There is required also a provision that distributive shares of partnership losses during the first 2 years of operations not exceed the amount of equity capital invested in the partnership. Creditors making nonrecourse loans must have no interest in the partnership other than as a secured creditor. Finally, the corporate general partners must have at least a 1% interest in each material item of partnership income, gain, loss, deduction or credit. This last provision is in addition to any interest due to ownership of limited partnership shares by the general partner.

It should be emphasized that these are merely rules governing favorable advance rulings, and not necessarily factors determining whether the partnership is taxed as a corporation. They appear to represent an effort by the service to discourage highly leveraged tax-shelter ventures employing a corporate general partner.

THE TAX BASIS OF PARTNERSHIP SHARES

Since a partner's interest in a limited partnership is a capital asset, he has a tax basis upon which the gain or loss is calculated in the event of disposition. But the importance of the basis transcends this consideration. Most partnerships are designed to provide a tax shelter for the limited partners, and each partner's share in these losses is limited to the adjusted basis of his interest in the partnership.

The Initial Basis. The general rule is that a partner's initial basis is equal to the amount he pays in cash plus his share of partnership liabilities and the adjusted basis of any other property he contributes to the partnership. Note that credit received in the partnership for the assets contributed is not the governing factor in determining the tax basis of a partner's interest. On the partnership books, for example, the partner is usually credited with the fair market value of any assets contributed. But the tax basis of his interest is increased only by the basis of the property contributed.

Example 11–3

Mr. Smith contributes to a newly formed partnership an apartment building with a fair market value of $250,000 and an adjusted basis of $100,000 (assume he owns the property on a free and clear basis). On the books of the partnership appears the entry, "Smith, Capital, $250,000." But the tax basis of Smith's interest is only $100,000. Should he subsequently sell his share to the other partners for $250,000 cash, for example, his gain would be $150,000:

Net selling price	$250,000
Less adjusted basis	100,000
Gain on disposal of partnership shares	$150,000

Example 11–4

Jones purchases shares in a limited partnership having a market value of $125,000. He pays $25,000 in cash and transfers title to property having a market value of $100,000. His adjusted basis for the transferred property, however, was only $20,000. Jones' basis for his partnership shares (market value $125,000), is only $45,000:

Cash	$25,000
Property, adjusted basis	20,000
Basis of property transferred to partnership, and of partnership shares received	$45,000

In these examples, the basis of partnership shares in the hands of the partner is the substitute basis of the property given in exchange. In the examples, no gain or loss is recognized on the transfer. The only exception to this rule is when a partner contributes services in exchange for a partnership interest. In this case, the partner performing the service is deemed to have received compensation in the amount of the fair market value of the shares received, and then to have contributed this compensation to the partnership in exchange for the partnership interest. The market value of the interest received is, therefore, taxable as ordinary income to the partner.

Example 11-5

An attorney forms a limited partnership and takes a 10% interest in exchange for his services in completing the legal work. The market value of partnership assets in excess of partnership liabilities is $200,000. The attorney is deemed to have received $20,000, taxable to him as ordinary income from personal services. If the shares are for services he has already performed, the entire $20,000 is taxable in the taxable year in which the interest is transferred. If only a portion of the services have been performed, with the balance to be performed in the future (perhaps upon sale of assets and dissolution of the partnership), then only the market value of that portion of the interest representing compensation for services actually performed is taxable when the interest is transferred. The balance is taxable as income from services when the rest of the services are performed, providing there are restrictions upon disposition of the interest in advance of completion of the services.

The depreciable basis of property acquired by the partnership through contributions by the partners is the adjusted basis the property had in the hands of the contributing partner. This is also the basis for figuring the partnership gain or loss on disposition. This remains the case without respect to the market value of the partnership interest received by the contributing partner, and without reference to his share of gains and losses as provided in the partnership agreement.

Example 11-6

A and *B* form a partnership, agreeing to share profits, losses, and cash distributions in the ratio of the market value of the property contributed by each. *A*'s sole contribution is $25,000 in cash. *B* contributes real estate having a market value of $100,000 and an adjusted basis of $50,000.

Annual depreciation deductions are based on the adjusted basis of $50,000, without reference to the market value at the time the property was transferred to the partnership. Assume that on this basis the first-year's depreciation allowance is $2500. Assume further that the partnership had revenues of $10,000 and other expenses of $2000. Finally, assume that just prior to the end of the year the partners sold the property for $100,000. The partnership's gain for the year is determined as follows:

Income From Operations		
Operating revenue		$ 10,000
Less expenses:		
Depreciation	$ 2,500	
Other expenses	2,000	4,500
Taxable income from operations		$ 5,500

Capital Gain From Sale		
Net selling price		$100,000
Less adjusted basis:		
Initial (partnership) basis	$50,000	
Less depreciation	2,500	47,500
Gain on sale		$ 52,500

Distributive Shares to Partners

Taxable earnings:

	Partner *A*	Partner *B*
Net operating income	$ 1,100	$ 4,400
Capital gain	10,500	42,000

If a partner assumes personal liability for a debt of the partnership, his basis is increased by the amount of the debt so assumed. If two or more of the partners assume the liability, each of them has his basis increased by his share of the debt. If, therefore, a limited partner transfers to the partnership property subject to an existing mortgage, his basis is increased by the amount of his adjusted basis of the property transferred, and decreased by the amount of the debt relief resulting from the transfer. This rule holds whether the partnership assumes the existing debt or takes the property subject to the debt.

Example 11–7

Mr. I. M. Quite exchanges property having an adjusted basis of $24,000 for newly issued shares in a limited partnership. The property transferred is subject to a note and first mortgage having a principal balance of $14,000. Mr. Quite is a limited partner and assumes no liability for partnership debts. The general partners do assume full liability for all debts of the partnership, including any mortgages on partnership property. Quite's basis for his partnership share is a substitute basis and is computed as follows:

Adjusted basis of property contributed	$24,000
Less debts assumed by other partners	14,000
Basis of partnership interest	$10,000

If the partnership incurs debts for which no partner has personal liability, then each partner's interest is determined by his ratio for sharing profits under the partnership agreement. This rule has particular significance for limited partnerships formed to hold real estate, because it applies to any mortgage on partnership realty where the general partners are exculpated from personal liability for the mortgage debt.

Example 11–8

Three investors form a limited partnership for purposes of investing in an apartment complex. Partner *A* is the general partner and assumes general liability for the debts of the partnership. For his role as the general partner, *A* receives a 10% interest in all profits and asset distributions, and bears 10% of all partnership losses. Partners *B* and *C* contribute cash to the patnership but assume the role of limited partners. The partners agree that *B* and *C*, who each contribute $20,000, each receive 40% of all profits or assets distributed and bear 40% of all losses up to the amount of their interest in the partnership. It is agreed that *B* and *C* assume no personal liability beyond their initial $20,000 investment. The partnership buys an apartment complex having a total market price of $150,000, paying $40,000 down and signing a note and mortgage for the balance of $110,000.

If the active partner in Example 11–8 assumes personal liability for any balance on the note that cannot be satisfied from partnership assets, then the limited partners' initial basis is $20,000 each (the amount invested in the partnership). Their cumulative losses from the partnership to be reported on their personal tax returns cannot exceed the initial basis for their shares. As a result of accelerated depreciation and favorable financial leverage, they might reasonably expect to have large tax losses in the early years coupled with substantial cash distributions by the partnership. When the cumulative tax losses and cash distributions to the limited partners equal the amount of their initial basis, their tax basis will have been reduced to zero, and additional operating losses may not be passed through to their personal tax returns. The losses in excess of their basis may be carried forward indefinitely, however, and charged off in future years when partnership profits result in an increase in their basis equal to the charges so deferred.

But the results are drastically altered if the mortgage securing the loan on the property in Example 11–8 contains a clause exculpating the general partner from any personal liability for the balance on the note (even though he remains liable for all other debts of the partnership). Since no partner has personal liability for the mortgage debt, each partner's basis is increased in the same proportion as they share in the profits. Each of the limited partners, therefore, has his basis increased by 40% of the mortgage debt, or $44,000. The adjusted basis of each limited partner's interest is now $64,000; the initial $20,000 of cash contributions and the $44,000 increase due to the assumption by the partnership of debt for which no partner has personal liability. Each limited partner may now experience cumulative reductions in his basis, because of cash distributions and tax losses through depreciation and interest expenses, of $64,000 before he has to begin carrying the tax losses forward to offset his share of partnership income in future years.

The exculpatory clause is simply a provision that the borrower be exculpated or cleared from any financial responsibility for the deficiency should the partnership default on the mortgage and the subsequent foreclosure action fail to generate sufficient funds to satisfy the balance due on the note.

Adjustments to the Partner's Basis. The basis of a partner's interest is adjusted to reflect the tax effect of subsequent transactions. His basis is increased by any additional capital contributions he makes. It is also increased to reflect his share of undistributed partnership income. A partner's basis may also be increased to reflect his pro rata share in newly acquired partnership liabilities. This would be the case, however, only if he assumes personal liability for his pro rata share of the debt or if *no* partner (including the general partners) has personal liability. The limited partner's basis is not affected by partnership debts for which the general partners are personally liable unless the limited partner also assumes liability.

Example 11-9

An investor contributes $10,000 in cash to a partnership under an agreement that entitles him to a 10% share of all profits, losses, and asset distributions. The investor is a limited partner, incurring no liability for partnership debts beyond the amount of his initial contribution. During the year the partnership acquires property subject to a mortgage of $1,000,000. The terms of the loan provide that the mortgagee not seek a deficiency judgment in the event of default. Therefore, no partner is personally liable for the $1,000,000 partnership debt.

Assuming no other activity in the partnership accounts, the limited partner's basis is $110,000, comprised of his $10,000 cash contribution and his pro rata share of the partnership debt (10% of $1,000,000).

The tax basis of a partner's shares is decreased by his pro rata share of partnership losses (without regard to whether the loss is an ordinary income of a capital item), by his share of partnership expenditures that are not chargeable either to expenses or to capital (e.g., for a charitable contribution), and by the amount of cash or the adjusted basis of noncash assets distributed to him.

Example 11–10

At the end of the first year of operations, the partner in Example 11–9 had an adjusted basis of $110,000. During the second year of operations, assume the partnership earns taxable income of $100,000 before accounting for depreciation and makes a charitable contribution of $1000. The depreciation allowance for the year is $140,000. The partnership distributes $10,000 in cash to the partners.

At the end of the taxable year the partner's adjusted basis is $104,900, determined as follows:

Adjusted basis at beginning of year			$110,000
Deduct:			
Distributive share of net loss:			
Depreciation deduction	$140,000		
Less income before depreciation deduction	100,000		
Net loss for year	$ 40,000		
Partner's distributive interest	10%		
Partner's distributive share of loss		$4,000	
Distributive share of contributions:			
Charitable contributions	$ 1,000		
Partner's distributive interest	10%		
Partner's distributive share		$ 100	
Cash distributed to partner (10% of $10,000)		$1,000	
Total deductions and adjustments			$ 5,100
Adjusted basis at end of year			$104,900

A partner's tax basis cannot be reduced below zero, however. Any distribution of cash in excess of his adjusted basis is generally treated as a taxable gain. A distribution of noncash assets does not result in a taxable gain due to the distribution, however, even if the value of the distributed property exceeds the partner's adjusted basis. The taxable event in this latter case occurs when the partner himself later disposes of the property.

The more important consequence of the rule that a partner's basis cannot be reduced below zero relates to his distributive share of losses. During the early years of ownership of depreciable real property, the accelerated depreciation rules generally result in tax deductible expenses greatly in excess of taxable revenue. The result is a net loss on the property that is offset against ordinary income from other sources. Since this loss is strictly due to the accelerated depreciation allowance (requiring no outlay of cash), it is a consequence that is greatly coveted by taxpayers having substantial amounts of taxable income from other sources. It is the anticipation of such tax-shelter losses that motivates many investors to enter into limited partner arrangements.

But these losses due to accelerated depreciation reduce the adjusted basis of the investor's partnership shares. And since the basis cannot be reduced below zero, any cumulative losses in excess of the basis cannot be used as an offset against income from other sources. The benefit of such losses in excess of the partner's adjusted basis must instead be deferred until such time as there are events that increase the partner's basis sufficiently that reporting the losses do not reduce the basis below zero. Generally, this means carrying the losses forward until the partner makes an additional cash contribution to the partnership or until the real estate venture begins to show a taxable profit due to the decline in the annual depreciation deduction.

REPORTING PARTNERSHIP OPERATING RESULTS

Since a partnership is not a taxable entity, it never incurs an obligation for federal income taxes (unless, of course, it is deemed to be a taxable association rather than a partnership). It must, nonetheless, file an information return regardless of the results of operations. The return gives a complete accounting of partnership operations for the year and shows how the partnership income or loss is distributed to the partners. The partners then report their shares of the partnership profit or loss on their own income-tax returns.

The partners must report their distributive shares of partnership income even if no cash distribution has been made. This remains the case even if the partnership agreement specifies that partners' income shares must be retained as partnership capital.

Example 11–11

Smith, a limited partner in the AAA partnership, receives 20% of the partnership profits and losses. In the taxable year, the partnership has net income of $18,000. In accordance with the partnership agreement, half of this is distributed to the partners and half is retained as partnership capital. Smith receives $1800 in cash distributions from the partnership but must report $3600 of partnership income on his personal income-tax return for the year.

How Conduit Status Affects the Partner's Income. Recall the earlier observation that partnership income and expense items retain their nature when passed through to the individual partners. To assure proper treatment of each item of revenue and expense, the partnership must segregate those items that merit special treatment on the partner's individual tax returns. The partnership return is so constructed that it shows each partner's distributive share of ordinary income and deductions, plus his share of credit and tax preference items. Each partner's separate share of each of these items is shown on a Schedule K-1, one such schedule being submitted for each partner. Examples of items that pass through the partnership tax conduit and must be reported on the partner's own individual tax statement include:

1. Ordinary income and interest income.
2. Additional first-year depreciation.
3. Net earnings from self-employment.
4. Short-term capital gains and losses.
5. Long-term capital gains and losses.
6. Section 1231 gains and losses.

The special items of income, deductions, credits, and tax preference items are distributed to the partners in the same ratio as they share ordinary gains and losses. If the partnership agreement provides a different ratio of sharing gains from that for sharing losses, the ratio used for distributing the special items depends upon whether the partnership had a gain or a loss for the taxable year.

How Partners Report Their Distributive Shares. Individual partners must report their distributive share of the ordinary income or loss of the partnership, plus their share of the special items, just as if the gain or loss and the special items had resulted from real estate held in the partner's own name. A partner may use his share of a loss to offset income from other sources. If he does not have sufficient income from other sources to completely offset his share of the partnership loss, he may carry the loss back or forward on his individual return for other years in the manner prescribed for income from any business or investment venture. But remember the earlier caution that the distributive share of losses used to offset ordinary income from other sources cannot exceed the amount that would reduce the partner's basis below zero. Any remaining loss must be carried forward and applied against the partner's distributive share of future profits, or until the partnership is liquidated.

Even though the partnership is not a taxable entity, it does choose the accounting method to be used in reporting the results of operations for purposes of determining the tax liability of the individual partners. These decisions are binding on all the partners. The partnership chooses which of the allowable depreciation methods is used, for example. It also chooses whether an item is deducted currently or capitalized, where such an option is permitted by the code.

The Tax Consequences of Self-Dealing. When a partner as an individual conducts business with the partnership, the transaction is generally treated as if it were between the partnership and an outsider. There are important exceptions to this general rule where the individual partner (or two or more individual partners acting in concert) own a substantial portion of the partnership shares and where the results of the transaction provide the individual taxpayer with a deductible loss or a capital gain. The rules for self-dealing are too complex and specialized to merit inclusion here. Taxpayers contemplating dealing with a partnership in which they have more than a nominal interest should first seek competent tax counsel.

SALE OR TERMINATION OF A PARTNERSHIP INTEREST

When a partner sells his interest in a limited partnership, the transaction is treated for tax purposes in the same manner as any other sale of assets held for business or investment purposes. The death of a partner (where this does not terminate the partnership) does not affect his interest in the partnership, although it may affect his basis. The distribution of assets to the partners upon dissolution of the partnership is treated as a sale of the partner's interest. Each of these situations is considered here.

Sale or Exchange of Partnership Shares. If the partnership agreement and the applicable state laws permit, a partner may sell or otherwise dispose of his interest in the partnership at will. His doing so does not affect the tax status or position of the partnership itself unless the partnership is terminated as a consequence.

The disposal of a partner's interest is viewed for tax purposes as taking place solely between the partner and the persons acquiring his interest. The partner's gain or loss on the transaction is simply the difference between the value received and his adjusted basis for the shares transferred. The exceptions that exist in the case of a less-than-arm's-length transaction (a "brother-in-law" deal) are the same as for disposal of real estate held solely in the name of the individual and are discussed elsewhere. The gain or loss is generally treated as a capital item. It is long- or short-term depending upon whether the partner has held the shares for more than 1 year.

Death of a Partner. Whether the death of a general partner terminates the partnership depends upon the provisions of the partnership agreement and upon the applicable state law. Assuming the partnership is not terminated by the death of the partner, his estate or other successor is treated as a partner so long as it (or he) is entitled under the law and partnership provisions to continue sharing in the profits and losses of the partnership.

The income-tax effects of liquidating the interest of the deceased partner are more complex than can be covered in the present treatise. They are similar to the treatment of a retiring partner, an eventuality that is also omitted on the grounds of materiality and in the interests of expediency. Specialized aspects of estate taxation are not well fitted to the do-it-yourself approach. They call for professional assistance.

Dissolution of the Partnership. Perpetual life is not a characteristic generally associated with the partnership form of organization. The day comes when the business of the limited partnership venture is complete, and it is time to distribute the remaining assets and close the books.

If the asset distribution involves only cash, the difference between the partner's adjusted basis and the cash received represents a taxable gain or loss in the year of the distribution. If the distribution involves assets other than cash, uncollected accounts receivable, or substantially appreciated inventory, no gain or loss is recognized as a consequence of the distribution.* The basis of the assets received is the adjusted basis of the partner's interest just prior to liquidation less any cash received in liquidation. If a partner receives more than one noncash asset upon liquidation, the basis

* Section 751 of the code provides special rules that apply when the distribution of residual partnership assets involves uncollected accounts receivable or appreciated inventory. These considerations are not generally relevant to the real estate investor considering a limited partnership entity.

of his partnership interest (less cash received on liquidation) must be allocated among the assets received.

PARTNERSHIP PITFALLS

The tax code is sufficiently complex to try the patience and comprehension of the most astute. The rules governing partnerships are not among the least trying. We have attempted to abstract from this complexity to provide guidance to real estate investors involved in or contemplating involvement in a limited partnership.

The danger of including sufficient detail so that the reader is not left dangling from an unsolved tax dilemma is that he may become entangled and strangle himself on the cords of complexity. Among the perils of oversimplification are that he underestimate the problem and do himself financial harm by running afoul of the code. We have tried to thread our way between these twin hazards by explaining the most relevant portion of the tax rules, ever mindful that the reader has no way of knowing whether we have succeeded until it is too late for him to benefit from his newly acquired wisdom.

We cannot overstate the importance of using this treatise only as a general guide in planning one's investment strategy. For your bank account's sake, seek specialized tax counsel before proceeding with any plan. Study the code itself plus any one of the excellent (and lengthy) tax courses available in order to gain the competence to engage in complicated tax deals.

We have alluded to several circumstances that could cause the partners to be denied conduit treatment. The more common of these are so serious and so commonplace as to deserve more specific attention. They are the focus of this concluding section.

Losses in Excess of Partner's Basis. Partnership losses reported on a partner's individual tax return as an offset against other income have the effect of reducing the adjusted basis of his partnership shares. Cash distributions have the same effect. But the partner's basis cannot be reduced below zero. When his basis is reduced in this manner to zero, his pro rata share of any additional losses must be carried forward and applied against his share of future partnership profits.

This limitation on conduit treatment for a partner's share of partnership losses usually creates no problems for the general partner or partners. The partner's share includes not only the basis of all assets he contributes to the partnership, but also all liabilities for which he is personally liable. And since the general partner is personally liable for all the partnership debts other than those from which he has been exculpated by agreement with the creditors, his basis almost always exceeds his cumulative share of partnership losses.

A limited partner's position is somewhat more precarious with respect to the relationship between his pro rata share of partnership losses and the adjusted basis of his partnership shares. Since limited partners do not have personal liability for partnership debts, such debts generally do not affect the amount of their adjusted basis. Their basis in this situation consists solely of assets contributed plus their pro rata share of undistributed profits. Given the amount of leverage employed in most real estate ventures, a limited partner's share of losses (due to accelerated depreciation and interest charges on mortgage debt) could easily exceed his basis during the early years of operation.

This problem can be avoided by assuring that *no* partner is personally liable for the mortgage debt of the partnership. When there is no personal liability on the part of any partner for a particular debt, each partner's basis is increased by his pro rata share of that debt. By including in the note and mortgage a clause exculpating the general partner from personal liability, the partnership can assure that the limited partner's tax basis is sufficiently large to enable him to claim currently his entire share of partnership losses.

Treatment as Taxable Association. Partnerships deemed to have more corporate than partnership characteristics are treated as taxable associations rather than partnerships. This means the partnership is taxed just as if it had been a corporation. Not only is tax conduit status denied, but the earnings are also in effect subjected to double taxation.

The safest way to handle this problem is to seek an advance ruling from the Internal Revenue Service. The procedure for such a ruling is discussed on page 27.

Investment Analysis and Tax Shelters. A very common problem is that investors become so enamored of the tax-shelter characteristics that they tend to slight the question of the economic soundness of a venture. Of what use is a tax shelter that never yields the partner a positive cash flow? The analysis should never focus simply on the anticipated tax shelter but rather on the after-tax cash flow. Also important is the question of timing of the anticipated cash flows and the amount of risk involved.

Any proposal that does not make economic sense in the absence of the tax circumstances should be viewed with a jaundiced eye. Make sure not to be the limited partner who ends up with the experience, while the general partner ends up with the money.

Conformance with Federal and State Securities Laws. Most states regulate limited partnership offerings to some degree. As a minimum, it is usually necessary to seek an exemption from registering partnership shares as securities on the basis of the size of the offering, the nature of the persons solicited, or some other basis provided for in the laws of your state.

If partnership shares are to be sold in a state other than that in which the property is located, the venture may have to be registered with the Securities and Exchange Commission. Federal securities law is exceedingly complex, and compliance is often prohibitively expensive. Seek legal help in conforming with the various regulatory bodies (including state agencies) and save yourself potential legal and financial headaches.

SUGGESTED READINGS

1. Anderson, Robert L., and Herschel M. Bloom, "Collapsible Partnership: The Complexities of Section 751," *Journal of Real Estate Taxation, 2* (4), 425–449 (1975).
2. Caruthers, Donald S., Jr., "Real Estate Tax Shelters: Special Retroactive Allocations Under the Tax Reform Act of 1976," *Journal of Real Estate Taxation, 4* (2), 119–146 (1977).
3. Fox, H. Lawrence, and Allen K. Halperin, "A Corporate Limited Partner in Limited Real Estate Partnerships," *Journal of Real Estate Taxation, 3* (4), 425–438 (1976).
4. Hyman, Milton B., and Peter M. Hoffman, "Partnerships and 'Associations': A Policy Critique of the Morrissey Regulations," *Journal of Real Estate Taxation, 3* (4), 377–400 (1976).
5. Kanter, Burten W., "Stop, Look and Listen–Some Current IRS Issues and Positions Affecting Tax-Shelter Real Estate Limited Partnerships," *Journal of Real Estate Taxation, 2* (2), 264–294 (1974).
6. Lane, Bruce S., "The Tax Reform Act of 1976: What it Means for Real Estate Limited Partnerships," *Journal of Real Estate Taxation, 4* (3), 195–213 (1977).
7. Saxton, John J., "Character of Income to Partnership and Partner," *Journal of Real Estate Taxation, 3* (3), 347–350 (1976).
8. Saxton, John J., "Partnerships," *Journal of Real Estate Taxation, 4* (2), 228–230 (1976).
9. Shillingsburg, J. Edward, "Winding Up Real Estate Tax Shelters: Problems and Solutions," *Journal of Real Estate Taxation, 2* (4), 405–415 (1975).

CHAPTER 12

THE QUESTION OF INCORPORATION

Double taxation of cash distributions and lack of conduit treatment have caused many investors to reject the corporation as a possible ownership entity. Their judgment may be faulty. Incorporation has advantages as well as disadvantages, the relative significance of each varying with the type of property involved as well as with the individual's tax status and investment objectives.

Chief among the advantages is the more favorable tax rate on corporate earnings. Instead of the steeply graduated rates applicable to individuals, corporations pay a flat 22% tax on the first $25,000 of net income, and 48% on all earnings in excess of $25,000.* In contrast, individuals are assessed at an incremental rate in excess of 22% on income of about $6000. The average rate paid by a single individual earning $25,000 is almost 29%. And individuals are taxed at an incremental rate of 50% or more on income in excess of $32,000.† An unmarried individual, for ex-

* The 1976 Tax Reform Act included temporary changes in the corporate tax rate. For all of 1977, corporations pay 20% on the first $25,000 of taxable income, 22% on the next $25,000, and 48% on all income over $50,000. As this book was being completed there were no indications whether this temporary change would be extended beyond 1977.

† Individual tax rate comparisons are based on the 1976 rate schedules. They do not take into consideration temporary surtaxes or tax credits that were in effect at that time. The reference to individual rates, unless otherwise stated, relates to an unmarried taxpayer's taxable income after all deductions and exemptions.

ample, pays a higher average tax than does a corporation at all income levels above approximately $12,000.

Married taxpayers filing joint returns fare somewhat better than single individuals, as do those qualifying as heads of households. But the difference is marginal. A special limitation on taxes applicable to personal-service income, discussed on page 9, alleviates this discrepancy somewhat. But since the maximum rate paid by corporations is below the maximum on personal-service income, the special provision does not eliminate the corporate advantage.

Offsetting the advantage of lower average tax rates on corporate income is the cost of transferring corporate earnings to shareholders. Corporate distributions are generally taxable as dividend income to recipients. And penalty taxes may be imposed on corporations seeking to avoid this double taxation by allowing cash to accumulate in excess of the "reasonable needs" of the corporation.

The double taxation problem does not necessarily rule out the corporation as an ownership entity, however. Other factors should be explored before making a final decision. This chapter provides the basic information needed to decide whether to incorporate.

Procedures are considered for calculating the corporation's income-tax liability. This is followed by consideration of how to take cash out of a corporation with minimum cost in terms of additional taxes to the shareholder. The individual tax liability that may be incurred upon dissolution of the corporate entity is then explored. The chapter concludes with a summary of special tax problems often encountered by those opting for the use of a corporate entity.

COMPUTING CORPORATE TAXES

Corporations are legal entities empowered to transact business in their own name. They can buy and sell, enter into contracts, and sue and be sued, in much the same manner as biological individuals. They are also tax-paying entities whose taxable income is computed in much the same manner as that of an individual. There are, however, special rules and special rates applicable to their earnings. These differences are very significant in determining whether the corporate entity is advantageous.

Capital-Gains Provisions. Corporate capital gains are computed in the same manner as for individuals: Short-term gains and losses are offset to compute *net* short-term gains or losses, and long-term gains and losses are similarly offset to compute *net* long-term gains or losses. A net loss in one category is then offset against any net gain in the other, before applying the applicable tax rate (see Chapter 8 for a fuller treatment of capital-gains computations). At this point the similarity in the treatment of capital items ends.

Corporate net short-term capital gains in excess of net long-term capital losses are included in ordinary income. Net long-term capital gains in excess of net short-term capital losses are either added to ordinary income in full or taxed at a rate of 30%, at the discretion of the corporate taxpayer. The corporation would choose to include the net long-term gains in ordinary income only if the resulting tax is less than 30%. Since the incremental tax rate is 48% on ordinary income above $50,000, the alternative rate is more advantageous for most corporations.*

For corporations earning less than $50,000 of taxable income before inclusion of capital gains, however, the best approach is less obvious. If ordinary income plus long-term capital gains total less than $50,000, the capital gains would, of course, be added in full to ordinary income and taxed at the 22% rate. But suppose ordinary income is less than $50,000, whereas ordinary income plus long-term capital gains total more than $50,000. In this case, adding the capital gains to ordinary income results in an average tax rate on the capital gains of something between 22 and 48%. The taxpayer would compute the tax both ways and opt for that approach resulting in the lower tax liability. This is illustrated in Example 12–1.

Capital-Loss Provisions. Unlike individuals, corporations may not offset capital losses against ordinary income. Instead, losses may be carried back 3 years or carried forward 5 years to offset capital gains in the years to which they are carried. The carried-forward or carried-back loss is always treated as a short-term loss in the year to which it is carried, without regard to its nature in the year incurred. This means it can be used to offset both short- and long-term gains, on a $1-for-$1 basis. Losses not fully offset within the 3-year carry-back and 5-year carry-forward period are simply lost: They have no further tax consequences for the corporation.

Effect of Ordinary Corporate Losses. Since partnerships are a tax conduit, any partnership loss is used by the taxpayer to offset income from other sources. This is not the case with a corporation. If a real estate corporation suffers losses (which is often the case due to the use of accelerated depre-

* The $50,000 threshold for the 48% incremental tax rate will revert to $25,000 in 1978 unless the "temporary" tax reliefs in the 1976 Tax Reform Act is extended.

Example 12–1

Corporations *A* and *B* each have taxable income of $52,000. Long-term capital gains account for $6000 of this total for corporation *A* and $10,000 of the total for corporation *B*. For corporation *A*, there is a $40 advantage in using the alternative capital-gains tax calculation, whereas for corporation *B* the alternative method results in $280 of additional tax liability. Here are the computations*:

	Corporation *A*	Corporation *B*
Taxable Income		
Ordinary income	$46,000	$42,000
Long-term capital gains	$6,000	10,000
Total taxable income	$52,000	$52,000
Income-Tax Liability		
Tax using regular method:		
Tax on $50,000	$10,500	$10,500
Tax on balance (at 48%)	960	960
Total tax liability	$11,460	$11,460
Tax using alternative method:		
Tax on ordinary income	$ 9,620	$ 8,740
Tax on capital gains (at 30%)	1,800	3,000
Total tax liability	$11,420	$11,740
Advantage (Disadvantage) of Alternate Method		
Tax with regular method	$11,460	$11,460
Less tax with alternate method	11,420	11,740
Advantage (disadvantage)	$ 40	$ (280)

* Example 12–1 assumes that the "temporary" tax rates in effect for 1977 are in fact extended. If these rates are not extended, then the problem addressed by Example 12–1 will occur when total taxable income exceeds $25,000.

---

ciation and high financial leverage), the losses are not available to stockholders. But the corporation may carry the loss back 3 years or forward 5 years in the same manner as described earlier for capital losses. The loss carry-back or carry-forward reduces the net taxable income in the year to which the loss is carried. Losses not fully used up within the carry-over period have no further tax consequence.

The law requires that losses be carried back to the earliest permissible year. Any remainder is carried to the next earlier year, and so forth. To illustrate, assume a corporation earned a profit in every year except 1978. The tax liability for 1975 would be recomputed, incorporating the 1978 loss. If there remained any portion of the loss not offset by 1975 income, the remainder would be used to recompute the 1976 tax liability. Any remaining loss would be used to reduce taxable income in 1977, 1979, 1980, 1981, 1982, and 1983.

Example 12–2

A corporation earned taxable income of $200,000 in each of the years 1975, 1976, and 1977. In 1978 the corporation experienced a net loss of $500,000. It used the carry-back procedure to recompute its taxes for the previous 3 years. All the taxes paid for the years 1975 and 1976 are refunded. The recomputed taxable income for 1977 is $100,000.

Example 12–3

The corporation described in the previous example suffers a net loss of $500,000 in 1979. Its average annual income for the next 5 years is $25,000. Of the net loss in 1979, $100,000 is carried back to 1977, reducing the taxable income for that year to zero. The remaining $400,000 is carried forward and used to offset the net income of the next 5 years. The $275,000 of net losses not used to offset income in other years have no tax consequences after 1984.

Many real estate investments offer substantial tax-shelter opportunities. A large net loss for the first several years of such an investment is not unusual. Indeed, it is to be desired, since the loss is merely a bookkeeping phenomenon that reduces the investor's tax liability on income from other sources and so produces a much larger after-tax cash flow. If the investment is held by a corporate entity, however, the tax loss can create problems. Unless the corporation itself has income from other sources against which to apply the tax shelter provided by its real estate investment, the only alternative is to carry the loss backward or forward for the allotted periods, after which the tax advantage is lost. A corporation holding several parcels of real estate acquired at various points in time can generally avoid this latter problem. Some of the property will always be substantially depreciated and so will be generating taxable income against which to apply the tax losses from other property.

CASH DISTRIBUTIONS

Corporate cash distributions are generally viewed as dividends and are taxable to the recipient at his incremental personal income-tax rate. This is the infamous double taxation problem that makes the corporate entity less popular than it otherwise might be. Some business enterprises can avoid this problem by taking advantage of the special provisions of subchapter S, which permits a closely held corporation to be treated as a partnership for tax purposes. But tax-option (subchapter S) treatment is not available for firms deriving more than 20% of their earnings from "passive" sources, including rents and interest.

Corporate strategies to minimize the tax liability on cash distributions include payment of salaries to shareholders or treating distribution as a return of capital. Both of these approaches contain possible tax-liability hazards as well as potential tax savings. The alternative of simply not distributing available cash may result in substantial penalty taxes. The limitations of each of these strategies are considered in the following discussion.

Shareholder Compensation. Corporations may pay "reasonable" salaries to stockholders who contribute services to the corporation. These salaries are tax deductible expenses to the corporation and are taxable income to the shareholders. If all the corporation's income is paid to the shareholders in this fashion, the double taxation problem is avoided. By varying the salary level, corporate earnings can be divided between the corporation and the major stockholders in whatever ratio results in the lowest overall tax liability. This is an opportunity not available in a partnership, where payments to the partners are not an allowable expense item.

There are limits to the corporation's ability to allocate its net revenue between the owner's salary and the corporation's net profit. Salaries in excess of reasonable compensation for services are treated by the Internal Revenue Service as a taxable distribution of earnings. The excess is then taxable to the corporation as net income *and* to the shareholder as dividend income. Should a controversy arise between the government and the taxpayer concerning the reasonableness of compensation for shareholder services, the burden of proof rests with the taxpayer.

Cash Distributions Treated as a Return of Capital. Taxable dividends may consist of any distribution by the corporation (either cash or other property) out of profits. The profits may be for the current year or they may be prior-year earnings not previously distributed. But what happens if a corporation has no accumulated earnings and earns no profit in the year of the cash distribution? To the extent distributions made under these circumstances do not exceed the adjusted basis of the shareholder's stock, they will be treated as a tax-free return of capital. The distribution so treated reduces the adjusted basis of the shareholder's investment in the corporation.

Example 12–4

A stockholder who has an adjusted basis of $12,000 for his shares receives a cash dividend of $8000. The corporation has no accumulated earnings, and has no net profit in the year of the distribution. The cash dividend is characterized as a return of capital and is not taxable to the shareholder. His adjusted basis is reduced by the amount of the dividend. The new adjusted basis of his shares is $4000:

Adjusted basis prior to cash distribution	$12,000
Less return of original investment via cash distribution	8,000
Adjusted basis after distribution	$ 4,000

During the early years of an investment, accelerated depreciation and high financial leverage often result in accounting losses coupled with substantial positive cash flows. Cash made available in this fashion might easily exceed the initial basis of the shareholder's investment. Even after cash distributions have reduced the basis to zero, additional distributions are not taxed as dividend income so long as the corporation has no accumulated earnings. But the distributions in excess of the shareholder's adjusted basis are taxable to him as capital gains. This is, of course, eminently preferable to incurring a tax liability at the ordinary income rate, because of the favorable treatment afforded long-term capital gains.

Example 12–5

A stockholder who has an adjusted basis of $12,000 for his shares receives a cash distribution of $14,000. The corporation has no accumulated earnings and no profit during the year of the distribution. Of the $14,000 received by the shareholder, $12,000 is treated as a return of capital and is not taxable. The remaining $2000 is taxed as a long-term capital gain. The shareholder's adjusted basis is zero after the distribution.

Example 12–6

Shareholder *A* owns a one-third interest in a corporation that during the current taxable year distributes $63,000 in cash to shareholders. At the beginning of the taxable year, the corporation had accumulated earnings of $5000 and during the current taxable year it earned a net profit of $10,000. Shareholder *A*, whose stock holdings have an adjusted basis of $3000, receives one-third of the cash distribution or $21,000. Of this amount, $5000 is a dividend (one-third of the sum of $5000 and 10,000). The remaining $16,000 received by shareholder *A* is treated as a distribution of capital, of which $3000 offsets his adjusted basis and is, therefore, not taxable. The balance of $13,000 is taxable to shareholder *A* as a capital gain. The calculations are:

Total corporate cash distribution		$63,000
Shareholder *A*'s interest in corporation		⅓
Cash received by shareholder *A*		$21,000
Less portion of *A*'s receipts taxable as ordinary income:		
One-third accumulated earnings	$1,667	
One-third current year earnings	3,333	$ 5,000
Balance, treated as capital distribution		$16,000
Tax-free portion of *A*'s capital distribution (equal to *A*'s adjusted basis)		$ 3,000
Amount taxable to *A* as a capital gain		$13,000

Cash distributions during any year in which there is a net profit must be treated as a cash dividend to the extent of the current income, even when the corporation has a cumulative net operating deficit. The cash so distributed is taxable to the recipients as dividend income, though the corporation itself might have incurred no tax liability on the earnings distributed because of net loss carry-overs from prior years. The rule is that cash distributions must be treated as coming from the most recently accumulated earnings before being attributed to distribution of capital.

Example 12–7

A corporation has a cumulative *net loss* of $50,000. During the current taxable year the corporation earns a net profit of $15,000 before carrying forward the net loss carry-over. It declares a cash distribution of $40,000. Of this amount, $15,000 is treated as a distribution of the current year's earnings and so is taxed to the shareholders as dividend income. The $25,000 balance is a distribution of capital, since the corporation has no cumulative earnings from prior years. The corporation incurs no income-tax liability for the current year (due to the $50,000 tax loss carry-over), but the shareholders must, nevertheless, report as dividend income a portion of the cash distribution equal to the corporation's current year earnings.

Distributions in excess of current-year earnings are next attributed to accumulated earnings from prior years, where such accumulations exist. If there remains a portion of the distribution not attributed to either current or accumulated earnings, the balance is treated as a distribution of capital.

COMPUTING THE SHAREHOLDER'S BASIS

Since the shareholder's adjusted basis determines the tax treatment of capital distributions received, factors affecting the basis are a matter of more than casual concern. In this section, we consider how the adjusted basis of the shareholder's interest is determined.

Computing the Initial Basis. When an investor or group of investors form a corporation in which they hold at least an 80% interest, no gain or loss is generally recognized on the transfer of assets to the corporation.* The tax basis to the corporation of the property so received, and the tax basis to the investors of the shares received in exchange, is the same as the adjusted basis the exchanged property had in the hands of the shareholders.

If a stockholder receives cash from the corporation in addition to shares in exchange for property transferred, he is considered to have received "boot," and both his and the corporation's basis are affected. If the fair market value of the property transferred to the corporation exceeds the shareholder's basis, he has a gain on the exchange that must be recognized to the extent of the boot received. The basis of the property in the hands of the corporation is the carry-over basis of the taxpayer plus the amount of cash or other boot paid by the corporation. But if the market value of the asset transferred is less than the shareholder's adjusted basis, no loss may be recognized as a consequence of receipt of boot from the corporation.

* "Control" implies ownership of at least 80% of the voting shares outstanding [Code Section 351(C)]. The control may vest in an individual or a group that transfers property to the corporation simultaneously.

Suppose the property transferred to a corporation has been depreciated by the shareholder using an accelerated depreciation method and would have been subject to "depreciation recapture" rules had the property been sold rather than exchanged for stock. If the shareholder receives no boot from the corporation, he need not recognize any of the gain, regardless of the extent to which the property is subject to recapture. But the corporation takes the property subject to the recapture potential it had in the hands of the shareholder. The recapture rules then become operative when the corporation disposes of the property.

If the taxpayer does receive boot he must recognize the gain to the extent of the boot received. And the gain so recognized must be reported as ordinary income to the extent it represents recapture of excess depreciation. Any recognized gain in excess of the recaptured excess depreciation is reported as a capital gain. Recapture of excess depreciation is covered more fully in Chapter 9.

Another exception to the rule providing for nonrecognition of gain upon transfer of property to a controlled corporation exists when the property transferred is subject to a liability that exceeds the shareholder's adjusted basis for the property.

Example 12–8

An investor transfers property worth $150,000 to a newly formed corporation in exchange for a controlling interest in its stock. The shareholder's adjusted basis for the property transferred was $50,000. The corporation assumes liability for the $125,000 balance on a note secured by a mortgage on the property received. The investor has a realized gain on the transaction of $100,000, determined as follows:

Market value of property exchanged	$150,000
Less adjusted basis of property exchanged	50,000
Gain on exchange	$100,000

Had the investor received no boot in the exchange, none of his gain would have to be recognized during the taxable year of the exchange. Debt relief in excess of the adjusted basis of the property exchanged, however, does represent boot. Accordingly, the investor must recognize as a taxable gain the $75,000 by which the mortgage balance exceeds his adjusted basis ($125,000 debt balance minus $50,000 adjusted basis).

The shareholder's substitute basis for the shares received in the exchange is zero. The calculation is:

Basis of property given in exchange	$ 50,000
Add recognized gain	75,000
	$125,000
Less debt relief	125,000
Substitute basis of property received	0

Adjusting the Shareholder's Basis. Since the corporation is a taxable entity in its own right, a distinction must be made between the shareholder's basis for his investment in the corporation, on the one hand, and the corporation's adjusted basis for its assets on the other. Adjustments to the corporation's tax basis have no necessary effect on the basis of the stockholder's shares in the corporation. Profits and losses experienced by the corporation, for example, do not affect the shareholder's tax basis.

Adjustments to the shareholder's basis is made for additional capital contributions to the corporation or for distributions of capital by the corporation. Additional contributions increase the shareholder's basis, whereas distributions decrease it.

If a shareholder performs services for the corporation, for which he receives additional shares of stock, the value of the shares is taxable to the shareholder as earned income and increases the adjusted basis of his interest in the corporation. The effect is the same as if the corporation had paid him in cash for his services, and he had then used the cash to purchase additional shares of stock.

Cash distributions that are not treated as dividends decrease the stockholder's adjusted basis. But his basis cannot be reduced below zero. Any additional distributions of capital to a shareholder after his basis has been reduced to zero are taxable to him as capital gains.

DISCONTINUING THE CORPORATION

When the time comes for liquidating the investment, a taxpayer who has chosen to incorporate faces another set of tax problems. He must determine the tax status of gains and losses on liquidation, and the resulting income-tax liability of both his corporation and himself.

The alternatives are to sell all noncash assets and distribute the proceeds to shareholders or to simply distribute the assets on a pro rata basis. By making the proper elections, one can so structure the liquidation that the difference in tax consequences of these alternatives is nominal. A more serious problem is the possibility of being designated a "collapsible corporation" and having all gains taxed as ordinary income.

Distribution of Noncash Assets in Liquidation. As a general rule, no gain or loss need be reported by a corporation that distributes its assets to shareholders as a liquidating dividend. There are exceptions for property on which there would have been recapture of excess depreciation if the property had been sold, for the sale of installment receivables on which ordinary gains would have been reported had the receivables been collected by the corporation, and for certain other properties generally not applicable to a corporation formed to hold income-producing real estate.

Unless an election is made under Code Section 333, the basis of the distributed property in the hands of the shareholders is its fair market value at the time of distribution. The shareholders, therefore, have a capital gain or loss if the market value of the property received differs from the adjusted basis of their shares in the corporation.

Example 12–9

Delta Corporation is wholly owned by one shareholder whose adjusted basis for the shares is $75,000. The corporation owns as its sole asset real estate having a market value of $750,000 and subject to mortgage debt of $500,000. It transfers its real estate (subject to the outstanding mortgage debt) to the shareholder in exchange for his stock. The corporation then retires the stock and goes out of business. Assuming that the corporation has no other income or expense in the year of liquidation, the results of liquidation are as follows.

Market value of assets distributed	$750,000
Less outstanding mortgage debt	500,000
Market value of distribution to shareholder	$250,000
Less adjusted basis of shares	75,000
Capital gain reported by shareholder	$175,000

The adjusted basis of the property to the shareholder is the fair market value of the assets at the time of dissolution. In Example 12–9, therefore, the basis of the real estate received from Delta Corporation is $750,000. Should the taxpayer elect to sell the real estate immediately, he incurs no further tax liability as a consequence of the transaction.

Example 12–10

Assume the same facts as in Example 12–9, but assume further that the shareholder immediately sells the real estate received at its fair market value. The results are as follows:

Capital gain or loss:		
Net selling price		$750,000
Less adjusted basis		750,000
Capital gain or loss		0
Net cash proceeds:		
Net selling price		$750,000
Less: Mortage debt	$500,000	
Capital-gain tax	0	500,000
Net cash proceeds		$250,000

One consequence of the provision that the difference between the market value of assets received and the adjusted basis of shares be treated as a capital gain or loss is that liquidation may have the effect of converting to a capital gain what would otherwise have been taxable as ordinary income. This is because *all* liquidating distributions are subject to capital-gain and -loss treatment, even though a portion may consist of corporate retained earnings, which if distributed prior to liquidation would have been ordinary dividend income to the shareholder. Substantial tax savings are sometimes possible, therefore, by allowing earnings to accumulate in the corporation until liquidation.

This strategy is subject to two strict constraints. The first is the possibility of a penalty tax on undistributed earnings in excess of legitimate needs of the corporation. The second possible unfavorable development is that the corporation might be deemed a collapsible corporation. Both these problems, and the possible tax consequences, are treated later in the chapter.

Tax-Free Distribution of Assets on Liquidation. Code Section 333 permits an elective treatment of a distribution of corporate assets on liquidation, which enables stockholders to avoid tax liability on much of the assets received. The liability is effectively deferred until the assets are subsequently disposed of by the shareholder. This elective treatment is *not available* if the corporation is deemed a collapsible corporation.

The main effect of this special provision is to enable "qualified electing shareholders" to receive appreciated corporate assets without recognizing a gain on the appreciation. The only gain that must be recognized is that relating to undistributed corporate income and to cash and securities distributed. The taxpayer is taxed (at the capital-gains rate) on the larger of his share of accumulated corporate profits or his portion of assets distributed that consists of cash or securities acquired by the liquidating corporation after 1953.

Example 12–11

A shareholder receives as a liquidating dividend real estate having a market value of $30,000 and cash in the amount of $2500. The shareholder assumes a $5000 corporate liability as a part of the liquidation. His shares, which he surrenders to the corporation, had an adjusted basis in his hands of $12,000. His pro rata share of undistributed corporate earnings is $1200. The net amount realized by the shareholder is $27,500, determined as follows:

Cash	$ 2,500
Real property (at market value)	30,000
Market value of assets received	$32,500
Less liabilities assumed	5,000
Net amount realized on liquidation	$27,500

The shareholder has a gain on liquidation of $15,500 ($27,500 less basis of shares of $12,000), which would be taxable as a capital gain in the absence of elective treatment under Section 333. A qualified electing shareholder need recognize only that portion of the gain attributable to the larger of the cash and securities received or of undistributed corporate profits. Since his share of undistributed profits is less than the amount of cash received ($1200 as opposed to $2500), the recognized gain is based on the cash received. Thus of the $15,500 gain, only $2500 is immediately taxable.

The basis to a qualified electing shareholder of the property received under this election is the same as his basis for the stock cancelled on liquidation, minus any cash received, plus any gain recognized. The basis is also increased by the amount of any corporate liabilities assumed by the shareholder. The total adjusted basis is then apportioned among the assets received on the basis of their respective net fair market values.

Example 12–12

Assume the same facts as in the preceding example. The basis of assets acquired by the shareholder is determined as follows:

Adjusted basis of stock cancelled		$12,000
Less cash received		2,500
		$ 9,500
Add: Liability assumed	$5,000	
Gain recognized	2,500	7,500
Basis of property acquired		$17,000

To qualify for this elective treatment of assets received in liquidation, a shareholder must file written notice of the election within 30 days of the date the liquidation plan is approved by the shareholders. A corporation that owns 50% or more of the shares in a liquidating corporation is excluded from the provisions of Section 333 and may not make the election. A further requirement is that the liquidation itself be completed within 1 calendar month of approval of the plan by the stockholders.

Sale of Corporate Assets Prior to Liquidation. If a liquidating corporation sells its assets prior to liquidation, it ordinarily incurs a corporate tax liability on any net gains from disposition. The gains may be taxed at the more favorable long-term capital-gain rate rather than as ordinary income, to the extent the assets were not held primarily for resale. Gains on assets held for resale may qualify for capital gains treatment if sold on a bulk basis, and primarily to one person.

Liquidating corporations can avoid liability for the capital-gains tax if they distribute all residual assets within 12 months of adopting a plan of liquidation. This special provision is found in Code Section 337 and applies to "involuntary conversions" during the 12-month period as well as to sales and exchanges. There are a number of exceptions to the no-gain rules spelled out in Section 337. They include:

1. Sale of inventory and property held primarily for resale, unless substantially the entire inventory is sold in a single transaction.
2. The discounting of installment receivables acquired by sales made prior to adopting the liquidation plan.
3. Ordinary income arising out of recapture of depreciation on the sale of depreciable assets.
4. Recapture of investment credit.

It is important to note that the provisions for nonrecognition of gains under Section 337 apply also to losses on disposition. If a corporation has a net operating profit at the time of liquidation and anticipates substantial losses on disposal of corporate assets, it is probably more advantageous not to avail itself of this special rule. By simply selling the assets, it can offset the losses on disposition against current operating income prior to liquidation.

The Collapsible Corporation Problem. The apparent magic of the complex provisions for liquidation of corporate assets is the potential for converting to capital gains what would otherwise be ordinary income. Under most of the rules discussed so far, the accumulated earnings of the corporation are treated as capital gains when distributed to the shareholders upon liquidation. This has a particular attraction for real estate investors who might hope to reinvest corporate profits for a number of years and then convert all the profits so invested into capital gains by distributing corporate assets as a liquidating dividend.

But isn't there always a catch? The liquidation must be carefully structured to avoid running afoul of the collapsible corporation rules. Code Section 341 contains wording to the effect that a corporation is deemed "collapsible" if formed principally with a view to enabling the shareholders to realize a gain attributable to corporate property before the corporation realizes a substantial part of the taxable income that could have been derived from the property. The result of having a corporation designated collapsible is that certain gains upon full or partial liquidation, which would otherwise have produced long-term capital gains, might instead produce ordinary income to the shareholder.

If the corporation is deemed collapsible under the provisions of Code Section 341, the gain from sale or exchange of its stock or from liquidation of the corporation is taxed as ordinary income to any shareholder who holds more than 5% of the outstanding shares if, (1) more than 70% of the gain is attributable to property produced or purchased by the corporation and (2) the gain is realized within 3 years following acquisition of the property.

While the provisions of Section 341 are tricky and potentially financially disastrous to the taxpayer, it is possible to avoid the collapsible corporation designation. If the designation is not avoidable under particular circumstances, it is still possible to greatly ameliorate the adverse consequences.

The general wording used by the code to describe a collapsible corporation (e.g., "principally," "view towards") leaves room for much disagreement and has resulted in extensive litigation concerning the status of corporations in liquidation. But there are guidelines as to when a corporation is not to be considered collapsible and when there is a presumption of collapsibility requiring the corporation to prove otherwise.

The basic intent of the rules is to prevent income that would normally be taxed as ordinary income from being accorded capital-gains treatment due to the use of a corporate ownership entity. If this possibility is not significant, then the collapsible corporation rules are not intended to apply. Subsection (e) of Section 341 provides an exception for situations where such gains are minimal. If, were the corporation to dispose of its assets in the normal course of business, the gain on disposal that would result in ordinary income is less than 15% of the corporation's net worth, then the corporation is not considered collapsible.

A major escape hatch is patience. Gains realized from the sale of stock or liquidation of an otherwise collapsible corporation are not treated as ordinary income if the appreciated assets have been owned by the corporation for more than 3 years. This rule is reasonably straightforward with respect to purchased assets. It is permeated with caveats, however, where the assets were constructed by the corporation. The difficulty lies in answering the question as to when construction was completed. The escape rule only applies if the asset is held for more than 3 years after construction is *complete.*

An investor who appears to have been boxed in by the collapsible corporation rules can sometimes avoid the unfavorable tax consequences by selling the corporation instead of liquidating. Subsection (f) of Section 341 provides that no ordinary income need result from the sale of the collapsible corporation itself, if the corporation files a consent to have the gain on ultimate disposal of the assets to be taxed as ordinary income to the corporation. It may be possible to find a buyer who, instead of simply purchasing the corporation's real property, will acquire the corporation as a going concern. The new owner can then look for additional depreciable assets that result in tax losses as a consequence of accelerated depreciation and interest on borrowed funds. The appreciated assets acquired by purchase of the corporate shell can then be sold in a year when the corporation has offsetting losses on subsequently acquired property.

THE PERSONAL HOLDING COMPANY PROBLEM

The relationship between individual and corporate income-tax rates creates a powerful incentive for high-bracket taxpayers to transfer assets to a corporate entity. Since the individual marginal tax rate exceeds that of corporations at income levels as low as $6000 (for single persons), a substantial portion of the employed population would benefit if they could hold their investments in the name of a corporate nominee and accumulate and reinvest all earnings. In addition to a car in every garage, there might be a corporation in every home.

Unfortunately, the Congress has deprived us of this opportunity. One measure to discourage the strategy, imposition of a penalty tax on accumulated earnings in excess of corporate needs, is discussed later in the chapter. An even more stringent rule applies to the income from corporations deemed to have been formed solely for this purpose. These corporations, called "personal holding companies," are first taxed at the regular corporate tax rate, on all income for the year. Then there is imposed an additional tax equal to 70% of the personal holding company income not distributed.

When the Penalty Tax Applies. The question of whether a corporation is a personal holding company is answered by applying two tests. The first relates to concentration of ownership; the second, to sources of income. If a corporation meets both tests, the holding company penalty is imposed on all undistributed income for the year. But if it can arrange to fail either test, the corporation can avoid the personal holding company designation. The rules outlined here are described in full in Code Section 544.

A corporation is not considered a personal holding company if, at any time during the last half of the taxable year, no more than 50% of its stock was held by less than six persons. Ownership is determined under "constructive ownership rules," which are concerned less with the name under which shares are registered than with who controls the shares. Thus an individual may be considered to be the constructive owner of all shares held by members of his family and by his business partners, or if he holds options or securities convertible into stock. "Family" includes brothers and sisters, spouse, ancestors, or lineal descendants. One is considered the constructive owner of a pro rata number of shares held by a corporation or trust in which one has an interest.

If more than 50% of the corporation's stock was (constructively) owned by less than six individuals at any time during the last half of the corporation's taxable year, it meets the "concentration of ownership test" for designation as a personal holding company.

The sources-of-income test for personal holding company designation is satisfied if 60% or more of the corporation's adjusted gross ordinary income is from sources classified as personal holding company income.

Example 12–13

One taxpayer owns 90% of the common shares in Alfa Corporation. Since more than 50% of the shares are, therefore, owned by five individuals or less (i.e., less than six persons), Alfa Corporation is considered a personal holding company if it also meets the "sources-of-income" test.

Example 12–14

Bravo Corporation had 9500 shares outstanding at one time during the last half of its current taxable year. Of these, 4500 were owned by various individuals having no relationship to one another and none of whom were partners. The remaining 5000 shares were held by 19 shareholders, as presented below:

Unrelated individuals		*A*	*B*	*C*	*D*	*E*
Number of shares held directly by individual		200	0	100	207	500
Number of shares held by:	his wife	0	500	0	200	500
	his son	100	50	0	0	0
	his daughter	100	50	0	0	0
	his mother	500	100	0	0	0
	his brother	50	200	0	600	0
	his grandson	50	0	0	0	0
	his partner	0	100	900	0	0
Totals		1000	1000	1000	1000	1000

Since individuals *A*, *B*, *C*, *D*, and *E* collectively have constructive ownership of 5000 shares, they meet the ownership test for treatment as a personal holding company. Thus if the sources-of-income criterion is also satisfied, the corporation is so classified for tax purposes.

To determine adjusted gross ordinary income for the year, first reduce the gross income by gains from sale of capital assets and property used in a trade or business. The remainder is gross ordinary income. This is reduced by certain deductions relative to rent and royalty income, and to income from oil and gas wells, as well as certain items of interest income, to arrive at adjusted ordinary gross income. The adjustments are:

1. A portion of rental income equal to allowable deductions for associated depreciation, interest expense, and property tax. Reducing rental income by these deductions results in "adjusted income from rents."

2. Income from working interests in oil or gas wells is reduced by related depreciation, depletion, taxes, interest expense, and rent.

Example 12–15

A corporation had gross income of $50,000 for the taxable year, accounted for as follows: $5000 in capital gains on the sale of a building used in operation of the business, $40,000 in rental income, and $5000 from sources not considered passive in nature. The corporation had depreciation deductions of $20,000 and interest deductions of $3000 and payed $2000 in property taxes, all relating to income-generating real estate. The corporation had adjusted ordinary gross income of $20,000, determined as follows:

Gross income		$50,000
Less capital gains		5,000
Gross ordinary income		$45,000
Less adjustments related to rental income:		
depreciation	$20,000	
interest	3,000	
property taxes	2,000	$25,000
Adjusted gross ordinary income		$20,000

The adjusted gross ordinary income is then divided by the corporation's personal holding company income. If the result indicates that personal holding company income is 60% or more of adjusted gross ordinary income, the corporation satisfies the sources-of-income criteria for designation as a personal holding company. If it also meets the concentration-of-ownership test, the penalty tax is levied.

Determining Personal Holding Company Income. Example 12–15 illustrates how to compute adjusted gross ordinary income, but leaves hanging the question of how much of this is personal holding company income. Personal holding company income is derived from rents, royalties, interest, dividends, annuities, and income from personal service contracts of specified types, as well as income from beneficial interests in estates and trusts. But not all income from these sources is necessarily included in personal holding company income. To be included, it must meet certain tests as to its significance in the total income of the corporation. The tests are somewhat involved and differ according to the source of the income.

Adjusted income from rent, dividends, interest, royalties and annuities, compensation for use of corporate property by a major stockholder, and income from certain personal service contracts are included in personal holding company income unless they individually equal at least 50% of total ordinary income.

Even where it passes the 50% test, rental income may be included in personal holding company income if all other personal holding company income, after adjustment for distributions during the year, equals more than 10% of ordinary gross income. This additional 10% test applies also to royalties from oil, gas, and other mineral leases as well as to copyright royalties. There are additional tests for income sources of less immediate concern to the real estate investor.

Example 12–16

A corporation formed primarily as an ownership entity for real estate investments has involved itself in mortgage lending operations with junior mortgages. During the current taxable year, it has adjusted income from rents of $80,000 and interest income of $10,000. If the corporation, which is wholly owned by less than six persons, pays no dividends for the year, all of its income is considered personal holding company income. This is because personal holding company income other than rents (i.e., interest) constitutes more than 10% of adjusted ordinary income, whereas total personal holding company income accounts for more than 60% of total income. To avoid personal holding company status, the corporation must pay dividends such that interest income less dividends equals not more than 10% of adjusted gross ordinary income.

1. If no dividends are paid:

Adjusted rental income	$80,000
Other holding company income:	
Interest	10,000
Adjusted gross ordinary income	$90,000

Other holding company income is more than 10% of adjusted gross ordinary income ($10,000/$90,000 = 11%), so adjusted rental income is considered holding company income. Therefore, 100% of adjusted gross ordinary income is personal holding company income.

2. If dividends are paid (say, $5000)

Adjusted rental income		$80,000
Other holding company income:		
interest	$10,000	
less dividends	5,000	$ 5,000
Other income distributed as dividends		5,000
Adjusted gross ordinary income		$90,000

Other holding company income less distributions is *less* than 10% of adjusted gross ordinary income $5000/$90,000 = 5.6%), and adjusted rental income is *more* than 50% of adjusted gross ordinary income. Therefore, adjusted rental income is *not* included in holding company income, and holding company income is less than 60% of adjusted gross ordinary income. The corporation is *not* a personal holding company.

The sources-of-income test generally presents no difficulty for the corporate structure created solely as an ownership entity for real estate, since income other than rents is incidental. Problems can arise, however, if other transactions are entered into by the corporation, which generate substantial amounts of passive income.

The moral of all this for the investor who chooses a corporate ownership entity is quite clear: During any taxable year in which rental income promises to represent less than 50% of adjusted gross ordinary income, or in which other income from passive sources such as interest approaches 10% of adjusted gross ordinary income, steps must be taken to avoid the possibility of having the corporation considered a personal holding company. This can be done by distributing sufficient income so that the other holding company income less distributions for the taxable year is less than 10% of the adjusted gross ordinary income.

The discussion serves to emphasize once again the importance of competent tax counsel during the planning stage and at all subsequent steps in one's investment program. The time to seek advice is in advance of action, not when notified of a tax audit.

OTHER CORPORATE TAX PROBLEMS

The popularity of the corporate entity among businessmen has spawned a virtual library of tax laws, rules, regulations, and precedents covering a multitude of corporate income-tax issues. This massive outpouring is matched by the ingenuity of attorneys and businessmen who constantly develop new tax avoidance strategies.

Every new strategy carries the seeds of its own demise. Success breeds widespread imitation, which in turn induces the Internal Revenue Service or the Congress to foreclose the strategy with new rules or revisions to the code. Investors who are unaware that a previously lucrative opportunity has been foreclosed can be caught by a tax audit that disallows tax deductions or tax treatment on which they were relying to make the investment financially viable. Two examples of changes of which many businessmen and investors still run afoul are the accumulated earnings tax and the problem of loans treated as capital contributions.

Accumulated Earnings Tax. A penalty tax is levied on corporations who allow earnings to accumulate for the purpose of preventing the imposition of the individual income tax on distributions to shareholders.

The accumulated earnings tax is intended only to prevent the accumulation of earnings as a tax avoidance strategy. It is not meant to penalize a corporation that retains sufficient of its earnings to meet legitimate business needs. The tax applies only to those earnings accumulated in *excess* of such legitimate needs.

"Legitimate needs" might include provision for expansion of operations, retirement of debt, acquisition of other firms, or loans to suppliers and/or customers where necessary to enhance the corporation's business connections. It would not generally include loans to shareholders or their friends or relatives for no legitimate business purpose, or for investments that are not related to the business of the corporation.

There is obvious room for disagreement concerning the legitimacy of needs for which the corporation accumulates earnings. Who prevails in such arguments? The Internal Revenue Service can, by following specified administrative procedures, shift the burden of proof to the taxpayer. The presumption of intent to avoid taxation must then be successfully rebutted by the tax-paying corporation if it is to avoid liability for the penalty tax. Rebuttal requires a *preponderance* of evidence that tax avoidance was not *one* of the purposes of the accumulation. It need not have been the dominant or impelling motive for the penalty tax to be assessed.

The penalty tax rate on earnings deemed to have been accumulated in excess of legitimate business needs is essentially confiscatory. The rate is 27.5% on the first $100,000 of accumulated taxable income and 38.5% on the remainder. Since this is in addition to the regular income tax on corporate earnings, the effective tax rate on such income is 75.5 and 86.5%, respectively.

Before determining the corporation's liability for the accumulated earnings tax, a number of adjustments are made to taxable income for the year, and there is allowed a lump-sum credit.

The deductions from taxable income made to determine accumulated income include:

1. All federal and foreign income taxes paid or accrued (not including the accumulated earnings tax or the holding company tax).

2. Unlimited deductions for charitable contributions.
3. Net capital losses that are not otherwise deductible.
4. Taxable long-term capital gains minus the capital-gains tax paid thereon (but note that the tax was already deducted in item 1).
5. Dividends paid.

In addition to the deductions from taxable income, to arrive at accumulated income for purposes of determining liability for the penalty tax, credits are allowed for that portion of the accumulated earnings that is deemed to have been retained for legitimate business needs (but this is reduced by the amount of the deduction in item 4).

The corporation may accumulate $150,000 in excess of legitimate business needs before incurring liability for the penalty tax.

Example 12–17

A corporation had accumulated earnings of $50,000 at the close of the preceding taxable year. Adjusted taxable income for the current taxable year is $140,000, out of which the corporation pays $25,000 in dividends for the current year. Because there are no other deductions available in determining accumulated earnings for the current year, the corporation opts to claim the alternative minimum credit of $150,000 minus accumulated earnings at the close of the preceding taxable year. Accumulated earnings for the current year are $15,000, determined as follows:

Adjusted taxable income for current year		$140,000
Less dividends paid or payable in 2.5 months		25,000
Accumulated income before accumulated earnings credit		$115,000
Tentative earnings credit	$150,000	
Less accumulated earnings at beginning of taxable year	50,000	
Accumulated earnings credit		$100,000
Accumulated taxable income for current year (before adjusting for any portion justified for legitimate business needs)		$ 15,000

A corporation with more than $150,000 in accumulated earnings, of course, has no further accumulated earnings credit. It, therefore, incurs a liability for the penalty tax on any portion of adjusted taxable income not distributed to shareholders, unless it can demonstrate that the accumulation meets a legitimate business need and that tax avoidance was not one of the purposes of the accumulation.

Example 12–18

Assume the same facts as in the preceding example, except that the corporation already has accumulated earnings of more than $150,000 in excess of its legitimate business needs at the close of the preceding taxable year. Assume also that the corporation cannot show a legitimate need to accumulate earnings for the current year. The accumulated earnings tax is calculated as follows:

Adjusted taxable income	$140,000
Less dividends payed or payable in 2.5 months	25,000
Accumulated income before earnings credit	$115,000
Less accumulated earnings credit	0
Accumulated taxable income	$115,000
Accumulated earnings tax:	
On first $100,000 at 27.5%	$ 27,500
On remaining $15,000 at 38.5%	5,775
Total tax (in addition to regular income tax)	$ 33,275

Loan Treated as Capital Contribution. A popular tax avoidance strategy is to make loans to a controlled corporation as a substitute for adequate capital contributions. The advantage of this strategy is that the taxpayer can then take cash out of the corporation and treat it as debt repayment rather than as dividend income. The cash so received affects neither the shareholder's tax liability nor his adjusted basis for the investment. Moreover, he can receive interest payments that are tax deductible to the corporation, thus avoiding the double taxation to which dividends are subject.

Example 12–19

A taxpayer forms two corporations, investing $100,000 of his personal assets in each. In corporation A, he makes a capital investment of $100,000, receiving common stock in exchange. He makes a capital contribution of only $10,000 to corporation B, however, and extends to the corporation a long-term loan for the remaining $90,000, at interest of 10%. Each of the corporations earn $15,000 before interest and taxes. The taxpayer wishes to withdraw $10,000 from each corporation. The results are as follows:

Corporate Operating Results	Corporation *A*	Corporation *B*
Income before interest on loan from shareholder	$15,000	$15,000
Less tax deductible interest on shareholder loan	0	9,000
Taxable income to corporation	$15,000	$ 6,000
Less corporate taxes (at 22%)	3,300	1,320
After tax corporate income	$11,700	$ 4,780
Net Cash:		
As interest on loans	$ 0	$ 9,000
As dividends	10,000	1,000
Retained in corporate account	2,700	4,780
Total before personal income tax	$11,700	$14,780

Both the interest income and the dividend income in Example 12–19 are taxable as ordinary income to the shareholder (subject to a $100 dividend exclusion). He is relatively indifferent, therefore, as to whether the cash is received as interest or dividends, but the difference has significant tax consequences to the corporation. Making a loan instead of a capital contribution enables a major portion of the income from the corporation to be distributed (as interest) without being subject to double taxation.

Moreover, the taxpayer in Example 12–19 can receive periodic payments on the principal of his loan to corporation *B*, without incurring a tax obligation on the receipts. Similar distributions from corporation *A* would be taxable as ordinary dividends to the extent they do not exceed accumulated earnings from past years plus the earnings of the current year.

Additional advantage accrues to the successful user of this tax strategy if the venture is less successful than anticipated. Losses of one's equity investment in a corporation are treated as capital losses rather than deductions from ordinary income. Bad debt losses, on the other hand, are deductible from ordinary income. Should the corporation prove unsuccessful, the shareholder would much prefer that the corporation default on a shareholder loan rather than have to write off an equity investment.

Recognizing the potential for abuse of the distinction between capital contributions and loans to a controlled corporation, the Congress, in Section 385 of the code, gave the Commissioner the authority to issue guidelines for distinguishing between bona fide loans and ostensible loans that are really contributions of capital. The major factors considered include the adequacy of the corporation's capitalization as reflected in its debt-to-equity ratio. If the evidence indicates that the ratio is unusually high, the Commissioner may rule that the alleged debt is in fact a capital contribution establishing an equity interest. In this event, the interest and principal payments on the alleged debt are treated as distributions of dividends and so taxable to both the corporation and the shareholder.

In determining whether a shareholder's loan to a corporation is a disguised purchase of an equity interest, the Service typically looks at several other factors and makes a decision on the preponderance of evidence taken as a whole. Other evidence that the "loan" was in effect a capital contribution might include failure to pay interest on the principal or the lack of any reasonable expectation of repayment of the principal. The intention of the parties and the use to which the loan proceeds are put are additional factors considered, as is the question of whether a disinterested third-party lender would have made such a loan.

SUMMARY

Investors who, because of double taxation of dividends, dismiss the question of incorporation may be missing a lucrative tax-avoidance opportunity. Double taxation occurs only when the investor takes funds from the corporation in the form of dividends, during a year when he has no offsetting losses from other sources. Several strategies are available for taking cash from the corporation without having it characterized as dividend income.

Advantages of using the corporate entity include a lower tax rate on corporate than on personal income, and the opportunity to distribute corporate earnings between corporate net income and personal income (as compensation for services rendered the corporation), in a manner that minimizes the total tax liability. It may be possible to further reduce the average tax bite by having the corporation employ family members who are in lower tax brackets or by distributing shares of stock to such family members who can then receive dividends subject to a much lower personal income-tax rate.

A major tax avoidance opportunity involves using the corporate entity to convert to a capital gain what would otherwise be taxed as ordinary income. This may be possible by selling the corporation rather than the underlying real estate, when sale of the realty itself would result in recapture of excess depreciation. This opportunity is constrained to some extent by the collapsible corporation rules.

Other problems encountered by investors using a corporate entity include compliance with rules to avoid the personal holding company designation and having loans from the corporation being characterized as dividends. These are problems that restrict an investor's freedom of action but that can be avoided with careful and informed advance planning.

SUGGESTED READINGS

1. Schwartz, Sheldon, "Liquidating a Real Estate Corporation," *Real Estate Review, 3* (1), 22–28 (1975).
2. Wasson, H. Reed, "Real Estate Investment Vehicles: A Comparison of Partnership, Affiliated Subsidiary, Subchapter S Corporations, and Ordinary Corporation as the Form of the Vehicle," *Journal of Real Estate Taxation, 4* (2), 167–205 (1976).

CHAPTER 13

TAX TRAPS

Throughout this book we introduce tax-avoidance strategies that flow directly from the factors under study. We show how large "accounting losses" can not only enable the investor to avoid taxes on the cash from his investment, but may also generate a tax shelter for income from other sources. Combined with measures to defer tax on gains from disposal, or to convert income to long-term capital gains, these strategies are designed to enable the taxpayer to build a substantial estate based on investment in real property.

But a monumental amount of careful planning and hard work can be rendered ineffectual overnight if one becomes ensnared in one of the many tax traps that beset the unwary. It is, of course, impossible to foresee every difficulty, and some unpleasant moments are inevitable for the ambitious and the adventurous. The more common (and costly) misadventures, however, can be avoided with adequate forewarning and a certain amount of foresight. It seems appropriate to conclude what has been a rather lengthy study with a final warning on the more notorious of these traps and with some suggestions as to how they may be avoided.

Most of the pitalls are encountered from ignorance or from greed. Trying to wring the last dollar of tax-avoidance benefit from a tax rule can be the downfall of the strategy. Such is often the case with a deflated mortgage, for example, as discussed in Chapter 6. Failure to state a sufficiently high rate of interest on promissory notes in connection with owner-financed sales can spring the imputed-interest trap. This is the first topic of this chapter.

We next revisit the entity trap, introduced in Chapter 11. Careful wording of partnership agreements can enable investors to avoid this problem, which involves having a partnership characterized as a taxable association.

The importance of avoiding "dealer" designation has been alluded to at several points in the book. Investors who fall into the trap of being characterized as dealers may lose the opportunity to claim their gains at the more favorable capital-gains rate. Even when one cannot avoid dealer status, however, it may be possible to support a claim that a particular deal does not represent sale from inventory and thus qualifies for exemption from this category. Where the gain on disposal is significant, this becomes a vital issue. Dealer status is treated as the third trap to be avoided.

The preference trap is a new problem for real estate investors. The minimum tax on preference items has been around since 1969, but only became a major tax factor with the 1976 Tax Reform Act. This very significant problem is the next issue covered here. We explain how the preference tax can alter the benefit of accelerated depreciation deductions and can reduce the value of the long-term capital-gain rules. The impact of the preference-tax rules can be minimized by careful timing of profit-taking to spread the preference items over a period of years.

The chapter concludes with observations on the danger of the illusion of permanency. We show how the tax rules have changed over time and how the changes can drastically alter the after-tax cash flows from a deal. The danger of relying on some particular aspect of the revenue code to make a venture profitable is emphasized by showing how suddenly such aspects can be altered by legislative fiat or administrative decree.

THE IMPUTED-INTEREST TRAP

When a seller takes back a credit instrument in part payment for his property, he, of course, expects compensation for the accommodation. Money has time value. The longer one must wait for payment, the greater the eventual payment is expected to be. The difference between the total amount actually received and the amount that would have been received had the seller insisted upon cash at the closing, is the compensation for waiting. The government intends that such compensation be reported as ordinary income.

But the additional compensation for waiting is not always explicitly identified as interest. It may be reflected instead in a higher price for the property than would otherwise prevail. Or it may be in part made explicit and in part represent other compensation such as a higher selling price. Chaper 6 discusses strategies that involve just this approach. Using a low-interest "deflated" mortgage combined with a high selling price enables the seller to receive the same periodic receipts, but to have a greater portion of the receipts taxable as a capital gain rather than as ordinary income. The opposite strategy of a deflated mortgage enables the buyer to have a greater portion of his payment characterized as currently deductible interest expense rather than as a part of the consideration.

Ideally, the seller who takes back a promissory note would like the selling price to reflect all the compensation, including that for accepting deferred payment. Then all the profit would qualify for capital-gains treatment. But this is not possible, because were the note to specify no interest the Internal Revenue Service would impute an interest rate and tax the proceeds accordingly.

Example 13–1

A taxpayer sells for $30,000 a parcel of income property having an adjusted basis of $4000. The terms of the sale are $9000 cash at closing and no further payment for 36 months, at which time the $21,000 balance is due and payable. No interest charge is specified.

In the absence of the imputed-interest problem, the taxpayer would have a $26,000 gain on the transaction in Example 13–1, all of which would qualify for capital-gain treatment. But because there is no provision for interest on the deferred payment, such interest is imputed. The Internal Revenue Service subtracts the imputed interest from the reported sales price. The portion of the payment representing interest on the deferred payment is taxed as ordinary income, with only the balance of the proceeds in excess of the adjusted basis qualifying for capital-gain treatment.

To illustrate, assume interest is imputed at a rate of 7% per annum on the note in Example 13–1. The $21,000 note is discounted at this rate to determine its present value. The discounted present value of the note plus the down payment represent the recomputed sales price of the property, for purposes of determining the capital gain. The difference between the discounted present value of the note and its face value represents interest income. The revised tax consequence of the transaction is as follows:

Reconstructed sales price:	
Down payment	$ 9,000
Present value of note, discounted at 7% *	17,084
Total sales price	$26,084
Less adjusted basis	4,000
Capital gain	$22,084

* The current rules provide for discounting at 7%, compounded semiannually. The calculation is $\$21,000/(1.035)^6$.

When the proceeds of the note are collected, the difference between the discounted value and the amount collected represents interest income, taxed at the incremental rate then applicable to the taxpayer's ordinary income. This might represent a rather severe financial shock.

But reduced rates of return and missed opportunities do not exhaust the potential adverse effects of the imputed-interest trap. Had the seller collected what he thought to be the maximum allowable percentage of principal during the year of the transaction, the result could have been that the transaction would not qualify for reporting under the installment method.

Remember from Chapter 9 that the major requirement for installment method reporting is that not more than 30% of the selling price be collected in the taxable year of the transaction. The seller in Example 13–1 received a down payment of 30% of the intended selling price ($9000/$30,000). The note is for the intended balance of the sales price or $21,000.

But if the Internal Revenue Service imputes interest at 7%, the present value of the note is $17,084. The sales price then is comprised of the $9000 down payment plus the $17,084 present value of the note, for a total of $26,084. And the $9000 down payment becomes 34.5% of the adjusted selling price. Since the down payment exceeds 30% of the selling price, the installment method cannot be used, and the total tax liability on the capital gain becomes due and payable in the year of the transaction.

The moral is clear: Avoid the imputed-interest trap, even if it means sacrificing a small part of the potential after-tax cash flow. As pointed out in Chapter 9, the way to avoid this trap is to specify an interest rate of not less than that which satisfies the Internal Revenue Service. In addition to specifying a minimum interest rate, it may be prudent to collect sufficiently less than 30% of the selling price during the year of the transaction so that imputation of a slightly higher rate does not reduce the selling price sufficiently to make the initial payments exceed 30%. If additional cash is needed by the seller on the front end, he can have the contract stipulate a substantial second payment on principle in the year following the year of the transaction.

THE TAXABLE ENTITY TRAP

An investor seeking the optimum combination of tax conduit treatment of operating results and limited liability for passive investors typically opts for either a straw corporation or a limited partnership entity. Both these entity decisions involve some risk of being characterized as taxable associations. Should this occur, the venture not only loses its tax conduit status, but any cash distribution to the investors is taxed twice–first as operating income to the entity, then as dividend income to the investors.

Recall that the significance of tax conduit treatment is that each item of income and expense, cash expenditure, and cash receipt retains its character when reported by the investor on his individual income tax return. Thus depreciation deductions reported by the entity are also reported as depreciation deductions on the individual's tax return, for example. The same is true for capital gains and losses, as well as for all other items. Since accounting losses often exceed operating income during the early years of the venture, conduit treatment is important to the investor who can use his pro rata portion of the accounting loss to offset taxable income from other sources. The benefit of pass-through treatment of long-term capital gains should be self-evident.

Loss of conduit treatment can render the investment financially disasterous for investors depending upon tax loss benefits to shelter income from other sources that would otherwise be subject to very high marginal tax rates. Without the shelter benefits, many investments make little sense for such taxpayers.

The taxable entity trap results from formation of an entity that has more corporate than noncorporate characteristics. This issue is analyzed at length in Chapter 11. Investors seeking tax benefits should avoid any venture whose existing or proposed organizational structure appears to flirt with this trap.

The safest way to avoid the taxable entity trap is to obtain an advance ruling to the effect that the entity is not characterized as a taxable association. Where tax benefits are a crucial element, prudence dictates a reluctance to invest in a joint venture that has not received such a ruling.

The popularity of limited partnerships, and the importance of tax shelters to their viability, resulted in a veritable flood of requests for advance rulings during the late 1960s and early 1970s. Like every good tax strategy, this one eventually became eroded by overuse. The preconditions for advance rulings (the so-called safe harbor rules) became ever more stringent. The rules (set forth in Chapter 11) are now so restrictive that it is often difficult for any but large public offerings to comply.

Even an advance ruling is not a grant of immunity from loss of conduit status. The entity trap can still be sprung by the active partner's failure to abide by the terms under which the advance ruling is issued. The situation obviously calls for vesting a great deal of confidence in the general partner–confidence that may not be justified until he has compiled an impressive track record on other projects.

THE DEALER STATUS TRAP

This pitfall causes anticipated capital gains to be taxed as ordinary income. A dealer is one who sells real estate in the ordinary course of his business, rather than on a casual or incidental basis. For the dealer, real property is inventory rather than a capital asset. Its sale is, therefore, not treated as a capital transaction, but as a regular business transaction that generates ordinary income.

The consequences of being treated as a dealer are obvious. Gains lose the preferential tax treatment associated with long-term capital transactions. Instead, they are included with ordinary income from other sources. This, of course, increases the tax on the gain. It may also move the taxpayer into a much higher marginal tax bracket, causing the tax on the gain to more than double.

Example 13–2

During the current taxable year an investor sells income-producing real property that results in a taxable gain of $24,000. The taxpayer, who is married and files a joint return, has net taxable income from other sources, after all exemptions and deductions, of $28,000.

If the sale qualifies as a long-term capital transaction only half the gain need be included in taxable income. In this event, the investor's net taxable income after inclusion of the gain is $28,000 plus $12,000 or $40,000. But if, due to dealer status, the gain is characterized as ordinary income, the taxpayer reports total taxable income of $28,000 plus $24,000 or $52,000. Because of the graduated nature of the income tax, this results in more than double the tax on the transaction. The calculations follow:

	Casual Sale	Dealer Sale
Income from other sources	$28,000	$28,000
Add taxable gain	12,000	24,000
Total taxable	$40,000	$52,000
Total tax liability (from Table 1-1)	$12,140	$18,060
Less tax on income from other sources	7,100	7,100
Tax on gain from sale of realty	$ 5,040	$10,960

Even where he is considered a dealer in real estate, an investor may often avoid this treatment with respect to the sale of a particular parcel of property. The question revolves about whether the property in question was held "primarily for sale." And dealers often hold property for investment purposes rather than primarily for sale.

Whether a property was acquired primarily for resale or for investment purposes becomes the dominant factor only when the investor is in the business of buying and selling property. For one not in the business, the mere fact that the property was acquired primarily for the purposes of subsequent sale does not mean that the gain is necessarily taxed as ordinary income. The question of whether one is in the business depends upon such factors as the frequency of transactions, the personal sales effort by the investor, and other activity involved in connection with acquisition and sale.

Frequent transactions hold the danger of being flagged as an indication of dealer status. When the question arises as to whether an investor's "sideline" activities in real estate constituted a business, the tax court considers the following factors:

1. Income test. The significance of income from real estate buying and selling relative to income from activities alleged to be the investor's real trade or business.
2. Activities test. The amount of effort involved in preparing the properties for resale (e.g., were the properties subdivided or improved prior to resale?).
3. Sales effort test. Did the investor pursue a marketing program in connection with the sale of the properties or were the sales a result of unsolicited offers to buy?
4. Sales continuity test. Is the investor involved in the purchase and sale of property on a regular and continuing basis?
5. Time test. How much time is devoted to real estate purchases and

sales relative to the amount of time devoted to activities alleged to be the investor's full-time trade or business?
6. Facilities test. Does the investor maintain special facilities or licenses designed to facilitate the sale of real estate?

The first line of defense against the dealer status trap is to avoid becoming tainted with the label. This unfortunately is not always a simple task for the investor seeking appreciation by imaginative "repackaging" of his property interests prior to their sale. The most common examples of this problem have involved investors who sought capital-gains treatment on the sale of land they subdivided or a building they converted to a condominium. Either activity threatens to taint the investor with dealer status.

A possible solution is the use of a controlled corporation. The land or the building is sold to the corporation who in turn carries out the subdividing and sale of individual plots or condominium units. The profit earned by the corporation is, of course, taxed as regular income to the corporation, but the gain on the sale by the individual to the controlled corporation has the prospect of beng taxed as a capital gain.

Attempts to claim a capital gain on property sold to a controlled corporation must run an intimidating gamut of judicial blocks, however. If the corporation is obviously no more than an agent for the individual, the sale is treated as a sham and all profits taxed as ordinary income to the individual. The same result transpires if the tax authorities can typify the transaction as more in the nature of a contribution of capital to the corporation. Finally, if the price charged the controlled corporation is excessive in view of the undeveloped nature of the asset being transferred, the basis of the property in the hands of the corporation may be reduced to the fair market value at the time acquired. Or the individual may be charged with having received a taxable dividend in the amount of the excess of fair market value paid by the corporation.

In summary, for the attempt to avoid dealer status by transferring property to a controlled corporation to be successful, very stringent requirements must be met. The property must be transferred at approximately its fair market value at the time of the transfer, the corporation must be adequately capitalized, and the property must have been transferred prior to completion of development work.

So far we have been concerned with avoidence of the dealer designation on the part of the individual for whom real estate is in the nature of a sideline activity. But even for the full-time real estate "professional," it is possible to avoid having the gains on disposal of particular parcels of property being taxed as ordinary income. Given that the individual is a dealer, there remains the all-important question as to whether the particular property being sold was a part of his inventory. If it was not being held primarily for sale to customers *in the ordinary course of business,* a capital gain may be possible.

A dealer who intends to claim that a specific property is an investment rather than inventory must be prepared to document his claim fully. A first step is to segregate all transactions relating to the property into separate accounts. In many instances, dealers have succeeded in attempts to claim capital gains on property held in their own name (where properties were generally held in a company name) and accounted for in separate books of account.

Of course, segregating property records into separate accounts does not in itself enable a dealer to avoid ordinary income. The tax court also looks at all the factors involved in the acquisition, ownership, improvement, and disposal of the property. But careful segregation of the property into books of account separate from those in which inventory property is recorded is an important step. Other factors considered by the tax court in cases of this sort include:

1. The purpose for which the property was acquired.
2. The purpose for which it was held.
3. The nature and extent of improvements to the property during the holding period.
4. The frequency, number, continuity, and substantiality of sales from the property.

THE PREFERENCE TAX TRAP

The concept and the computational rules involving the minimum tax on preference items was explained in Chapter 4. By way of review, recall that the excess of accelerated over straight-line depreciation and half of all long-term capital gains are included as preference items. To the extent that these preference items exceed the greater of $10,000 or half the regular income-tax for the year, they are subject to a 15% tax in addition to the regular tax liability.

The preference tax rules have stripped real estate of some of its tax-shelter allure, but careful planning can enable the investor to minimize the adverse impact. The taking of capital gains must be carefully timed so that they are spread over years when there are few other preference items. Where sale at the most opportune time significantly increases the preference tax liability, consider selling the property currently but deferring recognition of the gain by use of the installment method of reporting the transaction (see Chapter 9).

Perhaps the greatest impact of the new rules has been on the tax consequences of accelerated depreciation deductions. In some cases, taking accelerated depreciation can actually reduce the after-tax cash flow from an investment from what it would have been had the investor chosen to use straight-line depreciation. To see how this works, consider the tax consequences of accelerated depreciation instead of straight-line in the following example:

Example 13–3

An investor purchases new residential income property for $300,000, financing the acquisition with a $240,000, 8.5%, 30-year, first mortgage loan. Eighty percent of the value is attributable to the improvements, which have an estimated useful life of 40 years with no salvage value. The property generates net operating income of $27,000 per year throughout a 5-year holding period. The property is sold at the end of the fifth year for $300,000. The investor uses the 200% declining-balance depreciation method during the first 4 years of ownership, shifting to the straight-line method during the year of sale.

The investor, who is married and files a joint return, has $10,000 of preference items each year, before accounting for the effect of this investment. He has taxable income, after all other deductions and exemptions, but before including the results of this investment, of $55,000 per year.

Since the property in Example 13–3 is new residential-income property, it qualifies for the 200% declining-balance method of depreciation. In deciding whether to in fact use this accelerated method or to opt instead for straight-line depreciation, the investor considers the additional tax savings available currently from the accelerated method, and the additional tax liability upon disposal as a consequence of recapture of excess depreciation. This requires calculation of the additional depreciation resulting annually from the accelerated method, and application of the incremental tax rate to determine the annual savings.

The investor's taxable income after inclusion of the net operating income from the investment, but before deducting depreciation and interest expense, is $82,000. The first-year interest deduction is approximately $20,203, whereas that of the fifth and final year is approximately $19,459. Depreciation deductions range from a high of $12,000 in the first year to a low of $5430 in the last year. He is, therefore, in the 53% incremental income-tax bracket both before and after accounting for the effects of depreciation deductions in excess of straight-line.

Reasoning without the preference tax, the tax savings from use of accelerated rather than straight-line depreciation is equal to 53% of the excess depreciation. The annual savings before consideration of the preference tax are as follows:

	Year 1	Year 2	Year 3	Year 4	Year 5
Accelerated depreciation	$12,000	$11,400	$10,830	$10,289	$5,430†
Straight-line depreciation*	6,000	6,000	6,000	6,000	6,000
Excess depreciation	$ 6,000	$ 5,400	$ 4,830	$ 4,289	$ (570)
Tax savings (at 53%)	$ 3,180	$ 2,862	$ 2,560	$ 2,273	$ (302)

* The straight-line depreciation rate is 1/40, or 2.5% per annum. The original depreciable base is $240,000.
† The undepreciated balance when the investor shifts to the straight-line method is $195,481, and the remaining useful life is 36 years. The revised straight-line depreciation deduction is, therefore, 1/36 × $195,481 or $5430.

The investor's cumulative tax savings during the holding period is, of course, offset upon sale by the tax (at the ordinary income-tax rate) on recapture of the excess depreciation. But the taxes have been deferred for several years. The effect is as if the investor had received an interest-free loan from the Treasury.

All this, however, is reckoning without the effect of the minimum tax on preference items. And this is exactly what the usual analysis of the impact of accelerated depreciation does. As our continuing analysis of Example 13–3 shows, this reasoning from an isolated perspective can be very costly.

The preference tax rules now in effect introduce an additional tax liability in each year accelerated depreciation is claimed, reducing the funds provided by the depreciation deductions. This reduction in funds provided, with no corresponding decrease in tax liability from recapture of excess depreciation upon sale, constitutes an added cost.

Our example stipulates that the investor has preference items of $10,000 other than those resulting from the investment under analysis. Since there is a $10,000 exemption always available to the taxpayer, no preference tax liability would exist were it not for inclusion in preference income of accelerated depreciation in excess of straight line. But the entire amount of his excess depreciation each year is subject to the 15% tax on preference items. The preference tax liability from excess depreciation for each year of the holding period is:

	Year 1	Year 2	Year 3	Year 4	Year 5
Excess depreciation (from previous calculation)	$6,000	$5,400	$4,830	$4,289	$ (570)
Preference tax liability at 15%)	$ 900	$ 810	$ 725	$ 643	0

The annual increase in the preference tax liability partly offsets the decrease in the investor's ordinary tax liability due to the excess depreciation. The net effect is to reduce the tax savings from the excess depreciation by the amount of the increase in the preference tax due to the excess depreciation. The tax savings net of the preference tax liability, follows:

	Year 1	Year 2	Year 3	Year 4	Year 5
Tax savings from excess depreciation from page 270)	$3,180	$2,862	$2,560	$2,273	$ (302)
Less increase in minimum tax on preference items	900	810	725	643	0
Annual tax savings, after preference tax	$2,280	$2,052	$1,835	$1,630	$ (302)

Although the annual tax savings from excess depreciation are reduced by the imposition of the preference tax, the tax on the recapture of excess depreciation at the time of sale remains invariant. The cumulative depreciation taken over the life of the investment was seen to be $20,149 in excess of the amount that would have been taken had the straight-line method been used. This excess depreciation is 100% recaptured at the time of sale. Thus there is a tax of $10,679 ($20,149 times the 53% incremental tax rate) that would not have been imposed had the investor used the straight-line depreciation method. This additional tax is in effect a cost of having had the use of additional funds via the annual tax savings from the use of accelerated depreciation.

The cost of funds provided by the tax savings from excess depreciation then is the additional tax liability in the year of sale over the amount saved during the holding period. This cost can be expressed as an annual percentage rate (the same as an interest rate) by discounting all the cash flows at the rate that makes the present value of the tax savings from taking accelerated depreciation equal the present value of the additional taxes in the year of sale due to recapture of the excess depreciation. This can be expressed as:

$$\sum_{t=1}^{n} \frac{S_t}{(1+d)^t} + \frac{P_n}{(1+d)^n} = 0$$

where t ranges from 1 through 5, S_t is the differential tax effect of using accelerated depreciation rather than straight-line in year t, and P_n is the tax consequence of recapture of excess depreciation upon sale. The common discount rate, d, is the rate of interest on those funds. Solving for d results in a rate of discount of approximately 13%. It is important to note that this is an after-tax cost of making the funds available. Borrowed funds have an after-tax cost of

$$(1 - t)\, i$$

where t is the borrower's incremental tax rate and i is the rate of interest charged by the lender. Thus the after-tax rate on funds made available through the use of accelerated depreciation, to be made comparable with before-tax rates on borrowed funds, must be divided by $(1 - t)$. In our example the investor's incremental tax rate, t, is 53%, so $(1 - t)$ is 47%. The cost of deferring tax liability by use of an accelerated depreciation method is equivalent to borrowing money at an (before-tax) interest rate of 13/.047, or 27.7%! This would hardly be a worthwhile undertaking for most of us.

Our example is, of course, deliberately structured to generate the result achieved. The cost of taking accelerated depreciation is demonstrated, among other ways, by assuming a relatively short projection period. The longer the property is held the less the cost, as a per annum rate, of generating funds by claiming accelerated depreciation deductions. The cost also varies with the amount of other tax preference items, as well as with the level of the taxpayer's ordinary income. But whatever the assumptions employed, it is clear that the new preference tax rules have the potential to transmute accelerated depreciation benefits into an expensive proposition.

CAVEAT ON TRANSIENCY OF TAX RULES

Projecting the after-tax cash flows from a proposed investment over the entire anticipated holding period is a risky proposition. The risk is amplified by the possibility that tax rules may change in the middle of the game. Projections based on current tax law can be rendered worse than useless by a stroke of the presidential pen signing into law a major amendment to the code. If the anticipated tax consequences of a deal are a major determining factor in the decision to invest, a change in the tax rules can be disastrous.

This book incorporates the relevant portions of a 1500-page tax code amendment signed into law in 1976. When we first planned our manuscript (in 1975) there were only the faintest rumblings that such a revision might occur. And there was no way to determine what sort of bill might result when the issue was finally faced by the Congress. Similar major changes in the code occurred in 1969 and 1971. In each instance, the rules were so drastically changed that cash-flow projections based on prior tax rules were generally invalidated.

Does this mean that projections are useless? No. But it does imply that among the risk factors to be included in determining the minimum acceptable rate of return is the risk that changes in the code will adversely affect the results of the venture. Sensitive political antennae are required to anticipate such a major change. The investor and the analyst are wise to keep as current on political literature as they do on the literature of real estate and finance.

SUGGESTED READINGS

1. Aronsohn, Alan J. B., "Real Estate Investments After the Tax Reform Act of 1976," *Journal of Real Estate Taxation, 4* (2), 99–118 (1977).
2. Greer, Gaylon E., "Preference Tax Changes–The Sleeper in the 1976 Tax Reform Act," *Real Estate Issues, 2* (1), 13–21 (1977).
3. Schwartz, Sheldon, "Mortgages in Excess of Basis–the 'Back-end' Tax Problem in Real Estate," *Real Estate Review, 3* (3), 105–110 (1973).
4. Sills, Richard P., "The 'Dealer–Investor' Problem: Observations, Analysis, and Suggestions for Future Development," *Journal of Real Estate Taxation, 2* (1), 51–67 (1974).

INDEX